M3/5

# Mansex fine

MANCHESTER
UNIVERSITY PRESS

# Mansex fine

Religion, manliness and imperialism
in nineteenth-century British culture

DAVID ALDERSON

MANCHESTER UNIVERSITY PRESS

MANCHESTER AND NEW YORK

distributed exclusively in the USA by St. Martin's Press

*Published by* Manchester University Press
Oxford Road, Manchester M13 9NR, UK
*and* Room 400, 175 Fifth Avenue, New York, NY 10010, USA

*Distributed exclusively in the USA by*
St. Martin's Press, Inc., 175 Fifth Avenue, New York, NY 10010, USA

*Distributed exclusively in Canada by*
UBC Press, University of British Columbia, 6344 Memorial Road,
Vancouver, BC, Canada V6T 1Z2

*British Library Cataloguing-in-Publication Data*
A catalogue recored for this book is available from the British Library

*Library of Congress Cataloging-in-Publication Data applied for*

ISBN 9 7190 5275 0 *hardback*

First published 1998

05  04  03  02  01  00  99  98      10  9  8  7  6  5  4  3  2  1

Typeset in Charter with Dauphin
by Northern Phototypesetting Co. Ltd, Bolton

Printed in Great Britain
by Bookcraft (Bath) Ltd, Midsomer Norton

For Paul Pandolfo
and in memory of my Dad

# Contents

*vii*

# Figures

# Acknowledgements

Parts of this book have been published in different forms elsewhere. Elements of chapters 1 and 2 were originally published as 'An anatomy of the British polity: *Alton Locke* and Christian manliness', in Ruth Robbins and Julian Wolfreys (eds), *Victorian Identities* (Houndmills, Macmillan, 1995), and an earlier version of chapter 7 appeared as 'Momentary pleasures: Wilde and English virtue', in Éibhear Walshe (ed.) *Sex, Nation and Dissent in Irish Writing* (Cork, Cork University Press, 1997). I am grateful to Macmillan and to Cork University Press for allowing me to reproduce this material here. In the chapters on Hopkins I have used Catherine Phillips's Oxford edition of the poems, and I am grateful to Oxford University Press, on behalf of the Society of Jesus, for granting me permission to reproduce material still under copyright.

On a more personal level I would like to thank Linda Anderson, Dermot Cavanagh, Azzedine Haddour, Philip O'Neill, Laura Peters, Louise Purbrick, Jenny Richards, Mike Rossington and Linda Rozmovits for providing comradely encouragement and support over the years. Jonathan Dollimore, Norman Vance, and Éibhear Walshe all made valuable suggestions on a number of occasions, and Ian Willis provided me with references for material from *Punch*. Declan Kiberd and Jenny Bourne Taylor, who examined the D.Phil. thesis on which this book is based, were encouraging and constructive in their comments, and I have benefited from their advice. Shaun Richards, at Staffordshire University, provided much appreciated practical support whilst I was in the process of completing the manuscript. Seamus Deane, who read the manuscript for MUP, made a number of important and illuminating suggestions which I have done my best to take on board. My greatest debt, though, is to Alan Sinfield who supervised this book in its former incarnation, and whose attentive readings of my initial scripts were invaluable in helping me shape and refine inchoate ideas and arguments. I am, of course, solely responsible for the book's shortcomings.

# Introduction

IT IS a strange title, I admit. Many readers will recognise 'mansex fine' as a quotation from Gerard Manley Hopkins's poem, 'The Bugler's First Communion'[1] (though those to whom this is news will no doubt have found the title even stranger). I chose it for two reasons: first, because it draws attention to the veneration for the male body which is an integral feature of the imperial culture with which I am concerned; but also, because it derives from a poem which brings into play many of the principal, if apparently diverse, themes of this book – a book which is not organised in terms of a straightforward narrative, and which does not aim to outline the concerns of any particularly coherent group of writers. It is by way of an introduction to these themes, then, that I want to turn briefly to a discussion of Hopkins's poem itself.

'The Bugler's First Communion' is based on an incident which occurred in Oxford in 1879, whilst Hopkins was serving as a curate at St Aloysius's church. The post entailed acting as Catholic chaplain to the Oxfordshire and Buckinghamshire Light Infantry, stationed at the nearby Cowley Barracks, and the poem describes Hopkins's feelings on administering the communion to a young Catholic soldier. The result combines Hopkins's distinctive style with mostly conventional Victorian sentiments, since the poem is a patriotic expression of admiration for the figure of the soldier, who is made to embody a virtuous condition: 'Tongue true, vaunt- and tauntless; / Breathing bloom of a chastity in mansex fine' (ll. 15–16). Though 'mansex' to modern ears tends to suggest an erotic appeal, and though the description of the soldier in the rest of the poem is frequently sensuous, these lines will not sustain a queer reading – at least, not unproblematically – since the word is clearly intended to convey Hopkins's perception of the soldier as a flowering example of 'chastity' (and it is doubtful that even this refers exclusively, or even predominantly, to sexual restraint). It would be more appropriate to suggest that there is a pervasive tension between the sensuous depiction of the soldier and the moral and patriotic values which he embodies, a tension which is only resolved – or, rather, suppressed – in the later stanzas of the poem, where Hopkins moves from a celebration of what the soldier represents to an apprehension of what he will achieve, culminating in his death in some imperial battle: he 'Seems by a divíne doom chánnelled' (l. 41).[2] The soldier's first communion, therefore, is both a commemoration of Christ's sacrifice and an anticipation of his own, a parallel which clearly serves to sanctify imperial duty. Indeed, the soldier's very own 'regimental red' (l. 9), his 'scarlet' (l. 38), clothes him in the colour of a redeeming self-sacrifice. '"Were I come o'er again" cries | Christ "it should be this"', Hopkins wrote in another, later poem on soldiers.[3] All of this clearly demonstrates the extent to which Hopkins's attitudes were in keeping with more widely held convictions that the empire was both a Christian obligation and a providential reward, and in his veneration for the male physique and its sheer capacity to achieve imperial ends Hopkins evinces an indebtedness to the typical features of Christian manliness, a phenomenon I will be describing in greater detail in the following chapters.

But does this mean that 'The Bugler's First Communion' is simply a distillation of certain aspects of imperial ideology? Not quite, since the poem also demonstrates Hopkins's need to reconcile allegiances which were in tension, and which, during his lifetime, were exacerbated by major political events. There are important reasons for Hopkins's enthusiasm about this particular incident and this particular soldier. If England was felt to have a religious destiny in the nineteenth century, it was most frequently seen as definitively Protestant; and if the empire was, for many, the expression of providence, it was therefore the reward for the nation's commitment to the path of truth, in contrast with the religious allegiances of the majority of European nations. As a convert to Catholicism and a Jesuit priest – and Jesuits were the most despised Catholic order in England on account of their counter-Reformation origins – Hopkins was acutely aware of his country's heretical position and the implications of this in imperial terms. Writing to his friend and co-religionist Coventry Patmore, he claimed: 'Your poems are a good deed done for the Catholic Church and another for England, for the British Empire.' It is significant that these two ends are carefully distinguished here, and Hopkins goes on to lament their separation: 'That is the great end of Empires before God, to be Catholic and draw nations into their Catholicism.'[4] The figure of the bugler therefore achieves for Hopkins a symbolic reconciliation of divided loyalties; he embodies the poet's hopes for the future as much as his celebration of the present.

But this is not the only reconciliation of national and religious divisions attempted in the poem: the soldier is a

> boy bugler, born, he tells me, of Irish
> Mother to an English sire (he
> Shares their best gifts surely, fall how things will)
>
> (ll. 2–4)

These two nations – or races, as Hopkins regarded them – were, of course, long-standing antagonists in a colonial contest heavily mediated since the early modern period by religion. If Irish nationalism – despite progressive republican and nationalist strands from the 1790s on – has largely been associated with the cause of Irish Catholics, this is ultimately because English/British colonialism, which set the terms of the dialectic, was Protestant to a more or less zealous degree in the centuries following the Elizabethan reconquest. Anti-Catholicism had far from disappeared in the nineteenth century[5] – indeed, it had probably been reinvigorated by the Evangelical revival, and by antagonism towards Irish political demands[6] – and the Protestant Establishment in Ireland was only gradually dismantled over the course of that century. Hopkins's Catholic, half-Irish British bugler therefore appears to heal colonial wounds on emphatically Unionist, though not Protestant, terms. It is not entirely clear what gifts he inherits from each of his parents, but these lines do suggest a relatively passive role on the part of the Irish mother in delivering the child *to* his clearly virile father (creativity is generally a male activity in Hopkins, God himself being a fecund father).[7] The mother exhibits a proper colonised/feminine subordination, and the product of this exemplary union is a virtuous soldier who will sacrifice his unsullied existence to the imperial cause. Hybridity, in this instance, is a far from unsettling phenomenon.

Indeed the figure of the Irish soldier, even one of purely Celtic origins, was one which raised the prospect for many stalwart imperialists – Kipling, for instance – of a resolution of the age-old struggle on satisfactory terms. Even though most Irish soldiers were probably motivated by financial concerns rather than British patriotism,[8] their apparent submission to the British cause allowed them to be invested with great symbolic potential. This, for instance, is Charles Kingsley, prime mover of Christian manliness, at his most conciliatory towards the Irish in a note to his novel *Westward Ho!*, written at the time of the Crimean War:

> It has been reserved for this age, and for the liberal policy of this age, to see the last ebullitions of Celtic excitability die out harmless and ashamed of itself, and find that the Irishman, when he is brought as a soldier under the regenerative influence of law, discipline, self-respect, and loyalty, can prove himself a worthy rival of the more stern Norse-Saxon warrior. God grant that the military brotherhood between Irish and English, which is the especial glory of the present war, may be the germ of a brotherhood industrial, political, and hereafter, perhaps, religious also.[9]

This anticipation of a 'brotherhood' dictated on strictly English terms was clearly premature – the real reason for Irish passivity in this decade being post-Famine trauma, rather than English largesse – but the passage indicates the power the military appeared to possess for harnessing an inherent Celtic volatility which otherwise tended to find more politically destabilising forms. More generally, lawfulness, discipline, self-respect and loyalty – still less, Hopkins's tongue truthfulness – were not predicated of the Irish, and the Celt/Anglo-Saxon opposition is an important extension of my concern throughout this book with the Catholic/Protestant one.

These are the principal themes which have determined the concerns and direction of this book. Chapter 1 is a consideration of the ideological trajectory out of which Christian manliness emerged. Here I present a broader historical and political, as well as religious, context than is usually the case, analysing the significance attached by many to the Church and state alliance in the counter-revolutionary culture of Britain which dominated from the 1790s until roughly the mid-nineteenth century. Chapter 2 opens with a detailed discussion of Kingsley's novel *Alton Locke* – a text which lends itself to an account of Christian manliness as it emerged out of this counter-revolutionary period – and goes on to give a more general account of the subsequent institutionalisation and influence of what is generally acknowledged to be a major component of imperial ideology. I then turn to Kingsley's Catholic antagonist, John Henry Newman, considering the determinants of his religious and political development as well as the significance of claims about his 'effeminacy'. Newman, largely because of his religion, and despite his political inclinations, was more sympathetic to Irish nationalism than most English people, and those political and cultural determinants which generated the increasingly racial characterisation of the Celts on which English superiority was predicated are discussed in chapter 4. This also prepares the way for the final chapters on Hopkins – a demoralised Anglo-Saxon priest who spent the final years of his life in Ireland – and the self-styled Celtic aesthete who effectively repudiated the dominant ideology of manliness, Oscar Wilde. Consideration of male same-sex desire is almost ubiquitous in discussions of Wilde, and this account is no exception. The theme is not exclusive to this final chapter, though, since I am also concerned with the various relations between manliness, effeminacy and same-sex desire throughout.

Protestantism – an integral component of the dominant nineteenth-century whiggish historical narrative of British progress – was therefore a crucial determinant of perceptions of manliness in nineteenth-century England, though it is arguable that, in the course of that century, consciousness of this provenance lost its significance to the extent that religious values transmuted into secular common sense. This is one of the fundamental claims of this book, though it is also the premise from which I develop more detailed and specific arguments. Before embarking on these, therefore, I want to establish what manliness connoted, and precisely why I think it is necessary to look to the influence of Protestantism. Much of what follows is a synoptic account of the relationship between religion, nationhood and gender in English culture which may be more or less familiar to many readers. It seems to me, though, a necessary prelude to what follows.

## A Protestant polity

In 1849 a diary entry in *Punch* reviewed the proceedings of a meeting at Exeter Hall, deriding its illiberal, even hysterical, attacks on the Catholic faith: 'instead of Argument, I did hear Nothing but Abuse, which do always go in at one ear and out at the other'. In particular, the diarist noted, 'The Commotions on the Continent last Year laid much Stress on, and the Turmoils in Catholique and Quiet in Protestant States contrasted, as though there had been no Disturbance or Trouble in Prussia or Denmark, or any Tumult or Revolution in Belgium or Portugal.'[10] The entry is odd, because atypical in its scepticism about Protestant claims to greater rationality and political stability. However, not long after this the journal embarked on its own intemperate and sustained crusade against Catholicism. The cause of this *volte face* was the restoration of the Catholic hierarchy in England, or the Papal Aggression, as it became known because of its supposed infringement on British sovereignty. On Papal claims to jurisdiction, *Punch* demanded to know: 'will the POPE OF ROME ever be satisfied with the authority possessed by him in this country, 'till JOHN BULL becomes a Papal BULL entirely, and he has that stout and worthy gentleman – beaver, broadcloth, boots, breeches, crabsticks, watch, chain, seals, and all – at his foot, kissing his shoe?'[11] This prospect of a subservient John Bull (and there was a great deal of punning on Bulls in *Punch* during this controversy) was obviously intended to be laughably implausible, an impossible image of the archetypal freeborn Englishman bowing to Papal absolutism. At stake in the debate about sovereignty, then, were perceptions of national characteristics, as signalled too by the Prime Minister, Lord John Russell, who stoked the controversy in a letter printed in *The Times* warning of the advances of Rome: 'No foreign prince or potentate will be at liberty to fasten his fetters upon a nation which has so long and so nobly vindicated its right to freedom of opinion, civil, political and religious.' He ended, though, by alerting countrymen to internal dangers, especially those of ritualism within the Anglican Church, hoping that the English people would put a stop to these tendencies 'to confine the intellect and enslave the soul'.[12] *Punch* made similar accusations against the High Church Puseyite tendency: at a time when Rome was beating at the door – or, at least, jemmying the lock (see figure 1) – Anglo-Catholics appeared fatally mesmerised by the lure of the ancient faith (see figure 2).

The Aggression gives some indication of the extent to which Protestantism was still popularly regarded as a crucial component of Englishness and, by extension, Britishness.[13] According to one historian, 'The Pope, Wiseman and their supporters seemed for a few months to present a greater threat to national integrity than anyone since Napoleon.'[14] Throughout this controversy, fears for the manly condition of the nation's people constantly surfaced, fears which were bound up with profound and widespread convictions about the nation's history and destiny. In another sketch in *Punch* at this time, a petticoated Cardinal Wiseboy and his colleague Newboy (ushered in, with an obvious significance, by a 'poor, ignorant' Irish maid) confront Mr Punch with 'a *Little Bull*' (the Papal directive sanctioning the re-establishment of the hierarchy). Mr Punch restrains his dog from biting the Cardinal's ankles – 'I'll have no persecution' – but gives the Cardinal a lecture on the material progress of a Britain free from Catholic superstition: 'The railroad, the newspaper, free thought and free discussion, all of which privileges we have won in spite of my Lord Cardinal's petticoats, we intend to keep.'[15] The clothing is an obvious feminine taint, but the pun on 'boy' and 'man' in the visitors' names indicates that manhood was also associated with a maturity which valued liberalism and promoted enlightened progress; femininity and immaturity are, therefore, virtually synonymous here, connoting a developmental human stage prior to that achieved by the nineteenth-century English. In order to understand the basis for such perceptions we need to consider the significance of England's Protestant history.

Benedict Anderson has argued that the Reformation was a crucial moment in the founding of those imagined communities we call nations, as the sacral language of Latin was replaced by vernacular languages in print, a trend precipitated both by theological developments and by the needs of print capitalism to expand its markets (readers of Latin were comparatively few, though they were widespread).[16] According to Anderson, the massive explosion in the production and consumption of books in the sixteenth century was both the result of and a contributory factor in the growing belief in nationhood: finite, sovereign and horizontally conceived collections of people which displaced hierarchical and supra-national, cosmically conceived systems of religious authority. We might add to this by noting that Protestantism clearly styled itself as a revolt from below against the deceitful, corrupt and unjust system administered from Rome, and it did so in the form of vernacular languages which themselves materially signified opposition to a conspiratorially secret ecclesiastical system inimical to the individual and expressing itself typically in Latin. This sense of individual liberation from priestly control proved to be a durable component in the demotic rhetoric of the religion, and in the nineteenth century the authoritarianism of Rome was still popularly anathematised in these terms. Indeed, Reformation antagonism to the Catholic priesthood's mystification of the laity remained strong enough to keep the young John Henry Newman from the obvious step of conversion for years, and in his early verse – when he was more Evangelically inclined – prompted him to refer to Catholicism as

Mistaken worship! where the priestly plan
In servile bondage rules degraded man, ...[17]

If this aspect of Protestantism was a crucially important constitutive
element in an embryonic form of nationhood, then integral to this

THE THIN END OF THE WEDGE.

DARING ATTEMPT TO BREAK INTO A CHURCH.

FIGURE I   *Punch*, 19 (1850), p. 207

English identity was a sense of alleviation from mystery and superstition.

This religious individualism was also an important feature of a now widely acknowledged historiographical tradition which devel-

THE PUSEYITE MOTH AND ROMAN CANDLE.

" Fly away *Silly* Moth."

FIGURE 2    *Punch*, 19 (1850), p. 217

9

oped out of the Reformation and which culminated in the nineteenth century in specifically racial accounts of English history.[18] According to this tradition the distinctiveness of English social and religious development was founded on the 'genius' of the Saxon invaders who had brought with them an individualism in religion and forms of social organisation complemented by a virtually unique commitment to democratic government. Such claims for English society's Saxon roots were the basis of a pervasive constitutionalism[19] in eighteenth-century political attitudes which were capable of sustaining more or less radical inflexions. In this context, the reforms of 1688 which set consitutional limits to the authority of the (Protestant) monarchy came to be perceived as either the partial restitution of native freedoms or a very nearly definitive settlement (the controversy between Richard Price and Edmund Burke over the nature of the democratic rights of the English people in the wake of the French Revolution epitomises these opposing – though ultimately related – positions). For all, though, the symbolic importance of the Glorious Revolution was that it integrated protection from arbitrary power in the political realm with the definitive rejection of religious absolutism by prescribing a Protestant monarchy. Moreover, this popular commitment to constitutional principles throughout the eighteenth century and into the early nineteenth century was reinforced by successive wars with a France which was initially derided as Catholic absolutist and, following its Revolution, licentiously republican.[20] The unholy *rapprochement* of the Napoleonic Concordat, moreover, provided symbolic confirmation of a pervasive English assumption that the Revolution merely illustrated the viciousness of the French character which had been left uncorrected by Catholic teaching.

As all of this suggests, anti-Catholicism was more than a convenient propaganda tool against the French: specific doctrinal differences between the warring nations were important. In particular the central tenet of Protestantism was crucial to distinctions drawn between Catholic nations and Protestant England. Justification by faith entailed rejecting the authority of the Church as the only means by which the saving power of formal good works could be dispensed, placing the emphasis instead on individual conscience. In this sense those religious freedoms which rejected the mediations of Catholicism – good works, saints, the Virgin Mary, the rigidly hierarchical priesthood and the rest – were not incidental to the freedoms enjoyed by the Englishman. If Catholicism has been seen by Protestants historically as a repressive system, one inimical to the immediate relationship between the individual and God, and resulting in ignorance and a lack of conscientious virtue, this view became integral to representations of Catholic *nations*. Linda Colley cites the following eighteenth-century example, which – though it does not mention Catholicism directly – is indicative of the general perception:

> Let France grow proud, beneath the tyrant's lust,
> While the rack'd people crawl, and lick the dust:
> The manly genius of this isle disdains
> All tinsel slavery, or golden chains.[21]

The sense of freedom posited here in opposition to the physical oppression of the poor and in disdain of the spiritual corruption of the rich emphasises both gender and independence at the same time as it promotes the sense of a truly national Protestant community. *Manly* freedom, then, denotes autonomy and virtue, the two being inseparable in the Protestant experience. Moreover, virtuous independence is not merely characteristic of individuals, but is definitive of national maturity: 'manly genius' slips undecidably between reference to the individual and to the nation, emphasising the independence of both.

As the *Punch* sketches demonstrate, it was also popularly believed that Protestantism had conferred other related blessings on the nation, notably those of progress and wealth. Unlike Catholic nations, Protestant England had not placed substantial obstacles in the path of Enlightenment reason.[22] Indeed Enlightenment thought emerged logically enough out of the kind of anti-supernaturalism asserted by Protestant – and especially Anglican – theology, in its claims that God was not much given to miraculous interventions. The sixteenth-century Bishop of Winchester Thomas Cooper once claimed that nature 'is nothing but the finger of God working in his creatures',[23] and the natural theology which came to dominate eighteenth-century Anglicanism asserted that the world was governed by natural laws accessible to human reason. Moreover, these divinely constituted laws of nature, which necessarily resulted in a harmonious totality, also had a tendency to subsume those laws, or conventions, which governed society. For my purposes the most important exponent of this kind of thinking was Edmund Burke, notably in his response to the French Revolution – a response which forged out of established ideological trends a set of political values in every way antithetical to those of the French Republic and which, I will argue, fed crucially into the definition of manliness.

Appeals to a divinely constituted and therefore natural order tended to legitimate competing visions of society. Political economy, for instance, was a far from uncontested science, and those who did contest its growing influence in the early nineteenth century tended to appeal precisely to the sanctity of the established social order and of the mutual obligations which bound the classes together. But adherents of the new science, too, defended it on the basis that its laws were uncontestable because prescribed by a higher authority. When warning against state intervention in times of hardship, Edmund Burke affirmed: 'We, the people ought to be made sensible, that it is not in breaking the laws of commerce, which are the laws of nature, and consequently the laws of God, that we are to place the hope of softening the Divine displeasure to remove any calamity under which we suffer, or which hangs over us.'[24] In the nineteenth century Archbishop Whateley claimed as one of his motivations in accepting the Drummond Chair of Political Economy at Oxford his desire to reclaim the discipline for Christians, by 'a sort of continuation of Paley's *Natural Theology*, extending to the body-politic some such views as his respecting the natural'[25]. Charles Kingsley was one of the last-ditch defenders of natural theology,[26] as well as being originally a critic of *laissez faire* policies on the grounds that they violated the natural social order, but, once reconciled to bourgeois economics, he too argued that 'the laws of trade and of social economy, just as much as the laws of nature, are divine facts, and only by obeying them can we thrive'.[27] In the course of the nineteenth century – as Whateley's anxiety indicates – assertions of scientific laws tended to dispense with the need for divine legitimations, but the Protestant accommodation with nature assisted in asserting the ineluctability of 'natural' laws, and secularising scientific thinkers from the mid-century on acknowledged this. James R. Moore has noted that the dissident intellectuals – J. A. Froude, Francis Newman, Herbert Spencer and others – who challenged religious orthodoxies at this time saw themselves as engaged in a 'New Reformation', one which none the less developed organically out of established religious values.[28] The well-documented skirmishes over scientific threats to religious certainty in the latter half of the nineteenth century – the so-called Victorian crisis of faith – should not obscure recognition of underlying ideological continuities.

The relevance to my argument of this feature of Protestant culture again lies in its insistence on demystification. As Simone de Beauvoir has commented, man 'thinks of his body as a direct and normal connection with the world, which he believes he apprehends objectively, whereas he regards the body of woman as a hindrance'.[29] Though this reflects an ancient prejudice, the privileged access to 'truth' which manliness claimed in England over the course of the nineteenth century acquired particular inflections – the implications of which I trace in the following chapters – but, in so far as a stable society was believed to be founded on reasonable and natural – and therefore ineluctable – laws, it will be immediately obvious that manliness could acquire a conservative force predicated on the sure grasp of those laws. The revolutionary desire to overturn them was indicative of a feminine instability and disregard for those metaphysical forces which determined the proper, orderly course of history.

The most visible signs of national progress – itself the consequence of grasping the laws of development – were those of accumulating wealth and industrial supremacy, and these were, of course, popularly attributed to the work ethic.[30] The redemptive power and moral efficacy of work was widely regarded as lacking in Catholic nations, whereas England had prospered. Macaulay, in his *History of England*, struggles to repress illiberal anti-Catholic sentiments (a difficult task given the period he is dealing with), but none the less clearly attributes the power to effect economic transformation to the arrival of the Glorious Revolution's Protestant hero on English shores: Torbay, claims Macaulay, was once merely 'a haven where ships sometimes took refuge from the tempests of the Atlantic', but 'Since William looked on that harbour its aspect has greatly changed. The amphitheatre which surrounds the spacious basin now exhibits everywhere the signs of prosperity and civilisation.'[31] The work ethic which was the basis of this prosperity was mostly associated with the Evangelical or Nonconformist middle class, but praise for its benefits was, by Macaulay's time, clearly not confined to their ranks. Catherine Hall and Leonore Davidoff have provided an impressive account of middle class gender formations in relation to emerging family structures in the first half of the nineteenth century,[32] and it remains for me to distinguish my emphasis on Protestantism from theirs, since the argument I develop in chapters 1 and 2 relates mostly to a solidly Anglican tradition, one which sees its Church as symbolically central to the maintenance of order and the continuation of social and political traditions.

Protestantism, then, was perceived as the guarantee of English superiority, moral and material, and simultaneously of a rational freedom. It is in this context that the metaphors of maturity – of a fully individuated acquisition of the powers of conscience and reason against an irrational childishness dependent on external authority – came to potency and defined a national construction of manliness. In the context of the 1790s, however, this construction acquired distinctive inflections as a result of pervasive counter-revolutionary ideas – inflections which were to become inseparable from dominant nineteenth-century perceptions.

# I

## Manly freedom

MANLINESS, then, was bound up with the Protestant emphasis on autonomy in the pursuit of virtue; that is, with self-regulation and obedience to conscience. So far this claim has been a less than nuanced one about the connotations of the term in relation to British, and especially English, historical development. Protestantism, however, was never a unified phenomenon, and the value that was placed on autonomy was not an unproblematic one in terms of upholding social order, since the virtuous path of conscience could obviously lead to conflict with social conformity: obedience to conscience might, in certain circumstances, entail disobedience to the state, and in the revolutionary period stretching from 1789 to 1848 this was an urgent problem in the policing of the governed. The rhetorical power of Protestant rejections of an arbitrary and unwarrantable authority, for instance, found a significant place in the arguments of radicals. Thomas Paine argued that 'monarchy in every instance is the Popery of government',[1] and, as George Woodcock points out, amongst the English radicals of the 1790s were those Dissenting intellectuals whose 'resistance to religious authority inclined them to oppose secular authority'.[2] Later, in 1851, John Henry Newman – by this time an astute and profoundly conservative critic of Protestant culture – challenged Protestants to 'take your First Principles [of private judgement], of which you are so proud, into the crowded streets of our cities, into the formidable classes which make up the bulk of the population; try to work society by them. You think you can; I say you cannot.'[3]

Anglicans, however, were not unaware of the potential threat represented by too great an independence, and Anglican sensibilities became integral to English counter-revolutionary politics and culture: the Church of England was not merely the religious arm of the Estab-

15

lishment, it became, in many ways, the principal symbol of the moderate, conservative English character which was temperamentally antagonistic to the kinds of sweeping changes initiated in France in 1789. I want to indicate here some of the ways in which this ideology of Englishness fed into mainstream nineteenth-century perceptions, bearing crucially on constructions of gender.

### Feeling versus revolution

As with most accounts of English counter-revolution, Burke's *Reflections* are important to my argument, since not only does Burke establish the Church of England as the institution which sanctifies national development as he perceives it, but his defence of the established order develops important strands of Anglican social thought. Central to his defence, of course, is his depiction of English society as an organic whole, a complex and durable totality more suited to the population's real interests than any set of untested principles arrived at through mere reason. Integral to this representation, though, are the conventions and language of sensibility which had their roots in the Latitudinarian teachings of post-Restoration Anglican divines. This school commended moderate feeling as the basis of a sympathetic, charitable and moral disposition, challenging both the ascetic virtue prescribed by doctrinal puritanism and the Hobbesian rakishness which tended to be associated with the Restoration aristocracy. They were consequently an important influence on such important eighteenth-century moralists as the Earl of Shaftesbury.[4] As a *via media* between the stock characteristics of the vying middle and upper classes, sensibility promoted itself as the reasonable, and therefore natural, basis of social relations, constituting an intuitive, affective bond between the classes. Consequently it encouraged a view of society 'less as a mechanism and more as a system of relationships based on social sympathy'.[5] Directed downwards, sympathy taught pity for the poor,[6] thus bolstering paternalist relations. Directed upwards, it taught reverence for the nation's elite; or so argued writers such as David Hume and Adam Smith. Smith also claimed that sympathy was the force which produced familial and, by extension, regional and national solidarities.[7] The tradition of sensibility, particularly as it was developed by Hume and Smith, was therefore an important influence on Burke's thinking, ultimately determining his view of social relations. But, in drawing on this tradition of sensibility, Burke's entire argument came to rest on an apparent contradiction. On the one hand, he clearly evinces a conviction in the natural goodness of humanity – its potential for sensitivity – but, at the same time, he is also convinced that we are innately depraved creatures who need to be restrained for our own good. Unsurprisingly, for Burke, the contradiction is expressed in relation to class distinctions, with the upper orders exhibiting a genteel humanity and the lower orders a bestial rapacity.

This class division becomes apparent in the outrage he expresses at the revolutionary assault on the French Queen at Versailles. In this account Marie Antoinette becomes the vulnerable feminine principle of virtue in distress (a representation of her which became more widespread in the service of reaction after the executions of the royals).[8] Revolution therefore figures in Burke as a licentious masculine assault on feminine purity, and this epitomises his treatment of the demand for liberty not as an essentially political cry but as sinful human nature attempting to cast off all restraint. In the years which followed the Revolution liberty was overwhelmingly presented in such moral terms, and consequently as threatening to the socially vulnerable – frequently women – who were represented as the necessary casualties of any potential breakdown in checks on conduct. The sympathy which was encouraged for these vulnerable figures was therefore also an integral component of English conservatism.

Burke's own response to the Queen's plight is presented as an instance of human nature in its positive guise, since 'we are so made as to be affected at such spectacles with melancholy ... in events such as these our passion instructs our reason',[9] and this privileging of feeling over reason leads into his famous defence of English prejudices:

> In England we have not yet been completely embowelled of our natural entrails: we still feel within us, and we cherish and cultivate, those inbred sentiments which are the faithful guardians, the active monitors of our duty, the true supporters of all our liberal and manly morals ... We fear God; we look up with awe to kings, with affection to Parliaments, with duty to magistrates, with reverence to priests, and with respect to nobility. Why? Because, when such ideas are brought before our minds, it is *natural* to be so affected; because all other feelings are false and spurious, and tend to corrupt our minds, to vitiate our primary morals, to render us unfit for rational liberty ....
>
> You see, Sir, that in this enlightened age I am bold enough to

confess that we are generally men of untaught feelings: that, instead of casting away all our old prejudices, we cherish them to a very considerable degree; and, to take more shame to ourselves, we cherish them because they are prejudices; and the longer they have lasted, and the more generally they have prevailed, the more we cherish them ... Prejudice renders a man's virtue his habit, and not a series of unconnected acts. Through just prejudice, his duty becomes a part of his nature.[10]

'Manliness' is here associated with virtuous restraint, specifically with those checks which proceed from internal, yet cultivated, prejudices. It is this sensibility which forms an opposition with the uncivilised masculinity of the revolutionaries. This passage also demonstrates the importance of culture to Burke's argument, since he suggests that natural feelings have forged a social order which is itself a kind of second nature – one tested by use[11] – and which, in turn, serves to cultivate positive natural feelings to the extent that they become habitual. 'Habit', moreover, was a key word in the moral lexicon of the eighteenth-century ruling class, deriving from another, Aristotelian strand of Anglican social thinking whose influence continued well into the nineteenth century. Habit was prized as the means by which individuals became predisposed to proper conduct. The significance of the term is demonstrated in Bishop Butler's *Analogy of Religion Natural and Revealed to the Constitution of Nature*, one of the most influential pieces of Anglican thinking produced in the eighteenth-century, and a text which continued to be widely read throughout the nineteenth-century. For Butler there was no question but that civil society was a part of the natural order, and he compares the disciplining of children with the 'probation' of people on earth for their afterlife:

passive impressions made upon our minds by admonition, experience, example, though they may have a remote efficacy, and a very great one, towards forming active habits, yet, can have this efficacy no otherwise than by inducing us to such a course of action ... it is not being affected so and so, but acting, which forms those habits: only it must be always remembered, that real endeavours to enforce good impressions upon ourselves are a species of virtuous action.[12]

Active and repeated conformity in children produces a proper 'subjection and obedience to civil authority. What passes before their eyes, and daily happens to them, gives them experience, caution against treachery and deceit, together with numberless little rules of action and conduct, which we could not live without; and which are learnt so insensibly and so perfectly, as to be mistaken for instinct'.[13] There is an apparent, and familiar, contradiction in this argument: habit must be learnt, it is '*mistaken* for instinct', but it is the basis of conformity to the *natural* civil order. However, since the culture we acquire and which conditions our habits was believed to be the product of natural, yet ultimately social, impulses, the contradiction is somewhat diminished.

Burke's key emphases throughout the *Reflections* are on these mutually supporting qualities of sensibility and habit which together are constitutive of the organic society. It is precisely the habits of the majority in the new French National Assembly, on the other hand, which should disqualify them from government: 'The true lawgiver ought to have a heart full of sensibility. He ought to love and respect his kind, and to fear himself'.[14] Again, social sympathies should ideally hold in check individual recklessness. France's innovative legislators, though,

> seem to have taken their opinions of all professions, ranks, and offices from the declamations and buffooneries of satirists ... By listening only to these, your leaders regard all things only on the side of their vices and faults, and view those vices and faults under every colour of exaggeration ... in general, those who are habitually employed in finding and displaying faults are unqualified for the work of reformation; because their minds are not only unfurnished with patterns of the fair and good, but by habit they come to take no delight in the contemplation of those things. By hating vices too much they come to love men too little. It is therefore not wonderful that they should be indisposed and unable to serve them. From hence arises the complexional disposition of some of your guides to pull everything in pieces.[15]

Habitual cynicism towards the Establishment is therefore at the root of the revolutionary disposition and its essentially destructive character, but it also corrodes those affective relations integral to the healthy social order. Indeed the policies of the Assembly more generally undermine traditional habits, since they reflect the interests of factions rather than the judgement of the supposedly disinterested landed oligarchy which was Burke's ideal and whose passing in France he laments. Government by city-dwellers, for whom 'combination is natural',[16] leads inevitably to the dominance of sectional interests. Moreover, the centralisation of power in Paris and the repartitioning of the provinces has undermined local attachments, thereby breaking the bonds which generate true patriotism. Again, following Smith, Burke argues that our affections progress ineluctably from family to province to nation, since 'Such divisions of our country as have been formed by habit, and not by a sudden jerk of authority, were so many little images of the great country, in which the heart found something which it could fill.'[17]

This privileging of feeling – essentially moral feeling – has important implications when we turn to Burke's discussion of religion. Integral to the English prejudices he celebrates is the notion that religion should be the basis of civil society. Without this religious foundation 'we are apprehensive ... that some uncouth, pernicious and degrading superstition might take place of it'.[18] This claim anticipates a later element of his argument which was to become a consistent feature of counter-revolutionary thought in England: a comparison between Catholicism and republicanism. Burke's deeply felt anti-Enlightenment convictions lead him into a hatred of 'systems', since 'All our sophisters cannot produce any thing better adopted to preserve a rational and manly freedom than the course that we have pursued, who have chosen our nature rather than our speculations, our breasts rather than our inventions, for the great conservatories and magazines of our rights and privileges'.[19] The choice he presents here is between being guided by 'our breasts' – an interior, affective, moral guiding principle – and accepting the impositions of systems. He argues that the revolutionaries 'are so taken up with their theories about the rights of man, that they have totally forgot his nature ... They have perverted in themselves, and in those that attend to them, all the well-placed sympathies of the human breast'.[20] In this way the appeal to 'rational and manly' freedom is counterposed with conduct determined by theoretical abstractions, interiority with exteriority, authenticity with formality, drawing on the same antinomies which structured anti-Catholic sentiments. In fact, in his discussion of the treatment of the French monasteries by the new regime Burke considers the 'superstitions' of the old religion and those of the new social thinkers as almost equivalent, though he favours the established order on moral grounds.[21] This repudiation of systems makes genuine freedom in England dependent on the protection of the current order and reconciles conviction with conformity, manliness and independence with duty.

Burke, then, advocates a natural, yet cultivated, disposition in opposition to the authoritarian regulation of the individual which he predicts will be made necessary in France by the unleashing of an excessive liberty. Since he is defending the established order, Burke finds it necessary to absolve the French *ancien régime* of absolutism, whereas later commentators, such as Carlyle and Dickens, tended to blame that regime for provoking the Revolution. None the less, Burke's account of Catholicism betrays his sense that French society, even prior to 1789, was dependent in some degree on forms of regulation which were at odds with the natural humane disposition of the English.

In Burke, of course, the connection between morals and politics is explicit. In turning briefly to Austen – and also, at a later stage in the argument of this chapter, to Charlotte Brontë – I want to indicate how political concerns were effectively transmuted into moral questions, reflecting quite precisely the Burkean conviction that the English social order was grounded in cultivated sympathies; ultimately, that the social organism depended on the disposition of those individuals who comprised it.

### *Mansfield Park*: orderly habits

It has become conventional to read Austen's novels as being concerned with the defence of tradition and order, so I am conscious here of drawing on and contributing to well-established critical themes. *Mansfield Park* is a novel which rehearses debates about authority, liberty, conformity and the tensions between them, depicting an authoritarian regime – the Bertram household – which paradoxically makes possible, or at least is incapable of resisting, the increasing influence of certain dangerous cosmopolitan figures. This regime, though, is ultimately reformed and replaced by a more stable environment governed by sincere moral conduct, reflecting English ideals of an order based not on coercive authority but on supposedly natural sympathies rooted in familial and social bonds. The implication is that this represents society's best hope for achieving a reconciliation between freedom and conformity, and the novel ultimately vindicates the vital importance in this regard of the conscientious Anglican clergyman. Tony Tanner is therefore on the right lines when he observes that, following Burke, 'good manners ... became England's answer to the French Revolution'[22] and are thus integral to Austen's concerns, but *Mansfield Park* is also rather more complex than this suggests, highlighting the inadequacy – indeed, the potential duplicity – of mere manners.

Fanny Price represents Austen's ideal as I have outlined it, but Austen is clear that Fanny's moral ascendancy is not the unaided consequence of some innate virtue. What makes possible her social elevation from charity case to moral exemplum and clergyman's wife is the education she receives from Edmund himself, who inculcates in her those values which should be central to Mansfield Park, and which eventually – through Fanny – are restored to their proper place. Edmund's conduct towards her from the outset is exemplary in its manly virtue, its chivalrous sensitivity to the isolation in which she finds herself. It is Edmund whose sincere concern for her enables her to overcome her discomfort in her new environment and consequently attaches her to the virtues that his own 'excellent nature'[23] manifests. Edmund, we learn, 'recommended the books which charmed her leisure hours, … encouraged her taste, and corrected her judgement; he made reading useful by talking to her of what she read, and heightened its attraction by judicious praise'. In return for such attentiveness, 'she loved him better than any body in the world except William; her heart was divided between the two'.[24] In this way Fanny is cultivated by Edmund, her 'affectionate heart, and … strong desire of doing right'[25] making her a receptive student of his conduct and teaching. Fanny's virtue, then, is secured through the inculcation of a typically English sense of judgement transmitted via affective ties; it is not the product of impersonal pedagogy or dogmatic training. Consequently, the values which Fanny internalises in this almost imperceptible way become apparent only in particular situations, hence the emphasis throughout the book on the superior quality of her motivations and actions over those of other characters.

Austen is also clear that the virtue Edmund both teaches and, at least at this point, practises, is bound up with his vocation. Unlike that of any other character, his waywardness in the course of the novel is the product of strong temptation, rather than any inadequacy in his initial disposition. In the scene in Sotherton chapel, in which Mary Crawford demonstrates her cosmopolitan disdain for the Church, Edmund defends the moral integrity of the country parish, relating it to the moral condition of the nation: "'The *manners* I speak of, might rather be called *conduct*, perhaps, the result of good principles … it will, I believe, be every where found, that as the clergy are, or are not what they ought to be, so are the rest of the nation.'"[26] If there is any irony in this speech it lies principally in its relations to Edmund's future conduct and in no way undermines the speech's validity from the ideological perspective of the novel. What this reveals is Edmund's, and Austen's, belief in the value of the 'knowable community'[27] – the integrated country parish – as opposed to the anonymous, atomistic quality of city life which erodes determinate social relations and the sense of obligation and connection which goes with them. But it is not only city life that threatens to undermine social order. Maria Bertram's comments in the approach to Sotherton, for instance, reveal both a lack of social sympathy for the estate's inhabitants – whose cottages she judges, in purely aesthetic terms, 'a disgrace' – and, symbolically, a relief that the church and its intrusive bells are situated far from the house.[28] For her the value of Sotherton lies not in the organic cohesion of the estate but in the social status it offers her (contrasting, of course, with the Romantic-conservative feelings of awe Sotherton prompts in Fanny).[29] The lack of feeling Maria possesses for Mr Rushworth, not to mention the disregard she displays for his feelings in her flirtations with Henry Crawford, therefore epitomises her more general incapacity for sympathy, leaving the reader conscious of the checks a sensitive regard for others might have placed on her conduct. The loveless marriage she contracts with Mr Rushworth carries with it a strong social symbolism.

Although Edmund's behaviour towards Fanny is initially presented as commendably sensitive, for much of the later part of the novel he is subject to critical scrutiny, not only because he fails to live up to his ideals but because of the increasing insensitivity he demonstrates towards Fanny, the consequence of pursuing his desires rather than his responsibilities. His flirtations with Mary not only lead him to neglect Fanny, but his inability to appreciate the degree of Fanny's affection for him results in him unwittingly constraining her to witness his developing and partly improper relationship with Mary. Ultimately, and much worse, it leads to his involvement in the general conspiracy to promote Henry Crawford's ambition to marry Fanny. In this respect Edmund also fails in his duty of protection towards her. On one occasion, Edmund, in observing Crawford about to make 'a very thorough attack' on Fanny, retreats into his newspaper, leaving Crawford at liberty to press his suit and Fanny 'by every thing in the power of her modest gentle nature, to repulse Mr Crawford' as best she might. She is only saved from Crawford's intrusive insistence that he will win her over by the arrival of tea, delivering her 'from a grievous imprisonment of body and mind. Mr Crawford was obliged to move. She was at liberty, she was busy, she was protected.'[30] Fanny's liberty requires that Crawford's be checked, since he acknowledges no internal principle of restraint which might have resulted from a consideration of her feelings.

At this point Henry has enlisted the support of the rest of the Bertram family, whose financial insecurities no doubt determine the value they place on connections. Fanny is therefore left to resist him in isolation. Even Sir Thomas, for whom Fanny has become a favourite, accuses her of being a peculiarly modern woman, misreading her moralistic resistance to Crawford's proposal as wilfulness and independence, the consequence of the romantic imaginings of a 'heated fancy'[31] which has undermined her proper sense of duty, prudence and obligation. These, of course, are precisely the faults of the other women of the novel, and in particular Sir Thomas's outwardly dutiful daughters. The important point is that Fanny is unable to defend herself properly in this situation, because, in order to articulate what she knows of Crawford's character, she would also have to accuse Maria and Julia of impropriety. The position Fanny finds herself in is the product of her sincere sense of obligation in a world where, as we shall see, manners have become a social pretence made to serve ulterior motives. This returns me to a consideration of the operation of power at Mansfield Park.

Sir Thomas's bullying treatment of Fanny in his interview with her reflects his overall government of the house. Significantly he believes that proper conduct can be secured through diktat, suggesting to Mrs Norris, for instance, that it is possible to impose a correct line of conduct on his daughters in relation to Fanny, one based on formal guidelines rather than felt conviction: "'I should wish to see them very good friends, and would, on no account, authorise in my girls the smallest degree of arrogance towards their relation; but still they cannot be equals.'"[32] They are, then, to tread an absurdly prescriptive path between condescension and familiarity. Moreover, Sir Thomas's authority is itself detached, forbidding and peremptory, not rooted in the 'natural' affections of his family, and consequently serving merely to alienate his children. When he leaves for Antigua, therefore, he is not missed, and merely by his absence creates the conditions under which liberty can flourish to the extent that it threatens the moral integrity of the household.

The distance Sir Thomas maintains from his daughters results in their education being entrusted to Mrs Norris, who impresses on them the importance of their position without conferring on them a corresponding understanding of their responsibilities. Consequently, for them manners become merely self-serving:

> The Miss Bertrams were now fully established among the belles of the neighbourhood; and as they joined to beauty and brilliant acquirements, a manner naturally easy, and carefully formed to general civility and obligingness, they possessed its favour as well as its admiration. Their vanity was in such good order, that they seemed to be quite free from it, and gave themselves no airs; while the praises attending such behaviour, secured, and brought round by their aunt, served to strengthen them in believing they had no faults.[33]

It is clear from this that Austen regards manners without sincerity as insufficient guarantees of social attachments.[34] Manners may simply be performed for effect, and in this passage Austen ironically undermines each of the positive terms of the Bertram sisters' behaviour – that which appears natural is actually contrived, polite self-deprecation serves a vain hubris – demonstrating the girls to be actors in a social drama of inauthentic display and empty formalism. The climax to such processes of inversion is, of course, the famous episode of the theatricals where, paradoxically, the motivations of those who take part are revealed most transparently in the act of apparently adopting masks.[35] Even Fanny is gradually forced into complicity with this erosion of sincerity as she is painfully forced by the formal observance of manners to compliment Mary Crawford and Edmund after witnessing them act, whilst privately recognising that the love scene they have been rehearsing is a means of acting out desires which otherwise respect for propriety would require them to keep within limits. (Henry Crawford – significantly the best of the actors – and Maria Bertram similarly exploit the licence the theatricals offer them.) As Roger Sales notes, 'rehearsals allow some of the characters to play unrestrained versions of themselves'.[36] Acting, then, becomes a pretence of a pretence, and the insidious danger that this presents is demonstrated by Fanny's inability finally to resist becoming involved, and by the sudden, but necessary, restoration of order through the return of the patriarch, Sir Thomas. This is the only way out of the spiralling impropriety, but it is important to acknowledge that the theatricals are the consequence of Sir Thomas's absolutist rule and the void which is left by his absence.

In terms of the specifically religious values evinced by the chapters about the theatricals, Warren Roberts has argued that Austen displays her indebtedness to the dualistic morality of Evangelicalism: the theatricals function to 'establish a moral division, with one side representing right and the other wrong', a division which persists throughout the novel and forces individuals to line up on one side or the other.[37] Actually the significance of the theatricals is more complex than this suggests, demonstrating rather Austen's acute sense of the complexity of moral judgements and, ultimately, their inseparability from concrete social relations. This, as I have been suggesting, is in keeping with mainstream Anglican thought.[38] Edmund presents his capitulation as a means of saving the house's reputation, but we are expected to recognise this as the rationalisation of a decision prompted by desire rather than true judgement. The only person to attempt steadfast resistance is Fanny, but she, as a dependant, needs the support of Edmund if she is not to seem judgemental in relation to her social superiors. When Edmund twice entreats her to read Mrs Grant's role, then – neglecting to consider the strength and the nature of Fanny's opposition – even she must yield to the centripetal pressures which the theatricals exert. In these circumstances it would be wrong for her to resist. Certainly the theatricals have lasting effects throughout the novel, but their significance resides more in the way they highlight the stealthy progress of excessive liberty than in any explicit impropriety which they entail.

Henry Crawford's acting proficiency is part of a more general inauthenticity which indicates another significant fact about him: his arrogance and exaggerated manners, Sales suggests, mark him out as a Regency dandy.[39] Certainly he is a Society figure. This is important, a further sign of his cosmopolitan contempt for ordinary English decencies, since the Frenchified elitism which characterised Society at this time,[40] and which was embodied especially in the figure of the dandy, was popularly associated with a lack of patriotism which manifested itself in the pursuit of luxury and self-indulgence. This resulted in accusations of effeminacy, a term which, at this time, did not imply any tendency towards same-sex desire.[41] Attacks on the effeminacy of Society had been levelled for some considerable time, especially by middle-class radicals, as part of a critique of a social order dominated by an idle elite whose identifications were with France rather than with their own (Protestant) people and culture.[42] It was a critique clearly indebted to the discourse of civic virtue, so important to eighteenth-century politics, and one that implied that Britain's elite was governed by particularistic interests, rather than national ones, and that their devotion to luxury was symptomatic of their corruption.[43] A flavour of this radical rhetoric of effeminacy, and also of the manliness with which it was contrasted, can be found in Hazlitt's attacks on the purposelessness and extravagance of the rich and fashionable. He describes one of Beau Brummell's witticisms, for instance, in terms of 'a slippered negligence, a cushioned effeminacy – it would take years of careless study and languid enjoyment to strike out so quaint and ingenious a conceit';[44] and fashion in general he regards as 'a sublimated essence of levity, caprice and vanity, extravagance, idleness, and selfishness. It thinks of nothing but being contaminated by vulgar use.'[45] Against such an effeminate devotion to trivia and self-indulgence Hazlitt's work also reveals an emerging discourse of corporeal manliness, stressing an ideal unity of body and will which pre-empts certain emphases of Christian manliness. This is his admiring description of Michelangelo's figures in his essay 'On Gusto': 'His limbs convey an idea of muscular strength, of moral grandeur, and even of intellectual dignity; they are firm, commanding, broad, and massy, capable of executing with ease the determined purposes of the will.'[46] Britain's patrician governors took the charges of selfishness, luxury and effeminacy so seriously that, from the late eighteenth century, they made strenuous efforts to reform their image in order to promote themselves as a truly patriotic, even heroic, class of national leaders.[47] None the less, the Regency Society of Austen's time defied such reforms and continued to celebrate their Continental attachments.

Gerald Newman claims that central to the radicals' attacks on patrician corruption and display was the promotion of an alternative set of principles which might be subsumed under the term 'sincerity', and, though he argues that this was a secular ethic, if we consider those moral attributes which characterised sincerity – innocence, honesty, originality, frankness and especially moral independence[48] – it is not difficult to discern in them a Protestant provenance. Austen was no political radical, and therefore steers clear of the discourse of effeminacy, but she was clearly concerned about the moral integrity of her class, and the implications of its moral corruption in the eyes of the people. The nature of the danger she perceived is indicated in the incident in which Fanny's father learns of the flight of Henry Crawford and Maria Bertram by reading the newspaper: a class which disregarded the scrutiny to which they were now exposed was likely to lose the respect of their disorderly inferiors (the Portsmouth incident clearly indicates whose side Austen is on, demonstrating no sentimental illusions about the virtues of the less well off, the uncultivated). On learning of Maria's conduct, Mr Price notes that "'so many fine ladies were going to the devil now-a-days that way, that there was no answering for anybody'".[49] He even prescribes a severe flogging for Maria, demonstrating not merely his vulgarity but also his willingness to contemplate violence as a corrective for his social superiors' erring ways. As Terry Lovell has commented, Austen's 'urgent imperative is for the moral self-regeneration of her class to legitimate its ascendancy',[50] and to this extent, at least, it is possible that Austen was influenced by Evangelicalism.

It is clear, then, that at the heart of the moral danger which Austen is presenting in *Mansfield Park* is the separation of manners and conviction – precisely a lack of sincerity – and the extent to which these are seen as divorced in the behaviour of each character marks the degree to which they are morally culpable in the nicely graded judgement Austen demonstrates at the end of the novel. I am not arguing that characters fail to live up to what they recognise to be the true standards of virtue (though this is nearly true of Edmund) but that the corrupt motivations of individuals are frequently furthered by a merely formal observation of proper conduct.

As we have seen, Fanny's specific education is what enables her to achieve distinction in this respect, but there is another feature of her general demeanour which establishes her as the embodiment of Burkean principles, one partly bound up with her strong sense of obligation and social inferiority. After Fanny's rejection of Henry Crawford's marriage proposal, Mary Crawford instructs her she wishes to talk to her alone. Fanny cannot resist: her 'habits of ready submission … made her almost instantly rise and lead the way out of the room. She did it with wretched feelings, *but it was inevitable*' (my emphasis)[52]. Mary Crawford's habitual conduct, on the other hand, is one of irreverence for sincere and upright social conduct and for the national institutions which might secure it. Towards the end of the novel Edmund describes to Fanny the scene in which he breaks off his engagement with Mary on the grounds that her behaviour has been improper:

> 'She was astonished, exceedingly astonished … I imagined I saw
> a mixture of many feelings – a great, though short struggle – half
> a wish of yielding to truths, half a sense of shame – but habit,

habit carried it. She would have laughed if she could. It was a sort of laugh, as she answered, "A pretty good lecture upon my word. Was it part of your last sermon?"[53]

If Mary does retain any residual virtues, she suppresses them, yielding to her habitual and fashionable cynicism. 'Habit' therefore is foregrounded as the determining force behind social conduct, of conformity or nonconformity. It determines Fanny's almost instinctive virtue, which is the basis – the condition, even – of her rise through the relatively permeable ranks of English society.

The threat to moral propriety and sincerity manifests itself ultimately in the values various characters attach to marriage, as we have already seen in relation to Maria. The opening paragraph makes clear Austen's hostility to the marriage market, to the principles of social climbing and financial acquisition which determine marital choices. The language itself – at this point remarkably prosaic and unaffecting – conveys precisely her sense of the impersonality of such contracts. Fanny's marriage, though, could not be more different from this, the exemplum of a Christian union – loving, selfless, patriarchal, a true analogue of God's relationship with his Church. At the same time as Fanny achieves the triumph of her influence and an ideal union with Edmund, though, the other characters are, for the most part (Henry Crawford being the notable exception), meted out judgements which reassure us of an ineluctable process of justice practically indistinguishable from providence, as the characters' various social sins find them out.

It is important to recognise that *Mansfield Park* is not a defence of mere formal propriety as the basis of social order. Nor does it evince narrowly doctrinal religious beliefs on Austen's part. Such purely mechanistic values, indeed, are far removed from the novel's truly organicist and definitively English ideological project, manifest principally in the representation of a complex social order whose natural and divine legitimacy is a consequence of its dependence, not on abstract principles but on a delicate and sincere interplay of sympathy and obligation.[54] Fanny, of course, balances these qualities admirably, whereas it is the largely neglected duty of the distracted men of the novel to protect her, and all she represents, from the threats of duplicity, individualism and excessive liberty represented by the Crawfords.

## Cultivating the nation

Edmund's conviction in *Mansfield Park* that the clergy determine the moral condition of the nation is one that would have been appreciated by Coleridge, who argued for a revitalised role for the Church in ways which connect him with Burke's concerns. If ultimately unsuccessful, his arguments were none the less influential – not least on the Christian socialists, amongst whom were Charles Kingsley and Thomas Hughes. The importance of Coleridge's work for my purposes is twofold: Coleridge defines the proprietors of a national culture in definitively erastian – effectively Protestant – anti-Catholic terms; but he also makes culture the basis of an assimilative national principle. *On the Constitution of the Church and State* was first published in the wake of the Catholic Emancipation of 1829, though Coleridge began work on it some years before this. The Emancipation was made virtually inevitable as a consequence of the Union with Ireland, even if the measure was resisted and delayed. Though Ireland is not given lengthy consideration in *Church and State*, the extent to which Catholic Ireland posed anxieties for Coleridge is indicated by his view that Catholic affiliation represented an allegiance to an alien power, and that the only absolute disqualifications from membership of his proposed national clerisy should be the acknowledgement of a foreign principal of authority, and the vow of celibacy made on the basis of this loyalty.[55] In relation to Ireland, of course, this implied a defence of the continued establishment of the Church of Ireland and even suggests that Irish Catholics were unassimilable as citizens of the British polity, given the civic role Coleridge allotted to the clerisy.

Coleridge defines the Church as the third estate: ideally it should be the stabilising force in the dialectic of national development, the means of uniting the opposing (though, in this account, complementary) forces of land and continuity, on the one hand, and commercial progress and individual freedom, on the other. To adapt a metaphor from Gramsci, it was to be the suturing agent[56] in the development of a specifically national hegemony which would unite these classes by forging a common character. The national clerisy's role, according to Coleridge, should be a broadly educational one, and the means of achieving national unity would be specifically through the 'cultivation' of the population, a term which, as in Burke, refers to the inculcation of those standards of civility which were the prerequisite of citizenship. The role of the clerisy should be to ensure 'the harmonious devel-

opment of those qualities and faculties that characterise our humanity. We must be men in order to be citizens.'[57] This entailed: securing
the patriotic affections of the people through the dissemination of a
culture which bound past, present and future (a clearly organic principle); teaching a knowledge of rights and duties (the inculcation of a
sense of legality being a fundamental element of the clerisy's work);
and maintaining a civilisation at least on a par with those of other
nations.[58] The nationalist impulse behind Coleridge's project is made
clear in his description of the 'final cause' of the clerisy as being

> to form and train up the people of this country to obedient, free,
> useful, organizable subjects, citizens, and patriots, living to the
> benefit of the state, and prepared to die for its defence. The
> proper *object* and end of the National Church is civilisation with
> freedom; and the duty of its ministers, could they be contem-
> plated merely and exclusively as officiaries of the *National*
> Church, would be fulfilled in the communication of that degree
> and kind of knowledge to all, the possession of which is neces-
> sary for all in order to their CIVILITY. By civility I mean all the
> qualities essential to a citizen, and devoid of which no people or
> class of the people can be calculated on by the rulers and lead-
> ers of the state for the conservation or promotion of its essential
> interests.[59]

Coleridge not only perceives no conflict here between social control
and individual freedom, he actually recognises in the imperative of
state continuity the very condition of citizens' freedom. Through its
cultivating function, therefore, the clerisy would be the means of
securing individual subjection to a state whose organic development
was proof of a divine sanction.

In an unpublished fragment written several years after the essay
on *Church and State,* Coleridge clarified his understanding of the term
'civility', arguing that it implied an understanding of the individual's
duties to himself, his neighbours and society as well as an appreciation of 'the several Relations, social or natural, of Age, Sex, Rank,
Office, considered as so many Ordinances of the divine Providence'.
Finally, civility entailed

> a certain Discipline of the Will, a certain *Habit* of Thought, Feel-
> ing and outward Demeanour in accordance with this faith and
> knowledge. Now all these I – would comprize under the term,
> Civility, (as being the ground and condition) of each and every
> Native's comptence [*sic*] to discharge the duties, and conse-

quently of his claim to exercise the rights, of a Citizen and Subject.[60]

This is a clearly Burkean formulation in its emphasis on a certain
demeanour based on a sense of obligation, and on the importance of
recognising providentially determined social bonds. But more explicit
here than in Burke is the alignment of the individual will with social
and national demands. This emphasis on the will as the means by
which the (implicitly male) individual should 'freely' reconcile his
conduct with the divinely appointed requirements of society and
nation reflects an increasingly important strand in nineteenth-century
thinking which was to become a crucial element in the development
of Christian manliness.

In his arguments about cultivation and the harmonious development of the people in the interests of a stable polity, Coleridge prescribed for the Church an assimilative national role which for many
continued to be its main ideal function throughout the nineteenth
century, reconciling individuals to their position within a state which
represented the best hope they could have for freedom. Whereas
Coleridge saw the need to reconcile bourgeois and aristocratic classes,
later figures in this tradition also recognised a need to generate a
national consciousness amongst the working class and other potentially disruptive forces. Matthew Arnold was one of these, valuing an
ostensibly secular culture for its capacity to provide some social coherence in the face of class dialectics by counteracting the examples set
by the two dominant classes – the aristocratic, rakish Barbarians and
the insular and narrow-minded Philistines – but functioning also to
tame an assertive working class, the Populace. Arnold, whilst maintaining the Burkean hostility to systems, none the less also held to a
sacralised conception of the state. His career in the promotion of culture was, therefore, clearly anticipated by the tradition I have been
describing here, which is why it is possible to find many anticipations
of Arnold's arguments in writers who preceded him.[61]

Coleridge, then, developed the influential view that a national
culture should be actively disseminated in order to enhance social
cohesion. As the dust settled on the revolutions of the first half of the
nineteenth century, though, others expressed greater confidence in
the prospects for a stable polity, convinced that what protected England from the kinds of upheavals experienced elsewhere in Europe
was the racially determined disposition of its people. As racial expla-

nations of national characters became more entrenched in the first half of the nineteenth century, one of the dominant traits predicated of the English, the Anglo-Saxons, was precisely their disposition to observe the law. John Kemble's profoundly influential book, *The Saxons in England*,[62] first published in 1849, claimed that at a time when elsewhere 'thrones totter, and the deep foundations of society are convulsed' the British queen 'sits safely upon her throne, and fearless in the holy circle of her domestic happiness, secure in the affections of a people whose institutions have given to them all the blessings of an equal law'. Such security is the legacy of the Saxons, on whose principles current institutions of state rest and which have succeeded in 'uniting the completest obedience to the law with the greatest amount of individual freedom'.[63] What was so distinctive in the culture of these Germanic peoples was the original basis of their social organisation, the Mark (Gâ or Shire), and it is to this widely-recognised principle that Anglo-Saxons owe their commitment to freedom. The Mark combines several related meanings which together define 'a voluntary association of free men, who laid down for themselves, and strictly maintained, a system of cultivation by which the produce of the land on which they settled might be fairly and equally secured for their service and support; and from participation in which they jealously excluded all who were not born, or adopted, into the association'.[64] One meaning of the Mark refers precisely to this boundary which separates the community from other tribes – initially, an area of forest or waste ground considered sacrosanct. Kemble suggests that, over time, increases in population eroded the significance of the Mark in this latter sense, but that in a Christian society, where such superstitions were in any case redundant, the same guarantees were provided instead by the public law of the state.

This convergence of Anglo-Saxon sensibilities with an established religion which supports lawful process is also argued in Robert Knox's polemic *The Races of Men* (1850). Knox, like Kemble, demonstrates an acute consciousness of recent European events, which he interprets as inevitable, racially determined wars. He also supports the theory of the Mark as the original form of Saxon society, symptom of a specifically racial propensity for independence and freedom. Protestantism is naturally the religion which complements, or arises out of, this propensity. This might be expected to present a problem for Knox, since, of course, Welsh and Caledonian Celts are closely associated with Protestantism in some of its more austere forms. Instead he claims that these people are only 'seeming Protestant[s]',[65] all Celts being really Catholic 'even when not Roman', since they refuse to accept religion established by law.[66] What defines the Anglo-Saxon is the integration of religion with the rest of the polity, thereby reconciling freedom and duty. These claims were not idiosyncratic. In 1889 Isaac Taylor – a more moderate figure than Knox – also analysed the territorial habitations of Celts and Teutons: 'The Welsh and Cornishmen, who became Protestants by political accident, have transformed Protestantism into an emotional religion, which has affinities with the emotional faith of Ireland and Italy', whereas the English are 'neither Catholic nor Protestant, but Anglican'.[67]

### Destabilising the body politic

There is a final ideological trajectory emerging out of Burke's writings which I want to trace here. Burke suggested that Catholicism and republicanism were comparable, on the grounds of their devotion to dogmas and theories which overruled or ignored 'natural' moral ties. There was another, related way in which the innovations of the revolutionary French regime were stigmatised by him. According to the Burkean valorisation of the empirical over the theoretical, the 'real' over the invented, any inversion of these terms amounted to a form of madness, a consequence of the febrile imaginative faculty dominating the rational apprehension of fact and necessity. English history, for Burke, had been guided by an acceptance of real conditions, whereas France, by comparison, was now governed by abstractions and unprecedented innovations which were disdainful of established reality and traditional attachments, lending the new order the 'phantasmal' quality which Seamus Deane has suggested it acquires throughout Burke's account.[68] The repeated references to these abstractions, as well as to the inventions and speculations of the *philosophes* and revolutionaries, are clearly calculated to denigrate their prioritisation of the cerebral over the concrete. Consequently, madness and unreality go together in Burke's depiction of the Revolution, and this alignment is even more pronounced in Carlyle's later account. However, in turning to Carlyle a distinction clearly needs to be drawn with Burke, since, in his mature life, Carlyle was not a member of any Church and was no great defender of the institutions of the Establishment, even if he criticised those who attempted to change them. How, then, to account for certain continuities between his arguments and Burke's, and for his considerable status amongst a range of conservative and Anglican figures, including Kingsley and the Christian socialists? The answer to this resides largely in the fact that once he had liberated himself from the letter, if not the spirit, of his parents' Calvinism,[69] Carlyle too developed an antagonism to those 'systems' by which various groups of his time proposed to reconstruct the future: Fred Kaplan records Carlyle's objections to '"Puseyisms, Ritualisms, Metaphysical controversies and cobwebberies ... Universal Suffrages ... Nigger Emancipations, Sluggard-and-Scoundrel Protection Societies," [which] had no attraction for him'.[70] These forces – reactionary and progressive alike – were essentially similar in Carlyle's view: 'machinery', as he describes them in his influential essay 'Signs of the Times',[71] and therefore inimical to both individual spiritual growth and the natural ordering of society. Hence Carlyle rejected those attempts at the systematic, rather than moral, reformation of society, including those new principles – utilitarian and *laissez faire* – which were increasingly influential on government policies from the 1830s on.

What were the positive features of Carlyle's message? There is a strong conviction in his work that history is governed by divine laws as manifest in nature, and that any social order which does not acknowledge those laws is consequently doomed to apocalyptic change by way of readjustment. To a large extent – and this is what distinguishes him from Enlightenment perspectives – these laws are inscrutable, not susceptible to merely rational apprehension or delineation. The result is that they prescribe little more than a mixture of honest work and resignation – 'Our grand business undoubtedly is, not to see what lies dimly at a distance, but to do what lies clearly at hand'[72] – with the proviso that, in a just world, such honest work should receive its natural reward.

Carlyle's account of the French Revolution is distinct from Burke's, mainly because he is far more critical of the *ancien régime*, indicting its corruption as the cause of the Revolution. Carlyle's rhetoric and the sheer vastness of his project have provoked differing, even opposing accounts of his political perspective on its events,[73] but John Stuart Mill's appraisal still seems to me a fair summary: 'Mr Carlyle's view of the Revolution is briefly this: That it was the breaking down of a great Imposture: which had not always been an Imposture, but had been becoming one for several centuries.' Yet, Carlyle also subscribed to a Burkean conservatism in his conviction that the Revolution, though it destroyed what was bad, did so in favour of something as yet undetermined, and the result – 'with all man's boundless desires let loose in indefinite expectation, and the influences of habit and imagination which keep mankind patient under the denial of what they crave for, annihilated for the time' – was a chaos which could be suppressed only by a dictatorial regime.[74] This is consistent with Carlyle's own definition of revolution as it manifested itself in the French context: 'the open violent Rebellion, and Victory, of disimprisoned Anarchy against corrupt worn-out Authority: how Anarchy breaks prison; bursts up from the infinite Deep, and rages uncontrollable, immeasurable, enveloping a world; in phasis after phasis of fever-frenzy'.[75] The Revolution here takes on an inevitable, destructive character, one actually brought about by divine forces, since the law which determined the Revolution was 'that Man and his Life rest no more on hollowness and a Lie but on solidity and some kind of Truth. Welcome the beggarliest truth, so it *be* one, in exchange for the royallest sham!'[76] Consequently Carlyle occasionally appears to be sympathetic to the destructive forces of *sansculottism* (if only as 'the beggarliest truth'), but these sympathies emphatically do not extend to the theorists of the Rights of Man: the National Assembly, for instance, 'in so far as it sits making the Constitution … is a fatuity and chimera mainly'.[77] One falsehood, or 'imposture', to use Mill's revealing term, spawns another, and the greatest catastrophe to events in Carlyle's narrative is the death of the reasonable Mirabeau who might have rescued the situation had he lived. He, at least, was 'a Reality and no Simulacrum; a living Son of Nature our general Mother; not a hollow Artifice, and mechanism of Conventionalities, son of nothing, *brother* of nothing'.[78]

Once again this returns us to questions of gender. If individual control by external forces – whether Catholic or republican – could be stigmatised as unmanly because inimical to autonomy, madness was also conventionally associated with femininity. Hysteria was the condition which established this association, since it was considered bound up with the specificities of the female anatomy. It was not, though – even in the medical literature – associated solely with women. Peter Logan has described how, in the late eighteenth century, 'the body became redefined in terms of its nervous system rather than Galenic humours', a process which claimed for women's bodies a greater, though not exclusive, susceptibility to nervous disorders.[79] As with medical discourse, so with general perceptions: nervousness and hysteria were relatively disembodied conditions, bound up with and connoting femininity, but not limited to women. Their manifestation in males consequently denoted an unmanly lack of self-possession.

Those accounts of the French Revolution which characterised it as governed by insanity therefore tended to latch on to the prominent role played by women as almost emblematic of the uprising of unreason. The march to Versailles, led by women, figures prominently in both Burke and Carlyle.[80] Indeed this latter incident in Carlyle's narrative is sparked off by an event which is almost microcosmic of his interpretation of the Revolution itself:

> A thought, or dim raw-material of a thought, was fermenting all night, universally in the female head, and might explode. In squalid garret, on Monday morning Maternity awakes, to hear children weeping for bread. Maternity must forth to the streets, to the herb-markets and Bakers'-queues; meets there with hunger-stricken Maternity, sympathetic, exasperative. O we unhappy women! But instead of Bakers-queues, why not to Aristocrats palaces, the root of the matter? *Allons!* Let us assemble. To the Hotel-de-Ville; to Versailles; to the Lanterne![81]

The march to Versailles is therefore determined by the omnipotence of insubstantial thought, a consequence of the neglect of the body in both mother and child: hysteria results from genuine material oppression and an imbalance of mental and physical powers, finding its expression in revolt. It is a description which is consistent with influential medical models of the nervous temperament as outlined by Bruce Haley in his account of eighteenth- and nineteenth-century 'psychophysiology', a reductively materialist form of psychology. According to such models the nervous temperament was precisely one in which the mental and nervous systems had begun to dominate the rest of the body, and this, again, was a view which came to be widely disseminated and accepted in the nineteenth-century. One mid-nineteenth-century physician claimed that 'The nervous temperament is characterised by a highly developed nervous system; there is extreme sensitiveness to all impressions; the passions when evolved are impetuous, and the countenance animated and expressive; in such persons all is excitement and mobility.'[82] This extreme sensibility was far removed from the tradition of the calm, deliberative, yet sensitive gentleman-statesman idealised and promoted by Edmund Burke.

The stigma attached to energy, passion and excitement was therefore bound up with contemporary political sensibilities. Its reactionary legacy can be discerned in the typical Victorian depiction of Romanticism, and, in particular, its representation of the artist most passionately committed to libertarian ideals. For many post-Romantic writers Shelley came to represent the archetypal nervous temperament: afflicted by an unregulated and excessive sensitivity he was over-imaginative, and his poetry was consequently impenetrable by those who did not share his condition. John Stuart Mill's early essay on Tennyson, for instance, claims that 'nervous susceptibility seems to be the distinctive character of the poetic temperament', the basis of the vividness of the poet's associative powers. In this conservative, Wordsworthian account of the creative process, Mill argues that such a temperament should be controlled by culturally acquired powers of reflection. Shelley, lacking this moderating faculty, produced instead

> vivid representations of states of passive and dreamy emotion, fitted to give extreme pleasure to persons of similar organisation to the poet, but not likely to be sympathised in, because not understood, by any other person; and scarcely conducing at all to the noblest end of poetry as an intellectual pursuit, that of acting upon the desires and characters of mankind through their emotions, to raise them towards the perfection of their nature.

The fusion of nervous temperament and 'intellectual culture' in Tennyson, on the other hand, was the basis of his strength as a poet.[83] Charles Kingsley also discovered in Shelley's work evidence of a lack of control, but connected this more explicitly with his radicalism: Shelley the vegetarian is contrasted unfavourably with the manly, intelligible (and meat-eating) Byron who adhered to classical forms in his verse. In his sensitivity Shelley 'was tender and pitiful as a woman; and yet, when angry, shrieking and railing and hysterical as a woman'. This effeminacy was dictated by his nervous condition, his lack of control and inability to express himself with discipline, hence the oscillation in his writings between an excessive sentimentality and hysteria. He was also, like a child, 'inarticulate, peevish, irrational', and this essentially aesthetic disorder of both poetry and body is therefore aligned with, even a consequence of, his political convictions. Significantly Kingsley also goes on to make a connection with religion: 'if once his intense self-opinion had deserted him, [he] would probably have ended up in Rome as an Oratorian or a Passionist'. The obverse of radical hysteria, then, is a submissive obedience. Byron, despite his sins, aspired to occupy the English middle ground between enthusiasm and servility, understanding the importance of 'depending … upon a man's self, a man's own will, and that will exerted to do a will exterior to itself, to know and obey a law'.[84]

In the later nineteenth century this reactionary legacy continued, with secular influences tending to confirm Shelley's derangement. Writing in 1877, the Dublin critic Edward Dowden contrasted Shelley with both Byron – who, again, 'looked at times longingly towards the *via media* of moderated and justified desires, unambitious reason, and tranquil benevolence'[85] – and Tennyson. Arguing that the 'idea of human progress – itself subordinate to the conception of evolution' - was awakened in popular consciousness by the French Revolution, he notes that 'In English poetry [the idea of progress] did not manifest itself powerfully until it became the inspiration for the writings of Shelley'. However, 'the idea of progress with Shelley was the revolutionary, not the scientific idea', which latter principle only manifested itself in Tennyson, whose 'poetry exhibits a well-balanced moral nature, strong human affections, and, added to these, such imaginative sympathy as a poet who is not himself capable of scientific thought may have with science, a delight in all that is nobly ordered, and a profound reverence for law'.[86] Evolutionary logic, then, the ground of the scientific view of progress, sanctioned that political gradualism which had previously been predicated on religio-political principles, and provided a metaphysical basis for national law (the equivalent, apparently, of scientific laws). This potent ideological alignment between poeticism, femininity, nervous susceptibility, a deluded inability to grasp reality and a consequent political radicalism was the clear product of English counter-revolutionary culture, and true manliness became defined in opposition to such qualities.

### Anglicanism, nation and narration in Charlotte Brontë

If Fanny's and Edmund's marriage in *Mansfield Park* symbolises Austen's hope for a moral order centred on the Anglican Church, the marriage resolution of another, later novel also demonstrates the influence of the national religion on its moral argument and formal organisation. When Jane Eyre returns to the maimed Rochester in the place of a servant, carrying him a glass of water, she thereby declares, both by her actions as well as in her speech, her willing, because loving, subjection to him. The sacrifice she makes in agreeing to serve him is not the dispassionate service demanded by the various Evangelicals of the novel, but one genuinely mediated by love: "'To be privileged to put my arms around what I value – to press my lips to what I love – to repose on what I trust: is that to make a sacrifice? If so, then certainly I delight in sacrifice.'"[87] This declaration also represents the reconciliation of the compulsive oscillation between oppressive isolation and the desire for an excessive freedom which is Jane's experience of life up to the final chapters. Indeed, in this respect Jane finally achieves an ideal *via media* between these two alternatives, though, in terms of the book's broader ideological project, this represents more than simply a personal achievement. In *Jane Eyre*, then, Anglicanism is the key ideological force behind the pragmatic resolution of the triadic structure between protagonist, Romantic-radical and autocratic conservative which Terry Eagleton has suggested is paradigmatic of Charlotte Brontë's writing.[88]

The narrative is, as Eagleton implies, schematic, tracing Jane's progression from the repressive atmospheres of Gateshead and Lowood, through her initial relationship with the libertine Rochester and the rejection of the stern duty offered by St John Rivers's marriage proposal, before returning her to the conveniently maimed and tamed Rochester. Throughout this narrative of embattled virtue and sincerity there is the constant influence of Jane's inner, and explicitly Christian, voice. In her initial devotion to Rochester he threatens to come between her and her God (his language is persistently pagan and his desire for personal freedom threatens to subordinate her to a position of heathen slavery), and when Rochester is at his most threatening once their marriage has to be abandoned Jane instinctively calls on God,[89] from which point she finds the strength to resist her passions. Later, on the verge of accepting St John Rivers's offer of marriage, she entreats heaven to "'shew me the path'", and hears the voice of the now unthreatening Rochester calling to her. For this, again, she inevitably thanks God.[90]

But what are the threats which endanger Jane? Rochester is sullied by his contact with the foreign, and his libertinism derives from his French experiences: it was in France that he fathered his illegitimate child, Adèle, who retains her French coquetry up until, after the marriage of Jane and Rochester, 'a sound English education corrected in large measure her French defects'.[91] At the same time, though he is not actually a Catholic, Rochester has affinities with Catholicism – he regards his care of Adèle as justifying his licence: "'I keep it [i.e. Adèle

– he is comparing her to a 'floweret'] and rear it on the Roman Catholic principle of expiating numerous sins, great or small, by one good work'",[92] thus obviating any need to act on an internal principle of goodness. But his licence is underwritten by other French associations too. In explaining what drove him to France after transporting his Creole wife Bertha to confinement in England, he claims inspiration from a European wind: "'The sweet wind from Europe was still whispering in the refreshed leaves, and the Atlantic was thundering in glorious liberty; my heart, dried up and scorched for a long time, swelled to the tone, and filled with living blood – my being longed for renewal – and felt regeneration possible'".[93] The associations of France are therefore also with republicanism, with – to English sensibilities – an impulse to overturn the moral order and unleash desires which should properly be restrained by civil conduct: Brontë, in other words, transforms a Shelleyan political yearning into a Rochesterian personal and sinful sexual rapacity. Rochester represents a contradictory, yet typically English, composite of malevolent characteristics: an aristocratic libertine, he is none the less also associated with both republicanism and Catholicism, combining in one person extremes which might otherwise strike us as improbable.

If it is appropriate to regard Rochester as a masculine figure, rather than as tainted with a revolutionary hysteria, this masculinity clearly lies precisely in his disregard for conventional restraints on conduct. The project of the novel is to domesticate him, to restore his sense of moral relations and local attachments. We might call this Rochester's coming home. Maiming and blinding is a necessary, or at least appropriate, part of this process, since it is precisely his senses that have led him astray. His own moral will is unequal to plucking out his own eye, though, and therefore needs to be supplemented by what he comes to acknowledge as the workings of providence in the form of the fire which consumes both Bertha (madness) as well as the Gothic site of disorder.[94] Rochester is consequently purged of his raw, unbridled masculinity and is eventually reconciled to the real and the normal.

As I have already implied, Jane's fate is similarly allegorical, and the relationship of her condition to wider questions about the social meaning of freedom is made explicit in that passage which has become a ubiquitous focus for critical discussion, in which she asserts that 'women feel just as men feel; they need an exercise for their efforts as much as their brothers do; they suffer from too rigid a restraint, too absolute a stagnation, precisely as men would suffer'.[95] Sally Shuttleworth points out that this 'is not merely an isolated allusion, but rather raises to the level of explicit statement the implied parallels which run through the text'.[96] I agree, though it seems to me that this process of allusion does not dissolve the private/public, female/male division; rather, the private sphere is maintained as the analogue of the public, effectively ensuring that Jane's marriage resonates with a typically Anglican desire for a broader social unity based on Christian love.

Brontë's attitudes towards social unrest were mixed, but they demonstrate precisely the conviction which I have suggested is embodied in Jane's and Rochester's union. Her fears that Celtic revolutionary forces might spill over into England are well known, and they famously invoke bodily imagery of nervous contortions. However, Brontë also discriminated between European revolutions. Writing to Margaret Wooler, she expressed the view that

> insurrections and battles are the acute diseases of nations, and that their tendency is to exhaust by their violence the vital energies of the countries where they occur. That England may be spared the spasms, cramps and frenzy-fits now contorting the Continent and threatening Ireland, I earnestly pray
>
> With the French and Irish, I have no sympathy. With the Germans and Italians I think the case is different: as different as the love of Freedom is from the lust for License [*sic*].[97]

A combination of attitudes seem to be expressed here: Teutonic Germans and anti-clerical Italians are exonerated of the hysteria of those Celtic, and mostly Catholic, nations closest to England who had a record of revolutionary hostility towards it. This may also explain Brontë's convictions about the way in which indigenous revolutionaries should be handled: they were to be treated with firmness but also with sympathy, in spite of their rebellion against a social order which was believed to enshrine true freedom. In the days following the repression of the Chartists – and it is revealing that she acknowledges the repression that was involved – she wrote:

> their grievances should not be neglected, nor the existence of their sufferings ignored. It would now be the right time, when an ill-advised movement has been judiciously repressed, to examine carefully their causes of complaint, and make such concessions as justice and humanity dictate. If Government would act so,

how much good might be done by the removal of ill-feeling and the substitution of mutual kindliness in its place![98]

There are affinities here with Kingsley's response to Chartism in its conviction that Chartism addressed genuine grievances in a misguided way. (Indeed, Brontë did read and admire *Alton Locke*, though she thought his anti-Catholic poem *The Saint's Tragedy*, even better).[99] Her reformist response here, then, emphasises her commitment to an assimilative strategy based on humane sympathy.

Jane's *via media* is therefore the means by which she escapes 'cramps and frenzy-fits', the madness to which, as a woman, she is particularly prone. In an exemplary reading of the book Helen Small has argued that Brontë repudiates the Romantic past – symbolised, for Small, principally by Bertha's moral insanity – in favour of a sober Victorian realism, achieved through Jane's exercise of a controlling will guided by God.[100] Hence Bertha Mason, far from being the figure who covertly expresses Jane's anger,[101] acts as a warning: she is the embodiment of an excessive feminine licence which must be purged from the text in order to achieve the novel's reassuring closure.[102] So, when, in her solitary state musing on rebellion, Jane declares that she 'not unfrequently heard Grace Poole's [i.e. Bertha Mason's] laugh: the same peal, the same slow ha! ha! which, when first heard, had thrilled me',[103] this intrusive laugh is intended to alert us to the danger to which Jane has been exposed. The fact that she initially thrills to it merely highlights her impressionistic vulnerability within the Gothic environment of Thornfield Hall, an environment which clearly preys on her feminine predisposition to nervous excitement. Such a state encourages superstitious beliefs which are at odds with her rational Protestantism, so that, in the course of the novel, all of the Gothic trappings – the Gytrash, Bertha Mason, the insights of the 'gypsy', for example – have to be explained away, leaving only legitimate, because Christian, interventions from beyond the quotidian world.

The novel's final domestic setting, then, is integral to a more generally reasonable relationship between Jane and her environment, one purged of the sinister or the supernatural; and it is in this context that Jane sets about the re-education of Rochester, revealing to him a world which is beneficent and congenial (the Book of Nature?): 'He saw nature – he saw books through me; and never did I weary of gazing for his behalf, and of putting into words the effect of field, tree, town, river, cloud, sunbeam – of the landscape before us; of the weather round us – and impressing on his ear what light could no longer stamp on his eye.'[104] This reconciliation with the natural world is important to the general process of suppressing the licentious, superstitious and insane world of the Romantic past as represented by Thornfield (whose very name conflates malign nature with phallic sexual threat). Moreover, the venerable, yet modest and discrete, even enclosed, world of Ferndean not only acts symbolically to repudiate a Gothic-Romantic past superseded by Victorian stability; it also completes the exclusion of the foreign which is bound up with that past. The only acknowledgement of a world beyond English shores lies in the reference to St John Rivers's mission to India, but this, as Small notes, involves exporting Christian virtue,[105] albeit of an Evangelical kind which, we might speculate, was considered by Brontë more fitting for 'uncivilised' colonial contexts.

Of course, of all Charlotte Brontë's novels, *Villette* is the most clearly concerned with the antagonisms between English Protestantism and European Catholicism.[106] I have focused on *Jane Eyre* because this text more clearly demonstrates the alignment between the Romantic, the Catholic and the republican, and because the main protagonist of the novel achieves a satisfactory balance between the demands of duty and the passionate desire for freedom, a balance denied to Lucy Snowe whose repressive conscientiousness prevents her from ever attaining fulfilment, and who is consequently more of a problematic narrator. None the less, if further proof were needed of the common linkage of republicanism and Catholicism we need only look at Mme Beck, whose school regime combines a Napoleonic tyranny with a devout Catholicism (though admittedly this perception is mediated by the less than reliable eyes of Lucy Snowe). Mme Beck's 'system' combines a rigorous educational curriculum with management by surveillance, but this is indicative of a more deep-seated philosophy:

> interest was the master-key of madame's nature – the main-spring of her motives – the alpha and omega of her life. I have seen *feelings* appealed to, and I have smiled in half-pity, half-scorn at the appellants ... to touch her heart was the surest way to rouse her antipathy, and to make of her a secret foe ... Never was the distinction between charity and mercy better exemplified than in her. While devoid of sympathy, she had a sufficiency of rational benevolence: she would give in the readiest manner to people she had never seen – rather, however, to classes than

to individuals. 'Pour les pauvres,' she opened her purse freely – against *the poor man*, as a rule, she kept it closed. In philanthropic schemes, for the benefit of society at large, she took a cheerful part; no private sorrow touched her: no force or mass of suffering concentrated in one heart had power to pierce hers. Not the agony in Gethsemane, not the death on Calvary, could have wrung from her eyes one tear.[107]

It is interesting that Mme Beck is here regarded as rational – apparently the opposite of Roman Catholic superstition – but the reason stigmatised here is that of French republicanism rather than the common sense of Protestantism, and it is in opposition to feeling, an opposition which culminates in the validation of sympathy as the truly Christian principle of social relations. Rational, merely human systems always mediate Mme Beck's relations with others. We should not be surprised that in the next paragraph we find that 'madame was a very great and capable woman. That school offered for her powers too limited a sphere; she ought to have swayed a nation: she should have been the leader of a turbulent legislative assembly.'

Lucy Snowe's attitudes in *Villette* are typical of certain English Protestant convictions about the poor, convictions which stressed the importance of voluntarism in relation to relief, since state intervention reduced the potential for sincerity on the part of donors. Boyd Hilton argues that, amongst Evangelicals, such attitudes tended to underwrite *laissez faire* convictions.[108] However, if one strand of the Protestant antipathy to systems operated to erode social provision for the poor, another worked in the opposite direction. Many of those who were critical of the increasingly capitalist state of the 1830s and 1840s attacked it precisely on the grounds that it was driven by theories. Utilitarianism and political economy were regarded as innovative systems which threatened to undermine those natural sympathies between classes which cemented the established order and were essential to its stability. It is this tradition which informed the Christian socialism of figures such as Charles Kingsley.

# 2

## An anatomy of England: *Alton Locke*, Christian manliness and the games ethic

a man cannot be idle, for the need of his body drives him and he is compelled to do many good works to reduce it to subjection.

Martin Luther[1]

THE Evangelical asceticism of St John Rivers in *Jane Eyre* is symbolised at one point by reference to his body, to the physical strength by which he manages to repress his natural desires for Miss Oliver: 'His chest heaved once, as if his large heart, weary of despotic constriction, had expanded, despite the will, and made a vigorous bound for the attainment of liberty. But he curbed it, I think, as a resolute rider would curb a rearing steed. He responded neither by word nor movement to the gentle advances made him.'[2] Strength here equates with self-denial, the will to resist not simply temptation but physical urges in general as the inevitably fallen promptings of the material world. Christian manliness was, if not quite the antithesis of this, in part at least a reaction against such puritanical denial of created nature, whilst it also aimed at the suppression of the kind of licentiousness represented in Brontë's novel by the figure of Rochester. In terms of its religious content it was an attempt to resolve the tensions between corporeal existence and spiritual aspiration,[3] and, in this respect, its relationship to Protestant tradition is suggested in the quotation from Luther above. But its attempts to vindicate the corporeal body have also been connected with the growing seriousness in nineteenth-century attitudes towards physical health, stemming in large part from the rise of the biological sciences which promised to discover the laws of health, at the same time as the growth in towns and cities precipitated increased social anxiety about epidemic diseases (one of Charles Kingsley's abiding concerns). Bruce

Haley suggests that health was of greater concern to Victorians than the familiar topics of religion, politics, improvement or Darwinism,[4] and, whilst this represents an artificial separation of these issues, the statement is none the less indicative of the importance which was attached to physical fitness. Indeed, such was the perceived social significance of the body's well-being that in 1861 it seemed plausible to Herbert Spencer to argue that those who disregarded the laws of physical health were 'more or less flagitious' and that 'all breaches of the laws of health are *physical sins*.'[5] Christian manliness drew on and reinforced such imperatives, but the very name of the phenomenon serves to emphasise that physical health was not perceived in clinical isolation from religious, ethical and political concerns.

These, then, are some of the contexts in which Christian manliness has been discussed. My purpose here is to demonstrate its indebtedness to those features of English counter-revolutionary culture which I have already discussed, emerging, as it did, out of the Christian socialism of both Kingsley and Thomas Hughes. Christian socialism was a response to Chartism – the working-class campaign for political reform, including universal manhood suffrage – and represented an attempt to 'Christianise socialism'. In this respect it was heavily influenced by Carlyle's *Chartism* pamphlet (as well as by his other writings). In *Chartism* Carlyle attacks contemporary government policies on the same terms as he had condemned the French Revolutionary regime: it is a broadside against political economy as a theoretical infringement on the dominion of natural and divine laws, arguing that Chartism's origins lay in the renunciation of paternal responsibility by Britain's doctrinaire *laissez faire* rulers, resulting in a sense of injustice – of abandonment to economic chance – provoked in the governed: 'A deeper law than any parchment-law whatsoever, a law written direct by the hand of God in the inmost being of man, incessantly protests against [injustice]. What is injustice? Another name for disorder, for unveracity, unreality; a thing which veracious created Nature, even because it is not Chaos and a waste-whirling baseless Phantasm, rejects and disowns.'[6] Here the innate hatred of injustice is bound up with the natural abhorrence of disorder, and protestations against injustice are the inevitable response to perversions of the organic process. Similarly, 'socialism' to the Christian socialists was a term used to indicate their commitment to society – that is, to order and stability – rather than to anything approaching egalitarianism. Ideologically they were paternalists, the clerical counterpart of what Marx and Engels described as 'feudal socialism',[7] and their opposition to bourgeois economics continued the tradition of hostility to systemic innovation. The leading intellectual of the group, Frederick Maurice, regarded 'systems' as opposed to 'life, freedom, variety';[8] they were unEnglish and unnatural.[9] Kingsley followed Maurice in this, but he also made explicit the connection between the oppressive systems of Catholicism and those inaugurated by the French Revolution. Indeed, one provoked the other: the prime responsibility for the Revolution, Kingsley told one potential convert to Catholicism, fell on the Jesuits who actually

> caused the Revolution. Madam, the horrors of 1793 were the natural fruit of the teaching of the very men who not only would have died sooner than bring about these horrors, but died of them, alas! by them. And how was this? By trying to set up a system of society and morals of their own, they uprooted in the French every element of faith in, and reverence for, the daily duties and relations of human life, without knowing it – without meaning it. May God keep you from the same snare, of fancying, as all 'Orders,' Societies and Sects do, that they invent a better system of society than the old one, wherein God created man in His own image, viz., of father and son, husband and wife, brother and sister, master and servant, king and subject.[10]

In destroying natural social and moral relations, and thereby uprooting organic society, the Jesuits paved the way for the Revolution. Furthermore Kingsley here expresses a typical hostility to sectional – as opposed to national – interests, a hostility which is also crucial to his response to Chartism as it finds expression in *Alton Locke*. I want to consider this novel now, not for any influence the novel might have exerted at the time – though it certainly made its mark – but because it reveals how Christian manliness emerged from these concerns.

### *Alton Locke*: the body in English history

*Alton Locke* is an important text in the representation of the demise of Chartism as resulting from the movement's own ineptitude, petering out in the April rain never to be revived. John Saville comprehensively revises this long-standing view and meticulously details the repressive measures and ideological panic with which the state responded to the Chartist threat.[11] By 1848 the state had massively expanded its repressive apparatus – police constables, militia and volunteer groups (state forces available for action in London at the 10 April demonstration were nearly 100,000 strong);[12] also, by this time, it had initiated a range of legislation to deal with political threat – frequently in response to insurrectionary possibilities in Ireland – including, most significantly, the Crown and Security Act, which created a new offence of treasonable speaking. With the issue of a warrant for the arrest of Ernest Jones on 2 June the intimidatory political trials of the leaders of the movement began: 'Chartism was finally broken by the physical force of the British state, and having once been broken it was submerged, in the national consciousness, beneath layers of false understanding and denigration.'[13] The triumphalist press coverage in the wake of Chartism's defeat emphasised in particular three central aspects of counter-revolutionary ideology: the association of revolution with the foreign, the stupidity of egalitarian ideas and claims for the right to work, and, 'the most important and pervasive, the belief, which amounted to an article of faith, that in England the liberty of the subject had been assured by centuries of growth and development and that nowhere else in Europe were the practices of free speech and the possibilities of political change so self-evident as in Britain'.[14]

It is important to acknowledge all of this in an account of *Alton Locke*, not simply because of the way this novel influentially misrepresented the actual circumstances of Chartism's failure but precisely because of the centrality of these notions of English historical continuity and an ideal racial unity to Kingsley's sense of national community: he presents *laissez faire* state policies and the emergence of a politically conscious working class as causally related historical aberrations. His analysis of Chartism is therefore clearly indebted to Carlyle's, and Kingsley's denunciations of political economy were based on a sense of their betrayal of the moral economy, declaring as late as 1871 that he believed the feudal system – ideally, if not in practice – to be the most noble form of social organisation.[15] In 1852 he wrote to Thomas Hughes that

> I have never swerved from my one idea of the last seven years, that the real battle of the time is – if England is to be saved from anarchy and unbelief, and utter exhaustion caused by the competitive enslavement of the masses – not Radical or Whig against Peelite or Tory (let the dead bury their dead), but the Church, the gentleman, and the workman against the shopkeepers and the Manchester school ... A true democracy, such as you and I should wish to see, is impossible without a Church and a Queen,

and, as I believe, without a gentry.[16]

Democracy, to Kingsley, meant simply the opposite of the social disintegration which was implicit in the economic individualism advanced by the political economists, though he later changed his views on this. Here the spectres of anarchy, unbelief and national exhaustion represent a kind of diabolical trinity for him, all three being inextricably linked in his sense of the dangers to what was already an increasingly archaic – if still influential – ideal of nation-state formation.

Appropriately enough, one of the first scenes of *Alton Locke* to be written was Locke's final conversion.[17] The narrative is written from the perspective of the converted tailor, and describes how he came to reject his Chartist beliefs after a disastrous practical involvement with the movement brought about by the manipulation, at the hands of a range of embittered radicals, of his justified outrage at the treatment of his fellow workers. Retrospectively, Locke laments his failings, usually failings of conscience or perception. The telos of the novel is thus the message of the Christian socialists: the necessary moral reform of all the nation's citizens, the promotion of a Christian brotherhood across class divisions and the recognition of the central role of the clergy – a kind of Coleridgean clerisy – in the realisation of these ends. This is what Kingsley referred to as 'true democracy', and Eleanor – who preaches this message to Locke – exemplifies all of this when she speaks of Christ

> as the great Reformer; and yet as the true conservative ... the justifier of His own dealings with man from the beginning. She spoke of Him as the true demagogue – the champion of the poor; and yet as the true King, above and below all earthly rank; on whose will alone all the real superiority of man to man, all the time-justified and time-honoured usages of the family, the society, the nation, stand and shall stand for ever.[18]

The institutions and historical development of society are sanctified and vindicated as Christ is made to epitomise the two principles which had become the sacrosanct foundations of English historical development: reform and continuity. Somewhat problematically, though, this passage appears only at the end of a book which outlines the contemporary precariousness of that order which the novel suggests is coterminous with providence.

Both of the principal threats highlighted by the novel – revolutionary action and the lack of national fraternity on the part of the ruling class which precipitates it – are represented as originating from outsiders. Just as commerce at its most exploitative tends to be associated with a stereotypical Jew in the chapter on the sweater's den,[19] revolution is also consistently identified with malign foreign influences, with France and the Irish. Examples of this are obvious enough in the novel. The main Chartist leader – who at one point inflates the anti-Establishment rhetoric of a newspaper article written by Locke – is O'Flynn (a veiled reference to Feargus O'Connor), and in the lead up to the April demonstration of 1848 Locke claims that his friend Crossthwaite 'was always quoting French in those days'.[20] Later, when Locke and Crossthwaite arrive at the house of the Irishman Mike Kelly to find out about a claim – actually made by a government spy – that there are hundreds of men in government offices ready to support any insurrection, there is 'a hubbub inside Kelly's room of English, French, and Irish, all talking at once', and this is clearly symbolic of a chaotic confusion of national characteristics.[21] Kelly himself becomes symbolic of the ineptitude of the foreign-led movement, pre-empting the disaster of 10 April, by which time Locke is already disenchanted with the mendacity and lack of patriotism – towards *Britain*, that is – of the Irish.

The revolutionary characteristics of the French and Irish in contrast to the English are inevitably bound up with religious associations, and Eleanor becomes the mouthpiece for Kingsley's charge that revolutionary doctrine is analogous to Catholicism. She asserts that, if the people turn their attentions from God,

> there will be no lack of priestcraft, of veils to hide Him from them, tyrants to keep them from Him, idols to ape His likeness. A sinful people will always be a priest-ridden people; in reality, though not in name; by journalists and demagogues, if not by class-leaders and popes; and of the two, I confess I should prefer a Hildebrand to an O'Flynn.[22]

We are reminded here of O'Flynn's alterations to Locke's article on Cambridge, inflating its charges. The moderate truth spoken by Locke becomes lost in the rhetorical excess of O'Flynn, the garrulous Irishman. Indeed, throughout his involvement with radicals, Locke's sense of self – as Catherine Gallagher has noted – is constantly undermined.[23] But this is not, as she goes on to argue, the result of an irresolvable philosophical contradiction in the novel between material

determinism and a free will mysteriously reconcilable with providence. Still less is it a product of writing's capacity to demonstrate 'the
fictional nature of the singular identity',[24] a suggestion which improb-
ably attributes post-structuralist insights to Kingsley. Rather, throughout the novel Kingsley deliberately suggests Locke has an intuitive
sense of the falseness of his own thoughts and actions, an intuition
which makes his final conversion inevitable and confirms Eleanor's
conclusions about the nature of his compromise in the service of religious truth.

A case in point – demonstrating the Protestant alignment of truth
with inner conviction – is the key moment of Locke's 'fall' when he
agrees to 'emasculate'[25] his poetry, to censor its truths in complicity
with the demands of his 'aristocratic' admirers. This is performed
largely out of a desire to please Lillian: 'Could I not, just once in a way,
serve God and Mammon at once? – or rather, not Mammon, but
Venus: a worship which looked to me, and really was in my case,
purer than all the Mariolatry in Popedom.'[26] The reference to Mariolatry again insists on the falseness of mediated relations with God, and
Locke's love for Lillian is precisely a form of idol-worship (as the reference to paganism indicates), a form of enslavement. Lillian herself
proves unworthy – she goes on to marry Locke's Tractarian cousin –
and it is her sister, Eleanor, whose *formal* conduct leads Locke to consider her his enemy, who actually proves to be his guardian and the
true democrat (in the Kingsleyan sense). Indeed, once Locke has
become disabused of Lillian's character, Eleanor asks the rhetorical
question '"What was it that you adored? a soul, or a face? The inward
reality, or the outward symbol, which is only valuable as a sacrament
of the loveliness within?"'[27]

Lillian does not maintain her beauty, though, and the means by
which form and interior condition are made to correspond is of more
than passing significance in the context of the book's overall fascination with organisms. Late in the narrative, Lillian contracts typhus, but
recovers in a degenerate form. Her husband – Locke's cousin – dies of
the disease, as do one of his servants and the shopman who sells him
the coat which harbours the disease. The coat itself was the product
of sweated labour, made by a former workmate of Locke, Jemmy
Downes. Prior to its sale it was used to cover the bodies of Downes's
dead family, as Locke himself witnesses (Downes's family die of the
effects of drinking the water in which they also defecate). Locke comments that his cousin's death 'was the consistent Nemesis of all poor

George's thrift and cunning, of his determination to carry the buy-cheap-and-sell-dear commercialism, in which he had been brought up, into every act of life!'[28] The contamination of the fabric of the coat is both the means of contaminating the rest of society and a metaphor for that contamination – a reference to the *social* fabric – and therefore an insistence on the impossibility of denying social ties (a familiar theme of Victorian literature of this period). Kingsley is prone to mixing the metaphors which govern his thoughts, though, and the disease which traces the tortuous route from Jemmy Downes's house to Lillian inevitably returns us to a consideration of society as organism. Inner value and physical form finally correspond in Lillian, and she is made to stand for the degenerate body politic, a condition precipitated by the introduction of innovative political doctrines.

Other organisms feature prominently in Kingsley's narrative as victims of the system-building of humanity. Consequently they are rarely healthy. As a young boy Locke reveals an interest in natural forms of life, and his spontaneous natural theology has the effect of undermining the austere influence of his mother's Calvinism – he perceives that 'God's love shines out in every tree and flower and hedge-side bird'[29] – and this also distinguishes his appreciation of nature from the merely scientific naturalism of Lillian's and Eleanor's father, the Dean. The contemporary city, though, perverts nature. At one point, Locke imaginatively pictures the natural world of the tropical islands described to him in missionary tracts, and contrasts this with his own Cockney environment:

> one day, I recollect it well, in the little dingy, foul, reeking, twelve-foot square back-yard, where huge smoky party-walls shut out every breath of air and almost all the light of heaven, I had climbed up between the water-butt and the angle of the wall for the purpose of fishing out of the dirty fluid which lay there, crusted with soot and alive with insects, to be renewed only three times in seven days, some of the great larvae and kicking monsters which made up a large item in my list of wonders: all of a sudden the horror of the place came over me; those grim prison-walls above, with their canopy of lurid smoke; the dreary, sloppy, broken pavement; the horrible stench of the stagnant cesspools; the utter want of form, colour, life, in the whole place, crushed me down, without being able to analyse my feelings as I can now; and then came over me that dream of Pacific Islands, and the free, open sea.[30]

The constraining environment of the city produces its own aberrant organisms as well as a consequent intuitive desire for freedom in Locke in the form of a longing for an unspoilt natural environment. This is a demand to be able to develop naturally, physically as a man, in a way which is coterminous with divinely sanctioned growth (inevitably towards light). Freedom is not only freedom from the physical environment of the city, since there is a constant slippage between physical and moral description: Locke's desire for natural physical development is necessarily a desire to be able to develop morally.

Just as natural development is equated with true moral freedom, the city's perversion of organic forms precipitates their inner degeneration, and this is most pronounced in the conditions of the workers: the production of aberrant forms of the body results in corresponding aberrant convictions. On being told he is to become a tailor, Locke considers his compatibility with his environment:

> A pale, consumptive, ricketty, weakly boy, all forehead and no muscle – have not clothes and shoes been from time immemorial the appointed work of such? The fact that the weakly frame is generally compensated by a proportionally increased activity of the brain, is too unimportant to enter into the calculations of the great King Laissez-faire. Well, my dear Society, it is you that suffer for the mistake, after all, more than we. If you do tether your cleverest artisans to tailors' shop-boards and cobblers' benches, and they – as sedentary folk will – fall a-thinking, and come to strange conclusions thereby, they really ought to be much more thankful to you than you are to them.[31]

Political dogma solidifies into physical restraint, and this provokes unnatural mental stimulation. Kingsley's anti-intellectualism here is consistent with the same conviction that is demonstrated in Burke's characterisation of rational systems as 'inventions'. This association of sedentary occupation with revolutionary intellectualism is further reinforced in Crossthwaite, who

> might have been five-and-twenty; but his looks, like those of too many a working man, were rather those of a man of forty. Wild grey eyes gleamed out from under huge knitted brows, and a perpendicular wall of brain, too large for his puny body. He was not only, I soon discovered, a water-drinker, but a strict 'vegetarian' also; to which, perhaps, he owed a great deal of the almost preternatural clearness, volubility, and sensitiveness of mind … the marks of ill-health were on him.[32]

Crossthwaite, and tailors in general, therefore share certain characteristics with Kingsley's portrait of the hysterical Shelley: over-sen-
sitivity caused by disproportionate cerebral development – in
Crossthwaite's case the product of physical constriction – generates
political discontent. But Kingsley also believed that physiognomy
revealed an explicitly Christian condition: 'Body is that which
expresses the spirit to which it is joined; therefore, the more perfectly
spiritual the body, the better it will express the spirit joined to it', he
once wrote.[33] The spiritual condition which Crossthwaite's body
expresses, therefore, is a deranged radicalism, since spiritual condition, reason and bodily health should be aligned, symbolising healthy
national development. Perversions of organic form are again symptomatic of a departure from conformity with the reasonable English
polity.[34]

Amongst all these fears of national degeneration precipitated by
class conflict there is one moment of transcendence in the novel. This
is the moment at which Locke witnesses his cousin – who demonstrates a potential which he ultimately fails to realise – in a Cambridge
boat race:

> It was a noble sport – a sight as could only be seen in England –
> some hundred of young men, who might, if they had chosen,
> been lounging effeminately about the streets, subjecting them-
> selves voluntarily to that intense exertion, for the mere pleasure
> of toil. The true English stuff came out there; I felt that, in spite
> of all my prejudices – the stuff which has held Gibraltar and con-
> quered at Waterloo – which has created a Birmingham and a
> Manchester, and colonised every quarter of the globe – that
> grim, earnest, stubborn energy, which, since the days of the old
> Romans, the English possess of all the nations of the earth. I was
> as proud of the gallant young fellows as if they had been my
> brothers – of their courage and endurance (for one could see
> that it was no child's-play, from the pale faces, and panting lips),
> their strength and activity, so fierce and yet so cultivated,
> smooth, harmonious, as oar kept time with oar, and every back
> rose and fell in concert and felt my soul stirred up to a sort of
> sweet madness … My blood boiled over, and fierce tears swelled
> into my eyes; for I too was a man, and an Englishman; and when
> I caught sight of my cousin, pulling stroke to the second boat in
> the long line, with set teeth and flashing eyes, the great muscles
> on his bare arms springing up into knots at every rapid stroke, I
> ran and shouted among the maddest and foremost.[35]

This is the clearest exposition in the novel of what was to become known as Christian manliness. The ideal male body here becomes the symbol in which all classes can recognise themselves as part of a superior racial group whose achievement of an empire which surpasses the Romans' is their providential reward. The particular aspects of the body depicted here are important since they are made the principles of national unity: work, discipline, purpose, all manifest in the body's own lineaments and all functioning – at least potentially – in the service of nation. At the same time as this body is distinctly masculine, then, its self-control mitigates the potential of male energy to spill over into barbarism (it is 'so fierce yet so cultivated'). Just as it demonstrably shows signs of its own self-rule, it also conveys its ability to rule others – in particular, other, 'immature' races. Where the natural theology of Paley would have discerned in the body's musculature evidence merely of a benevolent design (an aspect of the body's constitutional orderliness),[36] Kingsley sees the natural expression of a divine and national purposiveness. It is this myth of national – indeed, racial – unity which Kingsley was able to forge from the state's defeat of Chartism and from the dual ideologies of freedom and continuity.

It should also be pointed out that the end of the novel – in which Locke dies whilst being transported – is no cop-out. In his analysis of the industrial novels Raymond Williams claims that the deployment of emigration to the colonies as a form of closure represents some kind of inability to confront the internal problems of England. Of *Mary Barton*, he suggests that 'a solution to the actual situation might be hoped for, but the solution with which the heart went was a cancelling of the actual difficulties and the removal of the persons pitied to the uncompromised New World.'[37] Similarly, in Alton Locke, 'the destiny of the hero is once again emigration'.[38] Yet the conclusion to Kingsley's novel emerges logically enough from its dynamic, and is determined both by a sense of the nation's internal growth and by a consciousness of its world position: the New World represents a space in which the expansive physical vigour of the English can find a proper outlet to perform the work of subduing the world to proper Christian rule. Locke's dreams of physical and moral freedom in foreign lands whilst he is constrained within the environment of the city lead naturally to this closure which also provides a sense of possibility, despite Locke's death.

Locke is headed for Texas. None the less, his journey intimates a natural capacity on the part of the English for conquest and expansion, a fundamental component of Kingsleyan Christian manliness which was, in many respects, its most enduring legacy. In the later *Westward Ho!* – set in the expansionist times of Elizabeth I – the novel's hero, Amyas Leigh, epitomises such traits, a figure of 'extraordinary size and strength' and explicitly 'a symbol of brave young England longing to wing its way out of its island prison, to discover and to traffic, to colonise and to civilise, until no wind can sweep the earth which does not bear the echoes of an English voice'.[39] It needs to be stressed that such a conception of the physical capacity of the Anglo-Saxon to realise his destiny was not peculiar to Kingsley. Others were arguing that the English were natural imperialists. Robert Knox's arguments about race, for instance, involved the claim that Saxons are 'tall, powerful, athletic ... the strongest, as a race, on the face of the earth', and this physique complements their 'applicative' rather than inventive nature:

> When young they cannot sit still an instant, so powerful is the desire for work, labour, excitement, muscular exertion. The self-esteem is so great, the self-confidence so matchless, that they cannot possibly imagine any man or set of men to be superior to themselves. Accumulative beyond all others, the wealth of the world collects in their hands.[40]

### The rule of Christian men

Within a few years of Chartism's defeat, Christian socialism lost its impetus, and this in itself is indicative of the group's essentially reactionary credentials. Kingsley became increasingly unmotivated in its cause, and from 1859 – when he preached at Buckingham Palace for the first time – embarked on a career as Establishment figure. In 1862 he censored most of his criticisms of Cambridge in *Alton Locke*, and in a new preface he wrote for the fourth edition of his novel *Yeast* he praised the effects of the notorious Poor Law Amendment Act for making labourers more independent, and of free trade for improving the diet of the workers.[41] This may seem to mark him out as a mere political renegade, but by the 1860s these were not the burning issues they once were, and the measures themselves were therefore assimilable into the narrative of progressive English historical development. In some ways, too, these apparent U-turns draw attention to his main and consistent concern: the moral and physical condition of the workers and their capacity to serve national and imperial interests (even after his desertion of Christian socialism he maintained an obsession with sanitary reform). After the early 1850s, indeed, the innovative aspects of Kingsley's writing were exhausted; there was nothing more to add to his message, only clarification and defence.

His – and Thomas Hughes's – ideal of the body did become influential, though, through its integration into the games ethic, as the public schools processed greater numbers of bodies from aspiring middle-class backgrounds and themselves grew in number in the second half of the nineteenth century in a culture still dominated by the ideal of the gentleman. By the early 1900s the number of public schools reached '- depending on the degree of exclusiveness or snobbery – anything between 64 and some 160 more or less expensive schools ... deliberately training their pupils as members of a ruling class'.[42] Games became increasingly central to the curriculum: their lengthy period of institutionalisation was 'extended and perfected' by 1900,[43] and their influence also extended into the universities (which by this time were, in any case, largely extensions of the public school system – four out of five Oxbridge students were products of public schools between 1855 and 1899, a greater proportion than ever before).[44] In 1869 Archibald Maclaren, founder of the popular Oxford Gymnasium, defined physical health in definitively Protestant terms as 'that condition of the body, and that amount of vital capacity, which shall enable each man in his place to pursue his calling, and work on his working life, with the greatest comfort to himself and usefulness to his fellow men'.[45]

Time after time the exaltation of games in sermons, doggerel, stories and novels by enthusiastic masters celebrated both the subordination of self in order to generate *esprit de corps* and the development of bodies whose musculatures were an index of the individual's capacity to perform virtuous work. Games were therefore an integral part of a training for what was expected of the individual after his graduation from school: team became nation, and work the practical business of spreading the interests of that nation. The contempt for both luxury and mere ascetic bodily denial, and the imperative of a discipline which also laid claim to being natural, remained the central moral features of this institutionalisation. Thomas Hughes's first novel was in many respects prototypical of later efforts. Though not dealing with curricular activities, Hughes's eulogy on pugilism in *Tom Brown's Schooldays* provides a good instance of the significance of physical activity. It has been defended on the grounds that his concept of 'fighting' is as much morally defined as it is physically defined,[46] but, though this may be a corrective to accounts of 'muscular Christianity' as mere licentiousness, it none the less misses the central feature of that crucial passage: the striking elision of self with nation, and the further elision developed between national service and the service of higher ends through a Pauline rhetoric which itself has a long tradition in English Protestant thought, and which took on a renewed significance in the militaristic atmosphere of the later nineteenth century:

> From the cradle to the grave, fighting, rightly understood, is the business, the real, highest, honestest business of every son of man. Every one who is worth his salt has his enemies, who must be beaten, be they evil thoughts and habits in himself or spiritual wickednesses in high places, or Russians, or Border-ruffians, or Bill, Tom, or Harry, who will not let him live his life in quiet till he has thrashed them.[47]

It is precisely the body's expression of a will subordinated to divine and national law that distinguishes the authentic message of Christian manliness, and it was fully preserved in the ideology of athleticism in the later nineteenth century. This physical manliness is important in *Tom Brown*, but, as in Kingsley, it is distinguished from barbarism and therefore bound up with an implicit historical trajectory. The narrative describes Tom's development from a fairly brutal rural primitivism to Christian manhood via the influence of Thomas Arnold's school, and especially the physically feeble but devout Arthur. Arthur therefore succeeds in reforming Tom, but this does not imply that 'in Hughes's estimation it is Arthur, not the pre-regenerate Brown, who epitomises "manliness"';[48] rather, a truly Christian manliness resides in a fusion of religiosity and corporeality, the one directing and channelling the force of the other.

In the schools themselves, enthusiasm for games grew as part of an increasingly explicit stress on imperialism. Few were more enthusiastic than Hely Hutchinson Almond – headmaster of Loretto School in Edinburgh from 1862 – who demanded in one sermon 'a holy alliance between the athlete and the Christian', in which the egotism of the athlete and the discipline of religion would find common cause against their joint enemies: 'intemperance, and indolence, and dissipation, and effeminacy, and aesthetic voluptuousness, and heartless cynicism, and all the unnatural and demoralising elements in our social life'. Examples of this ideal 'consecration of the body' included carrying 'the banner of the Cross to distant lands' and winning Christian victories 'among ignorant natives or coarse British traders', even 'protecting some rough colony from the inroads of civilised effeminacy and vice'.[49] Edward Bowen of Harrow placed an almost ineffable value on the practice of playing football, expressing a Tennysonian scepticism about the value of merely formal religion:

> when you have a lot of human beings, in highest social union, and perfect organic action, developing the law of their race and falling in unconsciously with its best inherited traditions of brotherhood and of common action, I think you are not far from getting a glimpse of one side of the highest good. There lives more soul in honest play, believe me, than in half the hymn-books.[50]

The body becomes a living expression of the ideal purposiveness of the 'race', rising above the potentially dead letter of the hymn; and that metaphysical appeal to the 'the law of their race' conflates the natural, national and divine.

J. A. Mangan argues that, as the century wore on, the public school emphasis on gentlemanly Christian virtue was largely superseded by the games ethic's emphasis on physical strength as the basis of natural leadership in the context of the empire, and he notes the 'precarious fusion' of the ethical imperative with social Darwinism – a fusion in which Christianity 'came out second best'. There may well have been instances in which this was the case, but Mangan's precise discriminations seem to me overly analytic, and his sense of social Darwinism is problematic: he defines it as 'the God-granted right of the white man to rule, civilise and baptise the inferior coloured races',[51] but there seems to be little that is distinctively Darwinian about this. None the less, his sense that the appeal to empire tended to eclipse any Christian content is neither improbable nor, in fact, entirely out of keeping with the emphases of Christian manliness. As we have seen, this tradition aligned from the start service to empire with service to God, and the degree to which either or both of these causes could be stressed was perhaps bound up with the particular religious convictions of masters and the increasing centrality of the empire to British self-esteem in the later part of the century. In this respect Christian manliness flexibly served the requirements of an expansive imperialist state which required metaphysical legitimation for that expansion.

There has also been demurral about the extent to which Kingsley and Hughes were responsible for the games cult and its relationship to imperialism. Vance notes that, though their heartiness 'could be adduced in ideological justification of the incidental miseries of later school life', on the whole 'neither Kingsley nor Hughes would have welcomed the institutionalising of games which made such a serious business of pleasure'.[52] It is unclear what the evidence is for Kingsley's probable disapprobation, but this may well be true of Hughes who in later life disavowed mere athleticism. In 1879 he published The *Manliness of Christ* as a contribution to the Christian Guild's attempts to diffuse the principles of Christian manliness amongst the northern working class in order to regulate their violence. The YMCA had been unsuccessful, Hughes noted, because its tone tended to suggest that Christianity was bound up with timidity and a lack of courage.[53] None the less, 'true manliness is as likely to be found in a weak as in a strong body ... a great athlete may be a brute or a coward, while a truly manly man can be neither'.[54] This, indeed, expresses a more widely-held anxiety about the developing cult of the body, and Hughes is mainly interested in re-asserting the moral component of Christian manliness. On the other hand, my concern here is not with the distractions of blame – whether Kingsley or Hughes can be held 'responsible' for the cult of athleticism – but with the more important question of ideological continuities. Again we must recognise the flexibility of this ideology and that, whilst Hughes is attempting to prioritise its religious content in this text, the overall emphasis was compatible with the greater insistence on physical strength; indeed such an insistence is to be found in Hughes's own earlier works.

Hughes's involvement with the Christian Guild is also indicative of a more general desire to extend to the working class those principles which had come to dominate in the public schools. This was increasingly the case in the later part of the century, and was explicitly precipitated by fears of a working-class degeneracy which would result in their incapacity to defend imperial interests. Though middle-class snobbery largely precluded the involvement of working-class, and even lower middle-class, men in the amateur athletics clubs which sprang up in these years,[55] proselytising agencies – often affiliated to the churches and incorporating militaristic features – did attempt to bridge the gap. The most prominent of these, and the one which proved most durable, was the Boy Scouts. Established in 1908, its founding tenets were based on the public school and imperial experiences of Baden Powell, whose aim was to inculcate principles of discipline, purity and patriotism amongst working-class youths who would be the cannon fodder of the future.[56] Other movements predated Powell's, the first being William Smith's Glasgow-based Boys' Brigade, whose aim was to promote 'habits of reverence, discipline, self-respect, and all that tends towards a true Christian manliness'.[57]

The specific moral fear to which Hughes was alluding in *The Manliness of Christ* – that of muscularity without Christianity – is the subject of Wilkie Collins's novel *Man and Wife*, published in 1870. This is in part concerned with the effects which Collins believed athleticism was having on young men, though it also targets the marriage laws of Ireland and Scotland for their openness to abuse. The principal athletic figure in the novel is Geoffrey Delamayn, and Collins is at pains to emphasise that Delamayn cultivates his body at the expense of moral or chivalric principles. Hence, Delamayn tries to reject the claims of Ann Sylvester, who he has promised to marry (having made her pregnant), by exploiting certain fortuitous circumstances – as well as Scottish marriage laws – to trap her into a marriage with his best friend (who, meanwhile, has actually married someone else). Delamayn has designs on a rich widow, Mrs Glenarm, but in the end both Delamayn and Sylvester are forced into a marriage neither of them wants (she recognises the threat of violence in his looks). Consequently Delamayn attempts to murder Sylvester but is thwarted by his own physical condition – his exertions have wasted his vitality, prompting him to have a fit whilst on the verge of suffocating Sylvester. He is finally finished off by his deranged landlady who strangles him (she has previously murdered her violent husband). The novel, then, emphasises the excessive cultivation of the body and how this leads to the abandonment of ideals, particularly those of chivalry towards vulnerable women. Paradoxically, athleticism also has the potential to waste the individual's finite physical energy. The following passage, describing Mrs Glenarm's admiration of Delamayn in training, conveys Collins's perception of the cult of the body:

> Dressed in a close-fitting costume, light and elastic, adapting itself to every movement, and made to answer every purpose required by the exercise in which he was about to engage, Geoffrey's physical advantages showed themselves in their best and bravest aspect. His head sat proud and easy on his firm white throat, bared to the air. The rising of his mighty chest, as he drew in deep draughts of the fragrant summer breeze; the play of his

lithe and supple loins; the easy elastic stride of his straight and shapely legs, presented a triumph of physical manhood in its highest type. Mrs. Glenarm's eyes devoured him in silent admiration.[58]

Collins manages to convey athleticist adulation of the body, but the moral principles which attend the Kingsleyan tradition are conspicuously absent. Indeed, one American reviewer described Delamayn as epitomising the character of 'the Muscular Pagan'[59]. Collins here presents a version of athleticism which simply celebrates the body for its own sake, and also conveys an eroticism at odds with the message of authentic Christian manliness.

Indeed, elsewhere Collins's writing evinces a commitment to some of the distinctive features of Christian manliness. In *The Woman in White* the main male protagonist, Walter Hartright, is a professional art teacher who falls in love with his pupil, Laura Fairlie (but his name, it might be noted, suggests a Protestant as well as romantic integrity). Such improper feelings for his student prompt him to leave England in order to forget her, but in the process he also leaves her vulnerable to the machinations of Sir Percival Glyde, her fiancé, and the Italian villain Count Fosco. In his narrative of events Hartright returns from Central America better prepared to rescue Laura from her fate:

> From that self-imposed exile I came back, as I had hoped, prayed, believed I should come back – a changed man. In the waters of a new life I had tempered my nature afresh. In the stern school of extremity and danger my will had learnt to be strong, my heart to be resolute, my mind to rely on itself. I had gone out to fly from my own future. I came back to face it as a man should.[60]

Thus Collins emphasises physical challenges. Indeed Hartright's physical triumph over the threat of a hostile alien environment – 'Death by disease, death by the Indians, death by drowning – all three had approached me; all three had passed me by'[61] – is the means of fitting him for moral conquests. This is a pivotal moment in the novel, since, as Jenny Bourne Taylor comments, the narrative largely centres on the reconstruction of Hartright's identity, 'how he learns to control the past and thus the present instead of being incapacitated by anxiety about the future … how he becomes both his own and Laura's moral manager'.[62] In this respect, of course, he is the antithesis of the degenerate, idle, nervously oversensitive and self-absorbed Frederick Fair-lie, the effeminate aesthete so unsuited to the patriarchal position he nominally holds.

Through the adoption of Christian manliness – or variants on it – by the pedagogical institutions of Britain's ruling class, it became integral to an ideal manliness up to the First World War – contributing substantially to the attitudes of Britain's officer class – and somewhat beyond. It was a major ideological factor in the legitimation of imperialism,[63] and at home contributed to, as it arose in part from, anxieties about national degeneration.[64] Except in the trashy outpourings of the public schools – where it was ubiquitous – its literary career was limited as a consequence of its didacticism.[65] But this in itself helped to reinforce the isolation of 'culture' from (moral, upright) society to the extent that art could become as self-absorbed and self-valorising (and consequently suspicious) as it did amongst the aesthetes.[66] As with any dominant ideology, Christian manliness was modified, resisted and challenged, but what is remarkable is the consistency of the writings of the schoolmasters who promoted it and the duration of the period in which it maintained – even increased – its ascendancy amongst the rulers of empire. Built on the myth of the natural integrity and durability of the English-dominated British polity, Christian manliness became symbolically central to that nation's claims to a uniquely blessed supremacy.

### Eroticised manliness

In *Man and Wife* Collins emphasises the erotic potential of the athlete. In this case the (fictional) gaze is that of a woman, but in most of the celebrations of the male body in the nineteenth century the eloquent, sometimes ecstatic, onlookers are men. Writings about the physical beauty of athletes provided a culturally sanctioned space in which to celebrate the sometimes naked male form; but how was it possible to distinguish manly celebration from erotic attraction? In the homosocial environment of the public schools, sexual relations between boys, or, worse, between masters and boys, were abhorred, but how could the lines between proper and improper responses to the virtuous athletic body be effectively policed? Eve Sedgwick claims that being 'a man's man is separated only by an invisible, carefully blurred, always-already-crossed line from being "interested in men"',[67] and this double-bind was one which became acute for some of those who perpetuated the legacy of Christian manliness. Moreover, this acuteness was compounded by the fact that games were not merely intended to prepare schoolboys for their role in the world, but, as part of this, were integral to the means of internally policing these institutions. Mangan argues that the development of games was the result of a need to instil discipline in unruly boys and, relatedly, to inculcate loyalty to the school.[68] Once established, one of their main supposed benefits was their contribution to the suppression of 'vice', a euphemism which referred principally to the unspeakable acts of masturbation – solitary or mutual – as well as to same-sex desire in general. Games were a means of producing self-discipline in this respect as in others. In a lecture on 'The Iniquity of Sodom' Hely Hutchinson Almond noted the recurrence of sensuality throughout history amongst 'men under whom there flourished a leisured, pampered, and cultured class' and instructed his boys that 'by the cultivation of modesty, temperance, and wise activity of both mind and body, your temptations to sins of the flesh will be subdued'.[69] Edward Thring of Uppingham, in a sermon on 'Courage, Manliness, Christian Chivalry', told his pupils that they were enrolled in a Christian brotherhood superior to medieval chivalry, though still based on the tenets of chastity, obedience, kindness and bravery: 'Look on yourselves as members of the nobility of the world; as having received the order of the knighthood in the kingdom of heaven, as Christ's champions and bodyguard.'[70] Bruce Haley records that in a letter survey conducted by Edward Lyttelton from Eton, assessments of the extent of masturbation suggested that between eighty and ninety per cent of boys were guilty, and Lyttelton believed that the eradication of the 'solitary vice' would put an end to the 'dual vice'.[71] This suggests that same-sex desire was generally regarded as a temptation open to anyone rather than the predominantly congenital disposition it was to become in the writings of the sexologists. Consequently the disciplinary effects of games were believed to be universally beneficial.

They were not universally successful; at least, not in the way they were intended to be. The ideal physique of the public schoolboy was held up for admiration not only in the declamations of the masters but in iconic representations in the schools' architecture (especially in the memorials to various imperialist battles), in stained glass windows and in the illustrations of their books[72] which exhorted boys to be like them, to admire them, even to love them. The Biblical love of David for Jonathan was constantly upheld as the prototype in this respect, and hero-worship, even romantic friendships between boys, could be encouraged, though from the 1880s there was an increased anxiety about such intimacies.[73] However, this same intense all-male environment actually helped to incite the desire it aspired to regulate. More than this, it actually structured the forms this desire took, as the very means of symbolising self-discipline became precisely the object of erotic attraction. In the writings of some of those writers labelled – somewhat indiscriminately – 'Uranian'[74] this tension between their own erotic response and the body's symbolic status as morally and physically healthy is both obvious and unresolvable. Vance records the examples of the Revd E. C. Lefroy – whose improbable attempts at a synthesis of manliness and aestheticism betray an anxious sexual attraction for the male body – and of W. J. Cory, a master at Eton who similarly enthused about young sports players, and ended by leaving the school under a cloud.[75] Such examples are perhaps not common, but they are indicative of a more widespread phenomenon, and they demonstrate the contradictions of the games ethic: designed to instil self-discipline, it could lead to the abominations associated more with the Greek gymnasium, which, in a sanitised form, was one model for Victorian athleticism.

The games ethic fed significantly into the writings of the Uranians. One of the more earnest of these, the Revd E. E. Bradford, erred on the side of purity. In his 1905 collection of *Stories of Life at Our Great Public Schools* – stories originally published separately in *Young England* – he continually aligns virtuous activity with physical muscularity. Often he writes of relationships between boys, as in the story he presents from Radley College, in which the older boy, Chris, constantly sacrifices his own interests to those of others, notably in the service of protecting the 'delicate little boy' Steevie Corda, finally dying as a result of saving Steevie from a fire in the school house. This is the picture of Chris(t) as he prepares to fight the school bully in order to protect Steevie:

> fair, curly hair, like little ringlets of gold, clustered around his broad white forehead. When his shirt was unbuttoned at the throat, and his sleeves rolled up above the elbows, as they soon were, Steevie could catch a glimpse of his deep broad chest, and see the muscles ripple all over his firm round arms at every movement that he made. But it was his eyes that struck his admirer the most ... They had a curious, fearless and loving look,

as if they heartily liked everything they rested upon. They wore it now as strongly as ever, though they were fixed full on Dobson; and from the first to last Steevie never saw their expression change.[76]

This confrontation with the school bully is a setpiece of public school fiction for which Thomas Hughes's homily on fighting was responsible. If the muscularity and beauty of the boy seem suspiciously prominent, one response might be that what seems to us a sexualised description of this earnest schoolboy is in fact the consequence of a change in our own perspectives. But if the muscularity of Chris is purposive and may therefore be countenanced within the limits set by Christian manliness, the possibility of disentangling the virtuous body from the eroticised figure is more difficult in the following poem by Bradford, 'May Flowers'. This body is nakedly aesthetic in its appeal:

> Deep in a sheltered nook; mid hawthorn trees
> Laden with a snowy blossom, on the grass,
> A lusty ploughman flung himself at ease,
> Close to a pool, whose waters seemed of glass.
> As, one by one, his russet rags he doffed,
> And let them drop like dead leaves to the earth,
> He showed a glowing form, as fair and soft
> As is the tender infant's at its birth:
> And when, at length, he stood in naked pride,
> A boy in beauty, but a man in might,
> He put to shame the blossoms at his side,
> As sanguine Dawn blots out anaemic Night;
>    No other bloom seemed half so sweet and fresh
>    As this majestic flower of the flesh.[77]

This is a more 'democratic' celebration of the body than in Bradford's public school writings, part of an increasing tendency which emerged towards the end of the nineteenth century – influenced by Whitman via Edward Carpenter – to celebrate same-sex relationships across class divisions. Unlike the celebration of the public schoolboy's physique, though, there seems to be no moral justification for this particular scene: the ploughman is actually resting from his work, and the only action he performs is that of discarding his 'russet rags'. This in itself is akin to striptease, having as its sole end the (eagerly) anticipated moment of revelation. Moreover, the suggestion of illicit – or at least covert – pleasure taken in this scene is emphasised by the viewer's privacy announced at the opening of the poem (even if the poem itself is publicly on display). At the same time, Bradford is careful to suggest innocence in his description of the lad, poised liminally between the purity of boyhood and the more knowing condition of manhood; and even manhood is depicted in terms of 'might' rather than sexual self-knowledge. The rural setting – and most 'democratic' relationships are set in the country – is intended to intensify this sense of innocence. Indeed elsewhere in his writings Bradford evinces a rather anxious need to distance himself from the erotic potential of the lads he describes, and, at the same time, from less inhibited contemporary legitimations of same-sex desire based on Hellenic models (Wilde's, for instance). In one poem he argued that

> ... passion freshened by a Northern breeze,
>   Gains in male vigour and purity.
> Our yearning tenderness for boys like these
>   Has more in it of Christ than Socrates.[78]

The fact that he needs to distinguish English pederastic relations from the Greek clearly indicates an anxiety – otherwise why should it occur to him? – and in other writings he adopts certain strategies which demonstrate his consciousness of sexual possibilities. In the poem 'Fomes Peccati' two poor, half-naked girls provoke lusts in one lad who is originally presented to the reader in a relationship with a younger boy. This male same-sex relationship is clearly not sexual but is none the less mediated by an intense physical admiration. Both the girls and the boys are distinguished by differences in age which denote differences of sexual awareness. As the poem progresses, the pairs meet. Of the girls, the younger is intimidated by the older boy's gaze whilst the older girl constrains her in order to seduce him. It is only when distant church bells ring that the older lad remembers with shame the imperative of purity in love, and the two male youths leave the girls to go to evensong.[79] The elder girl in the poem seems, therefore, a convenient presence on to whom (the poet's?) sinful desires may be projected, whereas the more ephemeral younger boy is a representative of spirit rather than mere flesh.

The attempt in Bradford's poem to associate sexual desire with women, whilst associating male love with purity and a greater spirituality, was not one peculiar to him. It was a particular strategy of many promoting same-sex love at this time, and represented a partial capitulation to prevailing gender definitions which emphasised the correlation between physical and moral health; consequently it was an always-compromised defence.[80] One of the major proponents of democratic love was Edward Carpenter, and his tract on 'Homogenic Love' – the title itself tactfully substituting a sense of mere compatibility for any reference to impure relations – argues against the emphasis placed on sexual love in modern societies. The scientific obsession with reproductive love, he claims, represents a 'materialistic and commercial phase of European history' in which 'the only form of love and love-union that it has recognised has been one founded on the quite necessary but comparatively materialistic basis of matrimonial sex-intercourse and child-breeding'.[81] Homogenic love, he argues, is more spiritual, and this is a train of thought pursued in an influential essay by Charles Kains Jackson, 'The New Chivalry', printed in the same year as Carpenter's in *The Artist* magazine. (The essay's influence is demonstrated by the fact that it provided Bradford with the title and the rationale for his 1918 collection of poems.) Again, the argument – an evolutionary one – is that the 'phallic filthiness' of cross-sex love was symptomatic of the materialism of bourgeois civilisation and that same-sex relations represented a higher, more spiritual form.[82] These arguments rest on the conviction that male same-sex love is, as Alan Sinfield suggests, *more* manly than relations between the sexes,[83] but it is also the case that the degree to which these relationships might be judged manly was bound up with the extent to which they disavowed specifically sexual relations. At the same time, cross-sex relations seemed necessarily to imply genital relations, since men and women were not considered intellectual or spiritual equals, attitudes which clearly reflect the specific homosocial educational environments in which these writers were brought up. Integral to many Uranian forms of apologia, then, was not only a denigration of sex – and therefore a form of self-reproach – but a denigration of women (Carpenter is a partial exception in this respect), since, logically, sex with a person implied a lack of respect for them, and women were 'naturally' the appropriate objects of sexual desire. Later, Alec Waugh – whose *The Loom of Youth* implied that sexual acts were commonplace amongst athletic boys – was to argue that the public school anti-sex ethic led a man to believe 'that the sexual impulse can only be gratified with a woman he does not love',[84] since respect enjoined sexual abstinence.

The emphasis on the games ethic, then, was one which encouraged but structured desire between men, whilst simultaneously defining sex as unclean and women as the appropriate objects of such base attentions (and in this we see something very different from the 'Angel in the House' ideology which has tended to dominate discussions of relations between men and women in the nineteenth century). English boys were exhorted to admire and to aspire to the physical condition of the exemplars of this ideal, but were simultaneously (if euphemistically) prohibited from achieving physical intimacy. Indeed the bodies themselves symbolised such proscriptions. Desire, in this context, could either be successfully controlled or suppressed – a natural, healthy and patriotic aspect of male bonding – or it could lead to guilty, secretive, even treacherous acts of sexual expression. E. M. Forster, in a moment of honesty and insight, describes one typical product of the public schools in *The Longest Journey*. Gerald Dawes was 'a young man who had the figure of a Greek athlete and the face of an English one. He was fair and clean-shaven, and his colourless hair was cut short. The sun was in his eyes, and they, like his mouth, seemed scarcely more than slits in his healthy skin. Just where he began to be beautiful his clothes started.'[85] Dawes, then, combines the athleticism of Greece with the repressive propriety of English culture; his very buttoned-upness acts as a silent reproach to the desiring and thereby subordinated gaze of the narrator.

The admiration for the male body which developed in this culture of physical manliness is something I want to return to in considering the patriotic appeal of such bodies for Gerard Manley Hopkins, since, as I have noted in relation to 'The Bugler's First Communion', this appeal precipitated in him too an awareness of the tendency of such admiration to evoke a sinful response: the male form 'does set danc- / Ing blood', he wrote.[86] Hopkins's consciousness of sin was clearly intensified by his Catholicism though it was not merely a product of Jesuitical scruples and, just as this religious affiliation conflicted with his erotic desires, it also sat uneasily with the patriotism which was mixed up with that same admiration for the body. For the moment I want to return to mid-century debates in order to consider more closely the anxieties which fed the persistent controversies over Anglo-Catholicism and 'perversions' to Rome, principally with reference to the man who received Hopkins into the Catholic Church, John Henry Newman.

# 3

## Out of unreality: J. H. Newman

IN THE first version of *Alton Locke* Cambridge is not simply the scene of manly displays of self-discipline and hard work; it is also the setting for Kingsley's portrait of a dissolute 'aristocracy' whose drunkenness, lack of faith and irreverence towards the institution itself Locke treats with disgust. The undergraduates view the University's traditions with cynicism and treat it as a place merely for making a name for themselves: 'They seemed to consider themselves in an atmosphere of humbug – living in a lie – out of which lie-element those who chose were very right in making the most, for the gaining of fame or money'.[1] However, in 1862 Kingsley revised the novel. He was now Professor of History at Cambridge and no longer the *enfant terrible* of the Church of England; also, the Universities themselves had been reformed as a result of the 1850 Royal Commission of Enquiry. The original criticisms were largely removed from the text, and Locke's attitudes to the students are made to seem merely an aspect of his unwarranted class resentment at their privilege. Kingsley also added to the novel, though, by including a brief account of Locke's cousin's Tractarian views, and this constitutes the major indictment of the Cambridge students after the accounts of their bawdiness were cut:

> He tried to assure me – and did so with a great deal of cleverness
> – that this Tractarian movement was not really an aristocratic,
> but a democratic one; that the Catholic Church had been in all
> ages the Church of the poor; that the clergy were commissioned
> by Heaven to vindicate the rights of the people, and to stand
> between them and the tyranny of Mammon. I did not care to
> answer him that the 'Catholic Church' had always been a Church
> of slaves, and not of free men; that the clergy had in every age
> been the enemies of light, of liberty; the oppressors of their

71

flocks; and that to exalt a sacerdotal caste over other aristocra-
cies, whether of birth or wealth, was merely to change tyrants.
When he told me that a clergyman of the Established Church, if
he took up the cause of the working classes, might be the bold-
est and surest of allies, just because, being established, and certain of his income, he cared not one sixpence what he said to any
man alive. I did not care to answer him, as I might – And more
shame on the clergy that, having the safe vantage-ground which
you describe, they dare not use it like men in a good cause, and
speak their minds, if forsooth no-one can stop them from so
doing.[2]

Kingsley here invokes the conventional accusations against Roman
Catholicism: that it is a conspiracy of a crafty clergy over a laity kept
in a superstitious and credulous thraldom in order to preserve ecclesiastical privilege. For Alton Locke such an ecclesiastical system represents the very type of privilege he, as a Chartist, rejects. Despite
changes in his own position and in Cambridge itself, the fact that
Kingsley should have incorporated this passage to replace all the other
criticisms of Cambridge is indicative of his view that the dominant
threat to the integrity of the social order came now, not from workers
who were turning their backs on traditional freedoms in favour of the
political theories advocated by foreigners, but instead from a ruling
class turning to Rome. Of course the major figure who exemplified this
tendency was the one Kingsley was to attack explicitly a few years
later: John Henry Newman.

What is primarily interesting about Newman for the purposes of
this study is the way in which he relates to perceptions of national
characteristics, including those associated with gender. The thinking
which drove him to convert to Catholicism in 1845, after years spent
as the figurehead of a Catholicising pressure group within the Anglican Church, was largely driven by the application of the very principles which were used to vindicate British social order. None the less,
this conversion was popularly derided – though it was also seen as
inevitable – and the ensuing outcry set him up as the most prominent
in a line of 'perverts' who were unEnglish and unmanly, and who have
since been closely aligned with homosexuality in various accounts of
(Anglo-) Catholicism.[3] It seems to me that there are various symptomatic confusions at work in such accounts, and that these actually
misinterpret the real significance of the debates about gender
prompted by the Oxford-led return to Rome.

In view of Newman's later defection, it seems ironic that the Catholicising movement of which he was the most prominent figure was precipitated by a hostility to Whig Church Reforms, notably the Irish Temporalities Bill of 1833 which effectively abolished two of the archbishoprics and eight of the bishoprics of the Church of Ireland. Newman saw this not in Evangelical terms as undermining the Church's mission in Ireland but as a capitulation to liberalism. Though he protested throughout his Tractarian career that he was always bound by obedience to the Church hierarchy – a matter of absolute principle for him which led to the suppression of Tract 90, his revisionary account of the Thirty-nine Articles – Newman's sense of the need to argue against the liberalisation of both the Church's ecclesiastical arrangements and its dogma was based on the grounds that they were undermining the nation's religious integrity. This resulted ultimately in his lengthy process of conversion to Roman Catholicism and a career spent mounting a deeply reactionary, but also – because it went against the grain – perceptive critique of Protestant society. Naturally, too, he became the focus of attack as the arch-'pervert' whose malign influence threatened to return Britain to Rome rule (to appropriate a phrase). Given what I have been arguing about the manly character of English religious self-consciousness, it should be unsurprising that accounts of Newman paid great attention to gender, referring frequently to his femininity or – when offence was intended – to his effeminacy, this latter quality designating an unnatural condition, another form of perversion.

The debate continues to the present day, with one of his most recent biographers explicitly attempting to rescue him from the picture painted of him by that of an earlier biographer, Wilfrid Ward: 'The "feminine" side of Newman's character has been much emphasised', writes Ian Ker; 'without in any way denying it, I have endeavoured to stress also the other highly "masculine" side of his temperament, which showed itself in an astonishing resilience and uncompromising toughness in the face of adversity, as well as in the kind of resourceful practicality one associates with the man of action rather than the thinker.'[4] In the book's index under 'Newman', Ker lists no fewer that fifteen references to 'toughness of'. He acknowledges, therefore, that the debate is not simply a trivial one, but only partly understands the accusation of effeminacy, as I hope to show. I suspect that Ker's real, if unstated, intention is to remove the stigma of ascribed homosexuality from Newman's name. He therefore places particular emphasis on repudiating the claim, made in Wilfrid Ward's biography, that, on the death of Ambrose St John, Newman lay all night on the bed beside him: 'Ward, who tended only to see the sensitive or feminine side of Newman's personality, presumably imagined or at least gave credence to a fanciful exaggeration of a normal priestly action, and in doing so typically missed the sheer masculine toughness which sustained Newman even at this darkest hour.'[5] This may be a corrective to the view that Newman desired physical intimacy with St John (though they were, after all, buried together), but it attempts to retrieve Newman's masculinity from accusations of effeminacy whose meanings have changed significantly over time. Not only was the increasing suspicion of close emotional relations between men largely a feature of the later nineteenth century,[6] but the accusations of effeminacy which were levelled by his contemporary critics were related to his religious affiliations rather than his sexuality. None the less, this debate is, I think, revealing in relation to certain modern perceptions of sexuality, and I return to this subject after considering what I think is genuinely at stake in the attack by Kingsley.

### A very English Catholicism

Newman's major criticism of Protestant culture was aimed at its rationalism, its conviction that all claims might be subjected to the scrutiny of the individual. Whilst still in the Anglican Church, he argued:

> The Rationalist makes himself his own centre, not his Maker; he does not go to God, but he implies that God must come to him … Our private judgment is made everything to us … The notion of half views and partial knowledge, of guesses, surmises, hopes and fears, of truth faintly apprehended and not understood, of isolated facts in the great scheme of Providence, in a word, the idea of Mystery, is discarded.[7]

In religious terms, there is a compelling logic to this: for Newman the decentring of the individual was a part of the necessary process of accepting a subordinate position in relation to the authority which was without origin, perceptible only in its effects, and which, for this reason, was inscrutable to human reason, or *mysterious*, to use a word fundamental to Newman's theology. That his religious affiliations were also precipitated by political convictions, though, can be seen in his increasing disenchantment with the liberal theology which was dominant in the Anglican Church and, in particular, pervasive amongst his fellows at Oriel College in the 1820s. After condemning the wickedness of the 1830 French Revolution ('they seem the most wicked nation on earth') in a letter to his sister Jemima, he went on to condemn the tendency of the age 'towards *liberalism* – i.e. a thinking established notions [not?] worth noting – in this system of opinions a disregard of religion is included … *moral* truth is not acceptable to man's religious heart; it must be enforced by authority', and the basis of this authority he concluded – contradicting the liberals – must be Apostolic Succession.[8] This doctrine ultimately became the basis of his reasoning that the Anglican Church must be heretical, and from this the vindication of Catholicism and its teachings – miracles and all – followed logically and, it must be said, with a genuine inevitability.

As we have already seen, Newman became profoundly sceptical of the possibility of basing a social order on Protestant principles; that is, of keeping the 'formidable classes' in line. The climax to the novel *Loss and Gain*, written whilst in Rome shortly after Newman's conversion, further demonstrates this desire for social cohesion. It culminates in the protagonist Reding's conversion after witnessing a Mass in which 'rich and poor were mixed together – artisans, well-dressed youths, Irish labourers, mothers with two or three children – the only division being that of men from women'.[9] This observation of the congregation acting 'as … one vast instrument or Panharmonicon, moving all together' provokes Reding to declare to himself '"This *is* a popular religion"',[10] and indicates the conservatism which was at the heart of Newman's thinking. Indeed, the work which, in its composition, finally precipitated his conversion is a peculiar piece of justification because of its unorthodox vindication of Catholicism; in its time suspicious alike to Old Catholics in England and to Rome. The main argument of his *Essay on the Development of Christian Doctrine* is a legitimation of tradition, but its dominant rhetorical strategies belie a specifically English understanding of tradition.

The *Essay* was received critically by many of Newman's new co-religionists – Wiseman considered it potentially in error, one former Unitarian attacked it as possibly giving legitimacy to certain Unitarian arguments, and many Roman theologians prepared refutations of it. Newman himself feared that the book might be placed on the Catholic Index of prohibited books.[11] The main problem appears to have been Newman's historicism, a feature of his argument which resulted in a

dependence on probability rather than certainty (though the emphasis on probability was also influenced in this respect by his reading of
Bishop Butler). Paradoxically, Newman's historicism is actually a
result of his desire for certainty, realising that the Protestant claim to
depend on the self-evident teachings of the Bible was both inadequate
and inconsistent – inadequate because the Bible could be interpreted
in many ways, and inconsistent because Protestants did in fact sup-
plement Biblical teachings with doctrines not explicitly to be found
there (original sin, for example). Certainty for Newman was to be
found in the true development of doctrine according to specific principles which demonstrate consistency. 'Development' in the title of his
essay therefore refers to the elucidation over time of an idea originally
implicit in the Bible but not fully revealed there. On this argument the
true Catholic Church has been consistent throughout history not
because it has not changed but because of its consistent, gradual
development of religious truth. A number of tests must be applied to
distinguish the proper development of this idea from corruptions of it,
but the basis of these tests is that of organic development:

> the corruption of philosophical and political ideas is a process
> ending in dissolution of the body of thought and usage which
> was bound up, as it were, into one system; in the destruction of
> the norm or type, whatever it may be considered, which made it
> one; in its disorganisation; in its loss of the principle of life and
> growth; in its resolution into other distinct lives, that is, into
> other ideas which take the place of it.

Corruption is distinct from decay in the sense that corruption 'hastens
a crisis, as a fever, or the disturbance of a system consequent on poi-
soning … whereas in decay there is a loss of activity and vigour'.[12]
Newman proposes seven not entirely discrete tests of development:
preservation of the essential idea, continuity, assimilation ('an eclec-
tic, conservative, assimilating, healing moulding process, *a unitive
power*, is of the essence … of a faithful development'),[13] precedence in
the original form of the idea, logical relations between innovation and
the whole, conservatism in innovation, and durability (since corruption – heresy – cannot last). The clear basis of the test, then, derives
from that organic ideal of development which had been established as
the chief ideological justification of the British polity. Newman had
come to regard Protestantism as heresy, a classic instance of disbodi-
ent rebelliousness; and order – essentially a religious dispensation for

Newman – could not be based on the disease which Protestantism had introduced. Newman's acceptance of that religion which in England was popularly considered the ultimate in servility was therefore an ironic product of his commitment to the rhetoric and sentiments which were pressed into service to defend the British state against radical change.

Newman goes on to argue that the accusations levelled against Christianity well into the fourth century by those outside it are the same as those accusations levelled against it now by those external to its organised form (Protestants, that is). This, in itself, demonstrates the integrity of the Catholic Church through history. However, this emphasis on the integrity of the Catholic tradition did not blind Newman to the traditions of Protestantism which, he argued, undermined the claims of individual Protestants to being independent, rational thinkers without dogma or a sanctioning authority – other than conscience or the Bible – for their views. His analysis of this in his response to the Papal Aggression controversy demonstrates his awareness of the ideological potency of Protestantism. In his *Lectures on the Present Position of Catholics* Newman argues that the 'First Principles' of Protestant society were an integral part of the individual's perceptions as a result of the accumulated effects of England's history since the Reformation: England had a Protestant Establishment, a Protestant law and a Protestant culture all largely founded, or substantially reinforced, by Elizabeth I. This culture is personified by Shakespeare, Spenser, Sidney, Raleigh, Bacon, Hooker, Milton and Bunyan, whose writings are so embedded in the nation's consciousness that the 'ordinary run of men find it very difficult to determine, in respect to the proverbs, instances, maxims, and half sentences, which are in the nation's mouth, which, and how much is from the Bible, and how much from the authors I have mentioned'.[14] Newman even describes Protestantism as

> a tradition floating in the air; which we found in being when we first came to years of reason; which has been borne in upon us by all we saw, heard, or read, in the high life, in parliament, in law courts, in general society; which our fathers told us had ever been in their day; a tradition, therefore, truly universal and immemorial, and good as far as a tradition is worth: I mean, requiring some ultimate authority to make it trustworthy.[15]

For Newman, though, legitimate tradition requires a metaphysical base, and this is precisely what English Protestantism lacks. Newman is clearly undermining the authority of private judgement by recognising its dependence on a process of socialisation resting not on Biblical teaching but on institutions, processes and an ensemble of writings which, for the English, have become not supplementary to but inseparable from the founding document of their religion. In this way he reinforces what I have been saying about the continuing ideological centrality of Protestantism to Englishness, not simply as the consequence of a negative relationship with certain European nations but through the positive dissemination of ideas which were constitutive of that culture. Protestantism established itself as a form of common sense, and Newman provocatively contrasts this Established, institutionalised religion with the denigrated Catholicism of Ireland, a religion he claims as genuinely popular because surviving in conditions of extreme adversity: 'Catholicism [in Ireland] has been, not only not established; it has been persecuted for three hundred years, and at this moment it is more vigorous than ever.'[16] Such comparisons were hardly calculated to endear him to his English audience.

Newman, though, had never really shared the general English antipathy towards Ireland. Though the Whig reforms of the Established Church in Ireland were the pretext for his Tractarianism, Newman's fear was more specifically the vulnerability of the Church to a range of anti-Anglican forces. At the time of the Catholic Emancipation he claimed this was merely symptomatic of, and the vehicle for, other forces:

> It is not a religious question. The Union will ultimately be dissolved, tho' Religion may seem [?] the cause for some time longer. Enlighten the Irish, Protestantize them – Macte tua virtute – it is right – but you only make them more formidable opponents. Again the Church in England will not (we will say) be injured by this very Emancipation, but here again Emancipation is the *symptom* of a systematic hatred to our Church borne by Romanists, Sectarians, Liberals and Infidels. If it were not for the Revolution which one would think must attend it, I should say the Church must fall.[17]

The Irish question is presented here as fundamentally political, unpacifiable by religious concessions, but this did not remain Newman's conviction. Conversion, a more direct experience of Ireland, and various historical developments shaped rather different attitudes later in his life.[18] His most revealing statements about Irish affairs display an ambivalence about the situation which reflects his position as English and Catholic, and as one whose attitudes were formed prior to the increased scientific racism of the second half of the century. In the 1880s Newman varied his views according to his correspondent: he chastised English bigots and warned of the dangers of separation to Irish nationalists. To Hopkins (one of the former) he wrote that 'Irish Patriots hold that they never have yielded themselves to the sway of England and therefore never have been under her laws, and never have been rebels'. Consequently 'there is no help, no remedy. If I were an Irishman, I should be (in heart) a rebel'.[19] The parenthesis is important. Earlier he had written to Dr Walsh, President of St Patrick's, Maynooth, asking advice on a theological point: that 'the Irish people has never recognised, rather have since the time of Henry ii protested against and rejected the sovereignty of England, and have seemingly admitted it only when they were too weak to resist; and therefore it is no sin to be what would be commonly called a rebel'.[20] Unsurprisingly – given popular English perceptions of Irish nationalists as being in thrall to priests – he asked Walsh to burn the letter (though Newman omitted to burn his draft), and in turn he promised to burn Walsh's reply. The premise of his suggestion is significant, since it recognises Irish nationalism as a kind of tradition and therefore not strictly sinful. It was this which differentiated the Irish from the French revolutionaries (as well, of course, as the latter's more thoroughgoing anti-clericalism), whereas for many of Newman's English contemporaries Celts generally were characterised by their predisposition to revolution.

On the other hand he did simultaneously regard the situation in Ireland as revolutionary,[21] and presumably therefore not to be condoned. He also suggested to Charles Gavan Duffy that separation might actually bring about a worsening of conditions in Ireland.[22] Nor was Newman without patriotic leanings. To John Rickards Mozley (as well as to others), he claimed that Home Rule would represent 'a blow on the power of England as great as it is retributive'.[23] Equally significantly, he wrote to Lord Blachford in 1888 claiming that his predictions about separation should not be taken for agreement with such aspirations, though he did believe that Ireland should have religious 'freedom and independence' such as the Scots enjoyed, and that there was no grounds for 'utterly ignoring [the Irish] claim to be under English law'. Home Rule, on the other hand, 'would destroy both themselves and us. You cannot have two supreme powers.'[24]

It is a striking paradox, then, that Newman's quintessentially

English commitment to tradition underwrote both his conversion to Rome and his sneaking sympathy for Irish rebels. Moreover, this latter sentiment can claim some genuine Burkean justification. Burke argued that, since Catholicism was the traditional religion of Ireland, the Establishment of a Protestant Church of Ireland represented an unjustified and destabilising disruption of organic national development. His arguments, though, were intended to provoke changes which would stave off popular discontent with the social order at a time when secular republicanism was a serious threat to political continuity in Ireland.[25] Newman similarly argued against the Ascendancy as a usurping power in Ireland, but his arguments were set in a context in which Catholicism had become more integral to Irish nationalism after the defeat of anti-sectarian republican influences and the ascendancy of O'Connellite nationalism.

### Kingsley versus Newman

The attack on Catholic movements within Cambridge in the later edition of *Alton Locke* was not an exceptional one in Kingsley's writings, nor was it merely a convenient substitute for the degeneracy of the Cambridge undergraduates he had earlier depicted. As we have seen, Catholicism was for Kingsley another threat to the natural freedom of the English, one comparable to, even prototypical of, the abstract systems of republicans and socialists. His attacks on Catholicism, though, often tacitly acknowledged that the object of his criticism was Newman, even before the apparently gratuitous, casual reference in *Macmillan's Magazine* which led to the celebrated controversy between them.

Kingsley's anti-Catholicism was always intense. In 1864 his review of J. A. Froude's *History of England* sparked off an historic row. His comments are rather opaque and therefore demand some lengthy consideration:

> Truth for its own sake, had never been a virtue with the Roman clergy. Father Newman informs us that it need not, and on the whole ought not to be; that cunning is the weapon which Heaven has given to the saints wherewith to stand the brute male force of this wicked world which marries and is given in marriage. Whether his notion be doctrinally correct or not, it is at least historically so.[26]

This attack resulted in the controversy which led to Newman's *Apologia Pro Vita Sua*. From the outset Kingsley foregrounded what for him were issues of gender and celibatarianism as central to the debate about truth, whilst consistently demonstrating that these debates were also about national anxieties. His final pamphlet – 'What then Does Dr. Newman Mean?', a response to Newman's own denials of the convictions Kingsley attributed to him, and a demand for evidence to support those denials – is notable in this respect not for its own veracity in its account of Newman's writings but for its frank display of what Kingsley thought was at stake.

This is a debate which has been frequently revisited, and recent accounts dovetail to an extent with my discussion here, though they come to different conclusions. Following David Hilliard's well-known account of the relationship between homosexuality and (Anglo-) Catholicism, Oliver S. Buckton has suggested that the underlying accusation against Newman is one of homosexuality, that this is contained in the epithet 'effeminate' which Kingsley applied to Newman, and, moreover – following an argument made by Susan Chitty in her biography of Kingsley – that this accusation was a defensive move by Kingsley resulting from his own ambivalent feelings towards men.[27] I want to consider briefly Buckton's and Hilliard's arguments, since together they are symptomatic of broader assumptions.

Alan Sinfield has convincingly argued that the term 'effeminacy' was by no means synonymous with homosexuality – it was, indeed, frequently associated with heterosexual libertinism – in the period prior to the Wilde trials. Only after this watershed did the two terms became virtually interchangeable.[28] This, of course, immediately problematises the arguments of those who depend on the validity of this correlation. Also, Buckton, in particular, attributes sexual connotations to the use of the word 'pervert' in the context of these religious debates. The term 'pervert' is, of course, significant in its application to Catholic converts, but not because of its sexual implications (if any). In his argument Buckton cites Jonathan Dollimore's work on the concept of perversion, claiming that the term carries an inherent charge of lack of manliness, since perversion is associated with the 'wayward woman'. More likely – since the Augustinian concept of perversion as Dollimore outlines it denotes an insidious turning away from righteousness[29] – what this really demonstrates is that the true path of Protestantism was considered coterminous with that of the English nation. Conversion to Rome was therefore a form of treachery, both to the nation and to the religion which had secured its destiny.

In his article on (Anglo-)Catholicism David Hilliard is conscious that the evidence on which his argument depends is at times sketchy, and that assumptions are inevitably based on innuendo. That there is now a cultural connection between (Anglo-) Catholicism and homosexuality in certain class-based English circles is undeniable, but the argument that this has always been the case is rather more dubious, even on the evidence Hilliard presents. For example, amongst the popular 'revelations' of the unnatural outrages of Catholicism, Hilliard includes those of the *Awful Disclosures of Maria Monk* and an 1864 incident in which a love letter from a Norwich monk to a choirboy was disclosed to the *Norfolk News* provoking popular outrage. These examples, though, do not exactly support Hilliard's case. Maria Monk's 'disclosures' were exclusively of outrages committed by monks on nuns and their illegitimate children (illicit sex, the disposal of unwanted babies and even the murder of the mothers). Moreover, the *Norfolk News's* response to the Norwich incident precisely does not align Catholicism with same-sex desire:

> We tell 'Ignatius' plainly, and we tell everybody else connected with this establishment who has the slightest powers of reflection, that the herding together of men in one building, with the occasional letting in of young girls – some of them morbid, some of them silly and sentimental – and of boys likewise, with soft, sensitive temperaments, cannot fail to produce abominations.[30]

Perhaps surprisingly, the first anxiety here is for the safety of girls, so the fear of monastic perversion is clearly not specifically connected with the fear of same-sex acts. What is indicated in these two pieces of evidence, therefore, is that the monks' denial of supposedly natural sexual relations was considered the cause of all kinds of abominations, amongst them – though perhaps particularly obnoxious – same-sex acts. The perception observed by Hilliard seems to have emerged later than he suggests, and there is little evidence that the specific charge of homosexuality is implied in that of effeminacy at this time.[31]

So, if Kingsley is not alleging same-sex desire against Newman, what is his agenda in this attack? I have already outlined what I take to be the main features of Kingsleyan manliness. His dislike of effeminacy, on the other hand, was a product of his hatred of all forms of 'manichean' religion, and that included, for instance, Nonconformity.

He once wrote to his wife from his Eversley parish, taking pleasure in observing the decline in Dissent and the corresponding increase in his own popularity: 'I find ... that the young wild fellows who are considered as hopeless by most men, because most men are what they call "spoony Methodists," i.e. effeminate ascetics – dare not gainsay, but rather look up to a man who they see is their superior, if he chose to exert his power, in physical as well as intellectual skill.'[32] Asceticism, then – not Catholicism alone – was the problem, and this further undermines any straightforward alignment of Catholicism, effeminacy and homosexuality. Kingsley despised the religious denigration of the body, emphasising instead its dutiful subjection to religious and national ends. The greater emphasis which Kingsley placed on the threat posed by Catholicism was a consequence of its indisputably alien character and a response to its increasing popularity amongst the educated.

In his pamphlet on Newman, Kingsley initially fastens on Newman's sermon 'Wisdom and Innocence', given in 1842 – to Kingsley's especial disgust – whilst Newman was still an Anglican clergyman. Kingsley interprets it as claiming that the rules governing earthly conduct are not directly connected with faith, faith being an inner assent rather than an outward conformity to law and secular morals. Consequently Newman appears to be arguing that deceit, evasion and apparent hypocrisy are legitimate means by which Christians should conquer the hostility of 'the world'. Indeed Newman suggests that these were, in fact, the means by which Christianity grew, means which were ultimately sanctioned by Christ himself. Moreover, the seeming artificiality of Christians is to be accounted for by their strict self-restraint '"which makes holy persons seem wanting in openness and manliness"'.[33] The division between Christians and the world depicted in this sermon, Kingsley therefore takes to represent the division between Roman Catholics and Protestants. The Christian values which Newman extols are those of monks and nuns, and amongst Christian doctrines he advocates celibacy of the clergy, sacramental confession and a relation of laity to clergy resembling that of subjects to rulers.

Kingsley's underpinning assumptions throughout all of this are that Newman does not respect conventional modes of behaviour, whilst Kingsley assimilates conformity to some form of higher truth. The differences between Kingsley and Newman in this respect are epitomised by Newman's ambivalent attitude towards the English ideal of the gentleman. Inverting Protestant wisdom that the Catholic Church enforced formal obedience whilst leaving the inner person unreformed, Newman, in his inaugural lectures to the Catholic University in Ireland, claimed that gentlemanly attainments were superficial: 'the "gentleman" is the creation, not of Christianity, but of civilisation … The world is content with setting right the surface of things; the Church aims at regenerating the very depths of the heart.'[34] For Newman – and for Gerard Manley Hopkins following him – the emphasis on conduct so important to English moral definition was not sufficient proof of a truly Christian disposition which was ultimately attainable only through Catholic teaching. Indeed Kingsley's claim in his pamphlet is that Newman actually exhorts people to defy worldly conventions – including the observance of national laws and customs – in pursuit of supposedly religious ends. What this demonstrates above all is Kingsley's abhorrence at what he perceives as Newman's disregard of the principles of civility and the observance of law. This abhorrence is brought out more clearly in the rest of his argument. In pursuing further Newman's 'perverse pleasure in saying something shocking to English notions', two especially provoke Kingsley's apoplexy. The first occurs in *Lectures on Anglican Difficulties* in the example of the Irish '"mere beggar woman, lazy, ragged, and filthy, and not over-scrupulous of truth"' who is none the less devout and whom Newman claims has a better prospect of heaven than the upright, but not particularly holy, state 'pattern-man'. Kingsley responds:

> What Dr. Newman may have meant to teach by these words I cannot say; but what he has taught the whole Celtic population, that as long as they are chaste (which they cannot well help being, being married almost before they are men and women), and sober (which they cannot well help being, being too poor to get enough whisky to make them drunk), and 'go to their religious duties' – an expression on which I make no comment – they may look down upon the Protestant gentry who send over millions to feed them in famine; who found hospitals and charities to which they are admitted freely; who try to introduce among them capital, industry, civilisation, and, above all, that habit of speaking the truth, for want of which they are what they are, and are likely to remain such, as long as they have Dr. Newman for their teacher – that they may look down, I say, on the Protestant gentry as cut off from God, and without hope of heaven, because they do their duty by mere 'natural virtue'.

Kingsley goes on to argue that the confessional also provides a place in which the Irish may be absolved of their crimes without incurring British justice. Altogether, Newman teaches that 'profanity, blasphemy, imposture, stealing, lying' are not prejudicial to the sanctity of the Roman Church, as works and faith are separable and faith is a result of supernatural influences. The practical effects of Newman's teaching of disregard for national laws is taken to be evident in Irish contempt for British laws. That Catholicism justified disobedience in Ireland was hardly a new claim, but we see in this context Kingsley's invocation of truth as legitimation of imperial law, and the consequence of this is that the mystified devotion of the Irish Catholics is one which blinds them equally to the acceptance of the rule of law and an understanding of their relations with the quotidian world. The consequences are their lack of industry and civilisation, and the devastations of famine from which the wealthy and benevolent English must rescue them. These were not attitudes peculiar to Kingsley.

The second troubling example for Kingsley from *Lectures on Anglican Difficulties* is Newman's account of a young woman with the self-inflicted marks of the stigmata, which, claims Kingsley, 'will arouse in every English husband, father, and brother ... the same feelings which it aroused in me':

> A poor girl, cajoled, flattered, imprisoned, starved, maddened, by such as Dr. Newman and his peers, into that degrading and demoralising disease, hysteria, imitates on her own body, from that strange vanity and deceit which too often accompany the complaint, the wounds of our Lord; and all that Dr. Newman has to say about the matter is, to inform us that the gross and useless portent is 'a singular favour vouchsafed only to a few elect souls' ... If he is to be on trial for nothing else, he is on his trial for those words; and he will remain upon his trial as long as Englishmen know how to guard the women over whom God has committed to their charge. If the British public shall ever need informing that Dr. Newman wrote that passage, I trust there will always be one man left in England to inform them of the fact, for the sake of the ladies of this land.[36]

The charge here is essentially the same as that made in relation to Newman's alleged irresponsibility towards the Irish: in his authoritative role he is encouraging those (congenitally) susceptible of failing to apprehend their real relation to the world, and in this rejecting truth. The clear inference is that Newman is undermining the rational, yet divine will whose truth is entrusted to patriarchal authority. This was an issue that was personally relevant to him, given that Fanny Kingsley was herself attracted to Puseyite teachings on virginity before meeting with Charles's corrective influence, but it needs to be stressed again that his response was not merely idiosyncratic. Anglo-Catholicism seems to have held a particular attraction for women,[37] and one persistent fear which this fuelled was that Catholicism represented an intrusion on the sacrosanct authority a man possessed over his wife. In the controversy generated by the Papal Aggression many cartoons and articles in Punch played on these fears. Women were presented as being vulnerable to the machinations of priests, who exploited women's susceptibility to hysteria. One cartoon depicts priests taking over a man's household (he is excluded at the door) and indoctrinating the women of the house, one of whom is clearly depicted in a state of agitated reverie (see figure 3).

There are further implications in Kingsley's comments, and here I want to consider the relevance of sexual abstinence to the debate. These implications are perhaps best demonstrated by a letter he wrote to John Stuart Mill in 1870 explaining his reasons for not overtly supporting the campaign for women's right to vote. Distinguishing those women who were 'brave, prudent, pure, wise, tried by experience and sorrow, highly cultivated and thoughtful too', he argued that

> foolish women, of no sound or coherent opinions, and of often questionable morals … are inclined to patronise us in the most noisy and demonstrative way. I am aware of the physical and psychical significance of this fact. I know, and have long foreseen, that what our new idea has to beware of, lest it should be swamped thereby, is hysteria, male and female. Christianity was swamped by it from at least the third to the sixteenth century, and if we wish to save ourselves from the same terrible abyss … we must steer clear of the hysteric element, which I define as the fancy and emotions unduly excited by suppressed sexual excitement … there will never be a good world for woman, till the last monk, and therewith the last remnant of the monastic idea of, and legislation for, woman, i.e., the canon law, is civilised off the earth.[38]

Celibacy is taken by Kingsley to be the root of hysterical symptoms and therefore of the kind of effeminacy he sees in Newman. Sexual relations (within marriage, of course) are correspondingly the root to healthy psychic development and therefore to a true relation to the world. This emphasis on the health of sexual relations is partly one personal to Kingsley – or, at least it finds one of its most vociferous exponents in him – but it is also one which had its roots more generally in Protestant culture.

From its origins Protestantism gave great symbolic significance to sexual relations as central to an understanding of the natural world purged of superstition. Luther argued that God 'wills to have his excellent handiwork honoured as his divine creation, and not despised', and that God's creation of men and women is complemented by his injunction to them to be fruitful and multiply. This, indeed, is both inevitable and natural: 'it is not a matter of free choice or decision but a natural and necessary thing, that whatever is a man must have a woman and whatever is a woman must have a man.' The consequence of resisting is that the sexual urge 'goes its way through fornication, adultery, and secret sins, for this is a matter of nature and not of choice'.[39] Luther sanctions a hydraulic model of sexuality, and his insistence on the irresistability of such drives is confirmation for him of a higher imperative. This emphasis on the natural as manifestation of God's will is, as we have seen, crucial to Protestant thought, not

FIGURE 3   *Punch*, 19 (1850), p. 227

87

least as it developed in England; the laws of nature were not something to be counterposed to God's will. In this way the natural was
imbued with a sense of divine legitimacy, though through this same
process it is also possible to discern a reciprocal legitimation of what
was considered natural as arbiter of what was moral. The contempt
for celibacy was no less a part of this vindication of the natural, and
the rejection of celibacy was bound up with a rejection of the greater
holiness once claimed by the priesthood, marking them off from the
laity.[40] Moreover, all shades of Protestant theology accepted that
mutual comfort and endearment were legitimate functions of sex
within marriage, an acceptance which, it has been argued, 'began the
slow separation of sexual pleasure from procreation that ended in the
late seventeenth-century spread of both contraception and libertinism'.[41] The Evangelical revival may have undermined the acceptability
of such libertinism, but it did not undermine the legitimate-because-
natural status of sex within marriage. As Michael Mason points out,
Protestant England held 'an almost universal distaste for chastity as a
deliberate and dedicated condition', and even such an Evangelically
inclined figure as Isaac Taylor persistently attacked early Christian
celibacy.[42]

Taking one popular literary example, we can see this vindication
of sexuality as a part of the natural world at work in Browning's 'Fra
Lippo Lippi'.[43] Lippi's endearing blokishness betrays Browning's own
sympathy with the natural eroticism which underpins both Lippi's
conduct – in the poem he is discovered in pursuit of his lusts, forced
into depravity by Catholic asceticism – and his aesthetic: he represents
the body as both naturally beautiful and, at the same time, intimating
something of the divine. Rejecting the priests' injunctions to desexu-
alise the figures he paints – "'Make them [the laity] forget there's such
a thing as flesh'" (l. 182) – he repeatedly describes himself as "'a beast'"
and insists "'The world and life's too big to pass for a dream'" (l. 251).
Instead Lippi views the function of art as being not simply to reproduce the world but to inspire in the viewer a sense of wonder at it:

> What's it all about?
> To be passed o'er, despised? or dwelt upon,
> Wondered at? oh, this last of course, you say
> But why not do as well as say, – paint these
> Just as they are, careless what comes of it?
> God's works – paint any one, and count it crime
> To let a truth slip. Don't object, 'His works

Are here already – nature is complete:
Suppose you reproduce her – (which you can't)
There's no advantage! you must beat her, then.'
For, don't you mark, we're made so that we love
First when we see them painted, things we have passed
Perhaps a hundred times nor cared to see;
And so they are better, painted – better to us,
Which is the same thing. Art was given for that -
God uses us to help each other so,
Lending our minds out.

(ll. 290–306)

So Browning, through Lippi, legitimates the *rapprochement* between religion and the natural world, a world to which sexuality is integral. Simultaneously, though, the poem serves to highlight the hypocrisy of Catholic monks by accusing them of a duplicitous materialism in contrast to Lippi's honest, forthright masculinity:

What would men have? Do they like grass or no –
May they or mayn't they? all I want's the thing
Settled for ever one way: as it is,
You tell too many lies and hurt yourself.
You don't like what you only like too much,
You do like what, if given you at your word,
You find abundantly detestable.
For me, I think I speak as I was taught –
I always see the Garden and God there
A-making man's wife – and, my lesson learned,
The value and significance of flesh,
I can't unlearn ten minutes afterward.

(ll. 258–269)

Of course the result is that the monks themselves are given to certain forms of self-indulgence which Lippi discovers as part of the monastic life. The monks enjoy

                    the good bellyful,
The warm serge and the rope that goes all round,
And day-long blessed idleness beside!

(ll. 103–5)

Moreover, the anti-Catholicism which underpins this monologue is consistent with much of the rest of the poetry in *Men and Women*, including the depiction of Bishop Blougram, a satire on Cardinal Wiseman in response to the Papal Aggression. Blougram's eloquence and duplicitous attachment to his lifestyle is similarly in contrast to the directness and honesty of Lippi.

Returning to Kingsley's pamphlet, we can see that his attribution to celibacy of a causal relation in hysteria – characterised by an unreal relation to the world – suggests that he is drawing on a more prevalent sense that celibacy had become emblematic of Catholicism's unnatural superstition. The Protestant tradition, on the other hand, had established – or, at least, confirmed – a new epistemological relation to the natural to which the legitimation of sexual relations was integral. It can be only in this light that Kingsley's original charge against Newman – that he made 'cunning ... the weapon which Heaven has given the saints wherewith to stand the brute male force of this wicked world *which marries and is given in marriage*' – makes sense. Marriage is part of that true relation to the world which is indicative of manhood. Newman, in not carrying out his duty of proper moral guidance towards women and the Irish, and instead encouraging their hysterical conditions, was not only refusing to face up to his role in the world as a man but was himself taking on the condition of femininity by participating in a religion which refused to validate the natural world as unfallen. As John Maynard suggests, Kingsley's sexual attitudes were integral to his whiggish historical sense.[44]

Theologically the root of Newman's alleged lack of respect for truth for its own sake is his acceptance of the doctrine of economy: since the mind of God is unknowable, our understanding must remain deficient, and therefore we must accept the teachings of the Church as authoritative, our only possible guide. Only through constant devotion can we begin to possess a knowledge of God, and this was not a directly communicable truth. For Kingsley this implies that truth is a 'virtue so lofty, as to be unattainable by man, who must therefore take up with what-is-no-more-than-a-hyperbole-to-call lies'. Consequently, Roman moralists 'have not seen that facts are not the property of man, to be 'economised' as man thinks fit, but of God, who ordereth all things in heaven and earth ... and that God requires truth, not merely in outward words, but in inward parts; and that therefore the first and most absolute duty of every human being is to speak and act the exact truth'.[45] Kingsley's facticity confronts the mystery which is at the heart of Newman's religious view in the form of manly maturity, a maturity which is symptomatic of a personal condition but which is underpinned by a profound sense of historical progression from the Reformation on (and even before this, since Kingsley's view is largely racial, based on a belief in Teutonic supremacy). Elsewhere Kingsley even equates the Enlightenment pursuit of truth with the truth of divine dispensation and suggests that the nineteenth century was a century of change as profound and of the same nature as that of the Reformation, and was similarly divinely inspired.[46] Newman's insistence on the unreal quality of corporeal existence and, consequently, his disdain for merely national law, is at the heart of his effeminacy as alleged by Kingsley. Indeed his rejection of custom and law was merely the obverse of the hysterical effeminacy Kingsley found in Shelley, who he suggested might end up at Rome, possibly as an Oratorian (Newman's order), if his egotism deserted him. In writing to Alexander Macmillan (the founder of *Macmillan's Magazine*) after the publication of Newman's *Apologia*, he gave as one of his reasons for not pursuing the controversy his unwillingness to be subjected to Newman's duplicitous oscillation between meekness and hysteria: 'I cannot be weak enough to put myself a second time, by any fresh act of courtesy, into the power of one who, like a treacherous ape, lifts to you meek and suppliant eyes, till he thinks he has you within his reach, and then springs, gibbering and biting at your face'.[47]

## Reality and homosexuality

In contrast to the Protestant acceptance of the world and its insistence on work as a means of bringing both that world and the self into subjection, Newman and other Anglo-Catholics cultivated a 'habit' of holiness which revealed in their very conduct their disdain for this world as a dream. This, indeed, had some impact on Anglo-Catholics' bearing towards the world. In 1858 Bishop Wilberforce at Cuddesdon College warned his students about their High-Church dress, and urged them not to 'walk with a peculiar step, carry their heads at a peculiar angle, and read in a peculiar tone'.[48] The perception of Newman's own effeminacy – his physical bearing which similarly suggested an 'unreal' interaction with the world – sometimes resulted in bizarre responses to him. Wilfrid Ward gave one account:

> The present writer's father – never one of the most intimate of the circle which surrounded Newman at Oxford – used to say that his heart would beat as he heard Newman's step on the staircase. His keen humour, his winning sweetness, his resentments and anger, all showed him intensely alive, and his friends

loved his faults as one may those of a fascinating woman; at the same time many of them revered him almost as a prophet. Only a year before his death, after nearly twenty years of misunderstandings and estrangement, W. G. Ward told the present biographer of a dream he had had – how he found himself at a dinner party next to a veiled lady, who charmed him more and more as they talked. At last he exclaimed, 'I have never felt such charm in any conversation since I used to talk with John Henry Newman, at Oxford.' 'I am John Henry Newman', the lady replied, and raising her veil showed the well-known face.[49]

As a dream, this was a gift for the psychological 'character study' of the Oxford Movement by Geoffrey Faber, first published in 1933, in which Newman's psychic development is regarded as the complement to his physiological 'femininity'. Ward's anecdote, Faber comments, is only one of many almost inevitable comparisons of him to a woman proceeding from his ability to charm, a trait which developed because of his need for the companionship of men, the complement of his sexual indifference to women. This is the most elaborate of all attempts to explain the determinants of Newman's femininity, and I want to consider it in detail not in order to attempt to restore Newman's reputation (I leave this to his hagiographers) but to discuss the book's assumptions, assumptions which give a new inflexion to those understandings of gender I have just been considering.

Faber's analysis of Newman depends on a conviction that Newman's life was determined from an early age by the strong moralism which his mother impressed on the plasticity of his infantile mind, producing an early repression which became manifest in his superstition, particularly his belief in angels which deceived him with the semblance of a material world. This repression remained all his life and resulted in the unnatural divorce of his intellect and emotions from his physical life: 'Newman's natural masculinity, if he ever had it, was quickly cauterized. As he might never be an ordinary boy, so he was never to be a whole man, and as a leader he was to prove a broken reed.'[50] Newman could thus never break with his dependency on his mother, a dependency at once strictly moral and simultaneously the source of a necessary love never satisfiable by anyone else because his permanent repression made transference impossible; the only other sources of emotional satisfaction were the celibate intense friendships which he developed with others throughout his life and which were always characterised by one particularly close one (notably those with

Hurrell Froude and Ambrose St John). Newman's progression towards the Roman Catholic Church is, in this account, the narrative of a return to the security of childhood via a revolt against the liberal orthodoxy of the Anglicanism of his time. This latter period, indeed, was the one in which he was 'most nearly a complete man',[51] though only because of the ferocity of a campaign which was itself a result of the attempted irruption of repressed instincts. His final conversion – one rationalised as an intellectual progression, though actually decided by emotional necessity – was one of self-abasement, of subjection once again to an absolute external authority. In Newman's account of the Monophysite heresy – in which Christ's nature is regarded as singular rather than both human and divine – Faber discerns in Newman's response to Pope Leo's authoritative voice a recognition of 'the veritable accents of power, severe, uncompromising, peremptory',[52] and considers Newman's own comparative image of the Anglican and Roman Catholic Churches to be revealing: 'he compared the Anglican conception of a detached and objective Truth to a Calvary, exhibiting Christ alone on the Cross; while he likened the Roman vision of Truth to the Child in the arms of a Madonna "lying hid in the bosom of the Church as if one with her, clinging to and (as it were) lost in her embrace"'.[53] This was the final result of a characteristic process of ambitious drive followed by self-abasement precipitated by his struggle to achieve a successful and complete repression.

Inevitably this psychological and physiological effeminacy also determines another aspect of Newman in Faber's narrative: his constitutional 'homosexuality'. This is a trait he shares with other Tractarians, notably Froude, and one manifest in their commitment to celibacy (in the *Apologia* Newman claims that at an early age he had a deep imaginative inspiration never to marry, an inspiration which 'strengthened my feeling of separation from the visible world')[54] as well as their intimacy. Froude is depicted by Faber as having sublimated his passion for male friendships into idealised and sanctified, if sometimes tormenting forms (even though, in strictly Freudian terms, sublimation or a problematic repression would not resemble the feelings which were being channelled or denied). Newman, on the other hand, was incapable of representing himself as other than a 'whole person', but the strong implication of him giving up entirely any desire to marry on meeting Froude implies to Faber a homosexual disposition. Normally, as with Whately, Newman was the lover rather than the loved – that is, he played the subordinate feminine role – but with

Froude he was the loved, and Froude's position was in turn occupied by Ambrose St John.

There are certain explicit and consistent aspects of Newman's thought which fit into Faber's scheme. A belief that the divine was also discernible in man – the specificity of gender implied here is intentional – was a part of Newman's aesthetics, and this to precisely the extent that each man disavowed his rationalist independence of spirit. Early in his life Newman claimed that a religious appreciation of the world enables us to recognise that 'our friends around are invested with an unearthly brightness – no longer imperfect men, but beings taken into Divine favour, stamped with His seal, and in training for future happiness'.[55] This conviction did not change: on becoming a cardinal, Newman took as his motto 'Heart speaks to heart'. Indeed this aesthetic sense was the intuitive route to faith for Newman, since rational systems – when used to analyse the natural world – reduced human comprehension of the religious ordering of that world. Whilst still vicar of St Mary's in Oxford he weighed in against the presumptions of science in ways which demonstrate the inadequacy for him of modest divine-watchmaker theories:

> if ... [man] conceives that the Order of Nature, which he partially discerns, will stand in the place of God who made it, and that all things continue and move on, not by His will and power, and the agency of the thousands and ten thousand of His unseen Servants, but by fixed laws, self-caused and self-sustained, what a poor weak worm and miserable sinner he becomes![56]

Newman's sacramentalism therefore generated a sense of the divine shadowing of the natural, and especially of humanity, which inevitably must have constituted an injunction against sin and especially against sexual activity of any kind. In this context, theories of repression or sublimation are unnecessary. For Faber, though, this sense of the divine represents a resort to magic in order to legitimate the repression inculcated in him by his mother, a form of repression by which Newman denied his real relationship to the world. The important conclusion which Faber's argument draws is an alignment between arrested development, homosexuality and a magical understanding of the world, and this is at the heart of Faber's account of the 'truth' of Newman as lying in his psychological and even physiological effeminacy.

At no point does Faber entertain the idea that Newman's philosophical position is anything other than mere delusion, an attempt to defend the outmoded beliefs of previous ages – despite the fact that his theology was (and, for Christians at least, remains) a real challenge to the rationalisations of Protestantism, to its prioritisation of reason in religion where faith should have the upper hand. This need to cling to outmoded but comforting beliefs is simply equated with Newman's need to preserve his repressed childhood condition, so that primitive superstition and an unmanly immaturity become synonymous. It is now also sexual maturity which is implicated directly in the definition of manhood as a psychic goal and the achievement of a 'real' relation to the external world. In this respect effeminacy is bound up even more intimately than before with this ensemble of values as a fact of the individual psyche – Newman's development is actually a regression.

Faber's account is clearly indebted to psychoanalysis, if not directly then at least through the psychological theory on which he seems to have drawn.[57] It is not difficult to see that Freud's own writings encourage a progressivist view such as Faber's, particularly in the text which sought to discover the origins of human morality through a study of 'primitive' societies by comparing the traditions of these societies to the state of mind of neurotics: *Totem and Taboo*, the work of which Freud remained most proud. This is a complex account of the integrated nature of ontogenetic and phylogenetic development, and in precisely this respect – in the intimacy of historical and personal evolution – it lends validity to the patterns of thought I have been outlining here. Freud argues that the founding moment of human morality lies in the attempts to expiate the sense of guilt generated by the murder and eating of the primal father by those males of the primitive horde previously excluded by him from sexual relations with the females of the horde, an act which corresponds on an individual level to the Oedipal drama in which remorse is felt at the desire to kill the father. This is productive of a fundamental ambivalence – the tension between the desire to commit the deed and the remorse at having felt such a desire – which in the individual is finally constitutive of the conscience, ultimately (in Freud's later writing) the superego, since in society the attempts at expiation for this repressed crime form religious and moral systems. In this way Freud deploys psychoanalysis to read anthropological history and vice versa, in a way which leaves uncertain which of the two is of primary significance.

Freud was in some ways sensitive to oversimplifications of his work and to attempts to use it to impose a normative pattern of development on individuals (though this sensitivity tended to be expressed in footnotes). This said, it is not difficult to see how normalising psychology was able appropriate his work in tendentious ways to validate conventional heterosexual relations as the most satisfactory outcome to a child's development[58] and also the proper attribute of a developed race, an aspect of the true, or truer, relation to reality, especially on the part of the man. Take, for example, the statement from *Totem and Taboo* aligning the phases of individual libidinal development and those of man (women, it seems, are without history):

> The animistic phase would correspond to narcissism both chronologically and in its content; the religious phase would correspond to the stage of object-choice of which the characteristic is a child's attachment to his parents; while the scientific phase would have an exact counterpart in the stage at which the individual has reached maturity, has renounced the pleasure principle, adjusted himself to reality and turned to the external world for the object of his desires.[59]

It seems that the 'religious phase' Freud has in mind here is Protestant; Catholicism resembles more the animistic, magical phase. The essential feature of this narcissistic early stage is, moreover, that of the unreal 'omnipotence of thought', the over-valuation of psychical acts which produces a belief in magical acts (significantly it is only in art, Freud claims, that such omnipotence persists). The turning away from self-centredeness is therefore the process by which, individually and historically, men have come to terms with the real world, and as part of this have come to discover sexual interest beyond both themselves (the stage of narcissism) and their original object-choices. In many normative readings of Freud homosexuality clearly figures as part of the narcissistic phase of the individual and therefore as arrested development.[60] In Faber's account Newman's superstition and his 'homosexuality' are, in turn, derived from the convictions which determined Freud's thinking, convictions which I have already suggested were perceptible in pre-Freudian contexts. The alignment of heterosexual relations with the reality principle pre-dates Freud and is vindicated by him; homosexuality's non-utility, its regressive characteristics and absorption in the pleasure principle, are tokens of its retreat from that real world, an always infantile individual condition.

This returns me to the question of authority. Part of Newman's contempt for the claims of rationalism was, as we have seen, for its self-centredness, its rejection of the kind of authority he undoubtedly craved. This was an aspect of his explicitly political convictions carried to their logical conclusion, though Faber portrays it as being his desire to return to a comforting state of domination by his mother. Over-extended parental authority and especially maternal domination are – according to one of Faber's sources – one source of 'individual and racial degeneracy' because they rob that individual of the independence of mind which is 'his birthright',[61] since mental health is constituted by a simultaneous respect for and willingness critically to examine tradition. Newman's spurned birthright was that which should have belonged to all Englishmen; its rejection was indicative of a malaise.

Inscribed on Newman's gravestone were the words *Ex umbris et imaginibus in veritatem* ('out of unreality into reality').

# 4

## Hysteric Celts

According to Terry Eagleton, Arthur Hallam in Tennyson's *In Memoriam* 'is nothing less than the empty space congregated by a whole set of ideological anxieties concerned with science, religion, the class-struggle, in short with the "revolutionary" de-centring of "man" from his "imaginary" relation of unity with his world'.[1] Yet, as Eagleton also realises, Hallam's status is finally replete with significance, and the renewed self-assurance, faith and sense of optimism at the end of the poem was made possible by nothing less than the British state triumph of 1848. The process by which Tennyson achieves this restitution, though, is a complex one, and the final sections of the poem manage to assert a pervasive sense of divinely ordained continuity which reconciles faith with evolutionary theory, whilst simultaneously contributing to the legitimation of the British polity. The means by which Tennyson is able to resolve his all-encompassing doubts is important, since it not only draws on and develops well-established ideological features of English culture but also contributes to that perception that the English were virtually unique in their rejection of revolutionary methods of change. This uniqueness, moreover, is presented as a racial propensity whose antithesis resides in the Celtic race.

Tennyson's grief over Hallam's death results from his inability to overcome his morbid fixation on the corporeal world of nature: death, in the early sections of the poem, is the material fact of inertia and decomposition. The Old Yew, for instance, is a metaphor for Tennyson's earth-bound, rooted obsession with physical loss:

> Old Yew, which graspest at the stones
> That name the under-lying dead,
> Thy fibres net the dreamless head,
> Thy roots are wrapt about the bones.[2]

This is the significance of the poet's imagined growing 'incorporate into thee' (i.e. the Yew): Hallam's physical death precludes any intimation of continuity between this life and the next, and the intensity of the poet's grief lies in his inability to overcome those doubts attendent on the clean break apparently represented by death. Such materialist morbidity in the overall context of the poem is connected with the influence of science, with its inability to apprehend the spiritual and metaphysical; and it is only Tennyson's intuitive perception of Hallam's non-corporeal presence which finally enables him to overcome his grief and simultaneously to surmount his fixation on the particular, to move beyond his hysteria in order to achieve self-mastery and a sense of perspective (these two being inseparable). As Elaine Jordan notes, this dynamic in the poem is generated by a specific contradiction: 'Emotional excess, heightened sensibility and expressive language, the stuff of poetry in the Romantic tradition to which Tennyson belonged are incompatible with manliness in its mid-nineteenth century definition'.[3] The process by which Tennyson overcomes this contradiction is demonstrated in section C of the poem, in which he achieves a panoramic survey of nature. Hallam's absence/presence is still felt, but memories of him are now 'gracious' – detached rather than overwhelming – and elements within the landscape appear to sigh ('breathe') with Tennyson without becoming embodiments of his near-derangement:

> I climb the hill: from end to end
>    Of all the landscape underneath,
>    I find no place that does not breathe
> Some gracious memory of my friend;
> ....
> But each has pleased a kindred eye,
>    And each reflects a kindlier day;
>    And, leaving these, to pass away
> I think once more he seems to die.
>
>                       (C, ll. 1–4, 17–20)

(The end of this section suggests a return to grief, but this is also bound up with the poet's retreat from the perspective he has gained at the opening.) If Tennyson's grief is intimately bound up with his relationship to nature, then, so is the means of overcoming that grief, as symbolised here by this more manly (because more self-possessed) relationship. As Tess Cosslett argues, it is plausible to see Tennyson in the poem 'as gradually adjusting his thought-processes into harmony with Nature, so that his inner life becomes an analogy or type of the ordered processes of the natural world';[4] hence the order he eventually finds in himself is a reflection of the order he finds in nature. Moreover, Tennyson's strategy throughout the poem exploits the evolutionary processes at work in nature in order to produce a synthesis of natural development and religious sensibility. It is this synthesis which vindicates the social order through an adaptation of the metaphor of organicism. Man's love and noble pursuit of 'Truth' seem to defy the brutalism of 'Nature, red in tooth and claw', and these superior qualities therefore intimate something of the divine in him (LVI). This intimation of greater things is finally personified in Hallam himself, and the logic by which Tennyson overcomes the apparent gulf between the present and the hereafter takes the form of a kind of moral and spiritual evolution, taking the potential which Hallam represents in earthly form to be capable of realisation only in the non-material world. Man is

> The herald of a higher race,
> And of himself in higher place,
> If so he type this work of time
>
> Within himself, from more to more
>
> (CXVIII, ll. 14–7)

The trajectory of the human, therefore, is to 'Move upward, working out the beast, / And let the ape and tiger die' (CXVIII, ll. 27–8). So Hallam pre-empts this higher self, and, in this way, Tennyson is able to reconcile evolutionary logic with the continuum between birth, death and the afterlife: ontogeny replicates phylogeny and also points to the evolution of pure spirit.

Crucially, the qualities which intimate this potential in Hallam – frequently passed over by critics, presumably as too embarrassingly particularistic in their Victorian patriotism – include those of statesman and gentleman, and Hallam's divination emerges quite logically from the poem's ideological re-working of science and theology:

> I doubt not what thou wouldst have been:
>
> A life in civic action warm,
> A soul on highest mission sent,
> A potent voice of Parliament,
> A pillar steadfast in the storm,

Should licensed boldness gather force,
   Becoming, when the time has birth,
   A lever to uplift the earth
And roll it in another course

                        (CXIII, ll. 8–16)

The social order is an integral part of nature (comprising 'the world') and has a proper direction which revolutionaries attempt to thwart. Whereas evolution is consistent with that gradualism which under-pins British development, the Celt is made to embody this anarchic desire to overturn such divine principles of order, his 'lever' consisting precisely in his licence. In contrast Hallam symbolises those charac-teristic English qualities of moderation which include, crucially, an attachment to manly freedom:

High nature amorous of the good,
   But touched with no ascetic gloom;
   And passion pure in snowy bloom
Through all the years of April blood;

A love of freedom rarely felt,
   Of freedom in her regal seat
   Of England; not the schoolboy heat,
The blind hysterics of the Celt;

And manhood fused with female grace
   In such a sort, the child would twine
   A trustful hand, unasked, in thine,
And find his comfort in thy face

                        (CIX, ll. 9–20)

In the last stanza here Hallam's partial feminisation is sufficient to enable him to develop familial bonds; it does not undermine those manly properties attributed to him in the preceding stanzas. The wholly feminised – or, alternatively, infantile – instability of the Celt, on the other hand, is a racial characterisation which is persistent in the poem: 'even though thrice again / The red fool-fury of the Seine / Should pile her barricades with dead', Hallam 'O'erlook'st the tumult from afar, / And smilest, knowing all is well' (CXXVII, ll. 6 8, 19 20). As with Tennyson's presentation of his own self-mastery, perspective and self-possession are integral to Hallam's assured and re-assuring manly objectivity, his distance from the disturbing immediacy of con-temporary events. Hallam comes to represent the metaphysical principle of order in continuity, derived from the ubiquitous analogy with nature; and natural continuity is demonstrated in the supposedly challenging principles of evolution which undermined certain (rudimentary) aspects of religious and political faith. Indeed Cosslett suggests that 'it is just as possible to see [Tennyson] recasting his image of the divine in the language of gradualist Nature, as to see him importing disruptive divine elements into the naturalistic world picture of science'.[5] The grounding principle of Tennyson's thought therefore is neither science nor religion, but gradualism itself, the definitive ideological feature of post-Romantic English culture.

### The laws of empire

Tennyson's deification of Hallam, then, invests the British state with a metaphysical legitimacy and destiny which is symptomatic of its successful emergence, reformed but essentially intact, from the years of revolution abroad and internal radical threat.[6] It also stigmatises the Celt as the racial antithesis of this principle of continuity, something entirely typical of mid-nineteenth-century racial thought, as we shall see. Tennyson's eye is clearly on the Celts of France, but Victorians did not perceive race as being coterminous with national boundaries; or, as Tennyson put it to his Irish friend William Allingham in a discussion on Fenianism, 'Kelts are all mad furious fools!'[7] Hence his attack on Celtic hysteria in *In Memoriam* held implications for the constitution of Britain. Since 1801 Ireland – with a population perceived as predominantly Celtic and overwhelmingly Catholic – was now a part of the Union, a political necessity precipitated by the republican uprising of 1798, which was by far the most substantial threat to British authority from within its empire during these revolutionary years. Moreover, the United Irishmen had demonstrated their Celtic allegiances by making common cause with France, and Ireland was strategically important to Napoleon as the place from which he might launch an invasion of England. As a consequence Ireland came under direct British jurisdiction whilst supervised by a heavy military presence, a presence which persisted as the main means of enforcing law – if rarely order – up to the official establishment of the Royal Irish Constabulary in 1836, themselves armed, unlike the British police introduced at around the same time. Thereafter the size of the British garrison in Ireland varied according to 'need', but such supposedly unBritish means of implementing the law were the clearest metonymic symbols of what seemed to the British ruling class an irrational, because unpacifiable, opposition to their reasonable government. Hardly a decade of the nineteenth century passed without some perceived major threat to political or social stability: secret societies, organised tithe and rent strikes accompanied by various 'atrocities', Catholic agitation, the Repeal campaign, Fenianism, Land Wars and Home Rule mobilisation all, despite their differing political complexions, repeatedly confirming the ungovernability of the Irish, and all being met with various degrees of repression. According to Oliver MacDonagh, only in around sixteen years of the period of the Act of Union was Ireland free from emergency legislation of one sort or another, and, in this respect, 'proximity appeared, not as an argument for union, but as an item in the catalogue of differentiation'.[8] As Charles Townshend notes, the 'composite concept "law and order" is one of the cornerstones of Anglo-Saxon political structures', a principle based, at least in part, on a racial perception of the basis of order and a conviction that 'abstract justice was ... an integral part of English law ... with the social corollary that since the English framed and obeyed just laws, Englishmen must naturally be just'.[9] For the most part English attitudes towards the Irish stressed the self-serving, double-binding logic that the Irish needed governing, and that nowhere was that need more clearly demonstrated than in their reluctance to be governed.

A great deal of this unrest was bound up with the peculiar legacy of colonial rule in Ireland. The defining moment, in this respect, was the colonialism of the Elizabethan period which set about the lengthy process of overturning the existing order of things in Ireland by integrating Protestant zeal into the suppression of a people, a process which over time involved brutally displacing the native Irish from their lands, instituting the Penal Laws and establishing a sectarian ruling class in the form of the Ascendancy. Religious domination, then, became indivisible from colonial rule. Despite this, Irish Republican politics of the 1790s attempted to overcome sectarian divisions, but after the defeat of 1798 such universalising aspirations dissipated in divisions largely fostered by powerful Unionist forces. In so far as nationalist politics in the first half of the nineteenth century were dominated by O'Connellite demands, there was a shift towards stressing perfectly legitimate Catholic grievances, but also towards the representation of these as *national* grievances, carrying with it the fatal implication that the Catholic people constituted the Irish nation.[10]

Amelioration of Catholic demands was clearly a more appealing prospect for the British state than a root-and-branch challenge to its authority, and this is largely the path which was taken in the nineteenth century. None the less, this was still not an entirely congenial route, for reasons which should be obvious enough from my argument so far. The social and political demands which Ireland generated over the course of the nineteenth century were far from unchallenging, and those statesmen who attempted to bring about reform in Ireland did so mostly out of pragmatic rather than principled motives, and frequently against strong opposition. A brief consideration of the nature of the reforms which were demanded and/or implemented suggests why this should have been the case, and it also gives some indication of just how anomalous Ireland appeared to those who had acquired prime responsibility for governing the country: concessions to Catholics threatened Britain's religious integrity which had ensured its stability and seemed to guarantee its destiny; concessions to political violence and even mass demonstrations challenged the rule of law; concessions to the starving were a sop to the indolent and undermined the laws of political economy which were increasingly dominant in informing British state policy; concessions to national autonomy threatened the Union as a whole and, beyond that, the empire; concessions to tenants were inimical to the rights of property and to the Irish landowning class who appeared to many to be the only representatives of civility in an otherwise barbaric land (and in this last respect it should also be noted that class ties frequently overrode religious ones: the younger Thomas Arnold – a convert to Catholicism, and one of Hopkins's colleagues at University College, Dublin – wrote to his wife in 1887: 'I would *never* give up the landlords; were I an Englishman I would shoot down the Irish like rats without the slightest compunction, sooner than that a single landlord should be unjustly despoiled'.)[11] Ireland, Christopher Morash has argued, was a standing affront to the sacralised nineteenth -century concept of progress,[12] a point I would strongly endorse. But 'progress' was not merely the fetishised product of an abstract Enlightenment commitment to the unfolding and accumulating benefits of reason, morality and scientific development; in England the concept was also bound up with specific social, economic and cultural features which were none the less prescriptive. One of my central arguments has been that England's success was considered the result of an accommodation with reality which had eluded other, less rational, mostly non-Protestant nations: England, it was believed, had grasped and observed natural and divine laws and had been rewarded by political stability, economic prosperity and an unrivalled empire. To contravene those laws on which this empire had been established was to offend against reality and truth. Hence the component features of the Irish stereotype – madness, drunkenness, garrulity without coherence – revealed problems which were far from trivial; they were the symptomatic features of a condition unreconciled to the real.

It is unsurprising, then, that the Union with Ireland should have disconcerted many commentators, since Ireland could no longer be forgotten about as a semi-autonomous off-shore island. If, as has been argued, the physical bestiality, alien speech and irredeemable incivility of the figure of Heathcliff in *Wuthering Heights* denotes his Irish provenance,[13] it is worth bearing in mind that the novel opens with a naked reference to the year in which the Union came into effect, and that at this moment the usurper is in possession. There are, though, other revealing characteristics about Heathcliff's depiction which pre-empt the themes of this chapter. Over the course of the nineteenth century, concepts of race became more, rather than less, fixed, and – though such compartmentalisation is no doubt overly schematic – commentators up to around the mid-century tended to be equivocal about the causes of what they saw as Irish degeneracy and disorder. Hence Heathcliff's Irishness may be further indicated by his combination of a naturally malign disposition with a constant justification of his behaviour on the grounds that he is returning like for like; the relative claims of nature and nurture – for which read race and history – to have brought about his condition are undecidable. Moreover, he eventually becomes a figure in (semi-)educated revolt against the social order, and someone whose anti-social desires reach out for satisfaction to an ungodly preternatural world, thereby representing another Victorian figure of the wild Romantic, licentious and threatening to civility, property and a rational, yet Christian, appreciation of the natural world: like Ireland itself, Heathcliff is an anachronism in the progressive whiggish Victorian scheme of things, a figure whose influence is purged only through the loving cultivation of Hareton by the young Catherine (and, as Eagleton observes, this is Arnoldian territory).[14] Hareton himself, though, appears to be a superior type to Heathcliff. He is, after all, a hybrid figure, and Nelly Dean suggests that the mature Hareton's physiognomy reveals his potential for cultivation, and therefore assimilation, since it provides 'evidence of a wealthy soil that might yield luxuriant crops under other and favourable circumstances'[15]

If, as a Romantic figure, Heathcliff resembles Rochester in certain respects, he none the less differs from Charlotte Brontë's protagonist in being a monster. This monstrosity is in certain respects typical of the representation of the anarchic Irish, who in the nineteenth century came to be represented as apes or (collectively) as Frankenstein's monster; even, on occasions, both. This is a phenomenon which has generated debate since at least the late 1960s when L. P. Curtis produced his extensive survey of the popular contempt of Anglo-Saxons for Celts, and followed this up with a discussion of cartoons of the Irish in *Punch* and elsewhere which betray specifically racial perceptions.[16] I refer to this debate not in order to state my allegiances (though I think Curtis's limitations have been greatly exaggerated, and largely for ideological reasons) but simply to make the point that monsters, as Chris Baldick notes, serve a purpose: 'in a world created by a reasonable God, the freak or lunatic must have a purpose: to reveal the results of vice, folly, and unreason, as a warning (Latin *monsere*: to warn) to erring humanity'.[17] These monstrous Irish were yet further embodiments of an irrational hostility to ineluctable laws.

This threat of Celtic anarchy to natural order is perhaps registered most strongly by Carlyle in his *Chartism* pamphlet. Here he is principally concerned with internal English developments, but the Irish serve as the antithesis to what he describes as 'the finest peasantry in the world'. They also present a lesson for a British ruling class which threatens to abandon its own workers to economic chance. It is important that Carlyle acknowledges the historic injustices meted out to the Irish, but goes on to argue that the degeneracy this has produced

> has gone far farther than into the economics of Ireland; inwards to her very heart and soul. Immethodic, headlong, violent, mendacious: what can you make of the wretched Irishman? ... Such people works no longer on Nature and Reality; works on Phantasm, Simulation, Nonentity; the result it arrives at is naturally not a thing but no-thing – defect even of potatoes. Scarcity, futility, confusion, distraction must be perennial there. Such a people circulates not order but disorder, through every vein of it; and the cure, if it is to be a cure, must begin at the heart: not in his condition only but in himself must the Patient be all changed.[18]

History has ossified into national character. The imputed traits of the

Irish are almost too ubiquitous to bear emphasis, but this account has clear affinities with Kingsley's account in his attack on Newman. The sense of Irish childishness is paramount, and their unreal relation to the physical world is productive of a legendary mendacity. The rewards for a true relation to nature are a decent standard of living, whereas the Irish are incapable of successfully cultivating even the staple food of their diet. Religion is never explicitly mentioned by Carlyle, but the claims he makes reflect familiar Protestant themes about the Catholicism of the Irish, and, significantly, the answer he prescribes for their condition is that of internal reform.

Carlyle suggests that one in three Irish people is on the verge of starvation through their lack of potatoes, personifying this statistic in the figure of Sanspotato who characteristically heads for England. That label is also a pun on the French radicals of the 1790s, themselves the epitome of destructive forces. Indeed Sanspotato makes his first appearance towards the end of *The French Revolution* as Carlyle is drawing lessons from the events he has just described:

> what if History, somewhere on this planet, were to hear of a Nation, the third soul of whom had not, for thirty weeks each year, as many third-rate potatoes as would sustain him? History, in that case, feels bound to consider that starvation is starvation; that starvation from age to age presupposes much: History ventures to assert that the French Sansculotte of Ninety-three, who, roused from long death-sleep, could rush at once to the frontiers, and die fighting for an immortal Hope and Faith of Deliverance for him and his, was but the *second*-miserablest of men! The Irish Sanspotato, had he not senses then, nay a soul![17]

As he was completing this work, then, Carlyle was designating those issues which would concern him in the future, seeing in Ireland a greater, because more abject, source of potential destructiveness. This was a perception which remained with him and finally compelled him reluctantly to visit the country in 1849 'as by the point of bayonets at my back. Ireland really *is* my problem; the breaking point of the huge suppuration which all British and all European society now is'.[20] This combines two of Carlyle's favourite metaphors for a degenerate society: Ireland is both diseased and waiting to erupt.

Surprisingly – and in contrast to other representations of the time – the Irish in Britain as they are depicted in *Chartism* are not entirely workshy. This is also partly the problem, since the danger is that they threaten to pollute the English working class by taking over 'their' jobs and undercutting the rates of pay they had achieved.[21] In this the Irish labourer is

> the sorest evil this country has to strive with. In his rags and laughing savagery, he is there to undertake all work that can be done by mere strength of hand and back; for wages that will purchase him potatoes. He needs only salt for his condiment; he lodges to his mind in any pighutch or doghutch, roosts in outhouses; and wears a suit of tatters, the getting on and off of which is said to be a difficult operation, transacted only in festivals and in the hightides of the calendar. The Saxon man if he cannot work on these terms, finds no work. He too may be ignorant; but he has not sunk from decent manhood to squalid apehood: he cannot continue there.[22]

This reference to apehood – in contrast to mature Saxon manhood – pre-empts those mostly later depictions of the Irishman as prognathous. Carlyle's representation combines Protestant rhetoric with a developing lexicon of race; it might be said to exemplify a transitional position in the movement from religious to secular grounds for contempt.

For Carlyle the ultimate threat is one of usurpation – in America the position of the superior Saxon has already been undermined by the Irishman, 'the ready-made nucleus of degradation and disorder'. The answer lies in the Irish being 'improved a little or exterminated',[23] since they threaten degeneration in England too. It is the market which has produced this levelling of clearly unequal races, giving the advantage to the more desperate: this is the apocalypse threatened by *laissez faire* policies. Moreover, the Union is clearly integral to the anxiety: 'Ireland is in chronic atrophy these five centuries; the disease of nobler England, *identified now with that of Ireland*, becomes acute, has crises, and will be cured or kill' (my emphasis).[24] In other words the more resolute English refuse to acquiesce in their immiseration, hence the rise of Chartism.

Carlyle's tour of Ireland during the famine was prompted and largely organised by Charles Gavan Duffy, who, after reading *Chartism*, came to the odd conclusion that Carlyle sympathised with the Irish poor and might, with persuasion, be inclined to support Irish independence.[25] This tour permitted Carlyle a detailed examination of the people and their native land, and in his observations of Irish physiognomies, living conditions and habits he sketches familiar pictures of degradation, but with characteristic Carlylean inflections. To a large extent landscape and people are integrated. This is Killarney: 'Ragged wet hedges, weedy ditches; nasty ragged, spongy-looking flat country hereabouts; – like a *drunk* country fallen down to sleep amid the mud.'[26] Ireland is at variance with reality in its very fabric, and the historic associations of its contours are merely memorials to the pointlessness of its people's struggles. On approaching Wexford Harbour, he regards Vinegar Hill 'not with interest, with sorrow rather and contempt; one of the ten thousand futile fruitless "battles" this brawling unreasonable people has fought, – the saddest of distinctions to them among peoples!'[27] Carlyle's descriptions are replete with the language of illusion, reverie and dramatic performance; and he complains of his periodic nervous and dyspeptic insomnia afflicting him with unusual severity for the duration of his journey. Constantly he refers to hungry 'spectral' figures: at one point, he witnesses a 'Phantasm in straw hat and rags, amid a small group of inhabitants' acting out some traditional supernatural tale;[28] Killarney is characterised not merely by a drunken landscape but by 'incarnated nonsense' amongst its population and 'dilapidation, beggary, *human fatuity*'[29] (my emphasis) along its lakeside shores. Elsewhere he perceives naked young beggars in theatrical terms: '*Dramatic* I take it, or partly so, *this* form of begging … Gave them nothing'.[30] Even a Church of Ireland service seems to him 'according to the English method, "decently performed" … in the midst of a black howling Babel of superstitious savagery – like Hebrews sitting by the streams of Babel'. But this 'weeping' Hebraic role reflects the distance between Ascendancy and people, and is also a form of self-delusion: 'take to working out your meaning rather than weeping it. No sadder truth presses itself upon one than the necessity there will soon be, and the call there everywhere already is, to *quit* these empty performances altogether.'[31]

The clear basis of this illusory existence is, as one might expect in an account by Carlyle, the pervasive lack of any purposeful employment. Artificial government schemes are actually undersubscribed by workers – they are 'extensive *hives* for which the bees are yet to be found'[32] – and the thousands of 'human swinery' (his persistent phrase) forced into the workhouses are made to work without productivity:

> Human swinery has here [Westport] reached its *acme*, happily:
> 30,000 paupers in this union, population supposed to be about
> 60,000. Workhouse proper (I suppose) cannot hold above 3 or
> 4000 of them, subsidiary workhouses, and outdoor relief the

others. Abomination of desolation; what can you make of it! Outdoor quasi-*work*: 3 or 400 big hulks of fellows tumbling about with shares, picks and barrows, 'levelling' the end of their workhouse hill; at first glance you would think them all working; look nearer, in each shovel there is some ounce or two of mould, and it is all make-believe; 5 or 600 boys and lads, pretending to break stones. Can it be a *charity* to keep men alive on these terms? In face of all the twaddle of the earth, shoot a man rather than train him (with heavy expense to his neighbours) to be a deceptive *swine*.[33]

Carlyle – the great critic of *laissez faire* – ultimately concurs with opinions expressed by those economists such as Nassau Senior that even the meagre state benevolence provided at this time could only perpetuate Irish anarchy; unreality is intolerable and unsustainable, if eradicable. The notes end with the advice he offered a group of Derry Irishmen: "'To cease generally from following the devil: no other remedy that I know of; one general life-element of humbug these two centuries: and now it has fallen *bankrupt*: this universe, my worthy brothers, has its laws terrible as death and judgment if we 'cant' ourselves away from following them.'"[34] On returning to Glasgow he is palpably relieved to find honest and productive work going on.[35]

Carlyle, the habitual prophet of doom, expresses himself with characteristic lack of reserve, but the notes from this journey, which were published only posthumously, could not have influenced contemporary responses to the famine. To characterise them as consequently idiosyncratic or irrelevant would be wrong, though, since one of the persistent features of English responses to Irish dilemmas has been to disbelieve native reports, viewing them as exaggerated or plainly untrue; if not exactly the products of fantasy, they were in need of verification by sound empirical sense. A typical impatience with Irish complaints was expressed by Tennyson in his second visit to Ireland in 1848, at the invitation of Aubrey de Vere. According to Emerson, Tennyson set certain conditions for his stay, including that 'there was to be no mention of Irish distress'.[36] Instead of witnessing a country going through the trauma of mass starvation and emigration, Tennyson brought Wordsworthian English attitudes to bear on his enjoyment of the scenery of Curragh, Kerry and Killarney, and managed to divorce the land from its people: looking out over the sea, he claimed that 'all the revolutions of Europe that were lit in 1848 had dwindled into irrelevance.'[37]

This suspicion of Irish claims was also a feature of more important, because directly influential, responses to the famine: both politicians and the *The Times* regarded Irish reports – and especially those of Catholic priests – as unreliable. At the start of the famine Peel dispatched a scientific commission to enquire into its causes, but also requested the Commission to ascertain the true extent of the loss, believing that 'there is such a tendency to exaggeration and inaccuracy in Irish reports that delay in acting upon them is always desirable'.[38] John Saville records the instance of a Mayo priest's letter to the *Freeman's Journal* in 1848 describing starving people feeding on weeds and being treated unsympathetically by Protestant administrators of the Poor Law. *The Times* editorialised on this letter, disputing the numbers of dead reported by the priest ('No rational man in this island believes a statement on the unsupported authority of an Irish Roman Catholic priest') and charging the Catholic Church in general with inciting discontent on the basis of 'extravagant falsehoods'. The famine itself represented 'the visitation of GOD',[39] and this latter view was also representative of a view held by many, including senior figures in the government, particularly in the Treasury, that the famine was the outworking of providence.[40] The famine points up acutely, then, the fatal association between Ireland and unreality. On the one hand this association could take on Romantic forms, as it did in Tennyson's association of the land with the spiritual, or it could take on more obviously malign ones, implying that its primitive people were at the mercy of an untrustworthy, falsifying priesthood who blinded them to the laws of cause and effect.

Despite all of this, one effect of the enormity of the famine was to call into question the universal applicability of political economy, resulting in a greater sense of distinctions between nations and suggesting to some the necessity of ruling them according to their particular characteristics.[41] Certainly this is a feature of John Stuart Mill's essay on *England and Ireland* which challenged the rights of property, though this proved also to be his most controversial essay, and the attacks made on him persuaded him to renege on many of the essay's most radical proposals.[42] Influenced by the Irish economist J. E. Cairns,[43] he argued against the 'superstitious' English conviction that ownership entailed absolute rights over property, claiming that the political economies of nations differed. His model for the rule of Ireland was British rule in India, which was 'now governed, if with a large share of the ordinary imperfections of rulers, yet with a full perception and recognition of its differences from England'.[44] This was, in other words, a strategy for maintaining the empire based on sympathetic rule, a conviction that gathered support in the later part of the century. Mill's conviction was that Ireland's independence would bring dishonour to England without materially benefiting Ireland, and along with this he maintained the usual scepticism about the maturity of Ireland to govern itself. Though Matthew Arnold would have found Mill's conclusions on land reform too radical – Arnold opposed legalising and generalising the Ulster custom to the rest of Ireland on racial grounds since the custom followed from Ulstermen being 'a strong race and Protestants'[45] – he none the less shared Mill's sense of the necessity of a more beneficent rule, a beneficence mostly confined to granting Catholic claims. Arnold's arguments, though, were explicitly based on racial theories, a consequence of the greater prominence of such ideas in the later part of the century.[45]

### Celticism

The response to Ireland for much of the first half of the century was dominated by a religious logic which prescribed specific elements of anti-Irish antipathy. None the less, as early as 1847, Alexander Somerville noted the emergence of secular prejudices:

> We once used to hear that it was the Catholic religion which disqualified the Irish for industrial enterprise. The people of Belgium, who are all Catholics, and at the same time marching in the front ranks of industry and civilisation, disprove that assertion; and we seldom hear of it now. But we hear now of the inferiority of the Celtic race to the Saxon. The leaders in Irish politics are, in some measure, to blame for provoking this odious comparison, at least for keeping it in activity.[47]

Despite this, anti-Catholicism did continue to be invoked against the Irish well beyond the mid-century. In the 1890s the *Birmingham Daily Gazette* sent a 'special commissioner' to Ireland to report on the condition of Ireland and to produce anti-Home-Rule propaganda. His reports depicted Irish peasants 'in the hands of priests and agitators … and their blind voting, their inarticulate voice, translated into menace and mock patriotism'. Tuam he described as a 'a depressing kind of place, and but for the enterprise of a few Protestants, the place would be a phantasmagoria of pigs, priests, peasants, poverty, and "peel-ers'".[48] Again in the 1890s, warning of the threat which ritualism within the Anglican Church posed to the nation's destiny, Walter Walshe, in his alarmist *Secret History of the Oxford Movement*, argued that '*Popery is an enemy to National Prosperity* ... Every part of Ireland is under the same government. Why, then, is it that the Roman Catholic portions of that unhappy land are those in which more poverty, dirt, disloyalty, and ignorance are to be found than in the Protestant portions?'[49] None the less, it is certainly true that racial theory became more influential, and its rhetoric more pervasive, in explaining social, political and cultural differences between Saxons and Celts in the second half of the century. According to such percep-tions Protestantism was the religion most compatible with the inher-ently freedom-loving nature of the Saxon race, whereas Catholicism was merely symptomatic of the Celtic race's need for more authori-tarian, external government. Nancy Stepan's analysis of racial science depicts a nineteenth-century trajectory away from the basically Chris-tian, monogenist assumption that all human races constitute one species, to quasi-polygenist accounts, dominant by about 1850,[50] which argued that different races effectively constitute different species. This does not imply that previous monogenist theories can be exonerated of racism, but polygenist accounts argued that the differ-ences between 'racial' groups were more absolute and more perma-nent than monogenists had considered them. For polygenists the whole superstructures of nations depended on these biological bases.

In this trend Stepan regards Robert Knox as 'a pivotal figure', one closer to Gobineau than to other British writers of his time. Signifi-cantly, his work only became popular after 1848, having been previ-ously confined to lecture tours of the provinces. Knox claimed that his analysis was not prescriptive; he simply believed that 'Race is every-thing: literature, science, art – in a word, civilisation, depends on it'.[51] What is particularly important in Knox's work, though, is his convic-tion that 'races of men, differing as widely from each other as men do; inhabit, not merely continental Europe, but portions of Great Britain and Ireland'.[52] Thus Knox turns from a concentration on racial differ-ences between Occident and Orient to an internal analysis of Europe, and this contributed significantly to a trend in racial science, given that, according to Robert J. C. Young, 'interest in European races, "stocks", developed alongside more global analyses of racial differ-ence'[53] which have received wider critical attention. One of the prominent features of the ethnological and anthropological writings of the 1860s was the familiar opposition between Celtic mendacity and Saxon truthfulness.[54]

Knox's views on the Celt are drawn from historical incidents, specifically from revolutionary events which demonstrate that 'the Celtic race does not, and never could be made to comprehend the meaning of the word liberty'.[55] His analysis involves him in characterising the Irish amongst the family of Celts:

> Furious fanaticism; a love of war and disorder; a hatred for order and patient industry; no accumulative habits; restless, treacherous, uncertain: look at Ireland. This is the dark side of the character. But there is a bright and brilliant view which my readers will find I have not failed to observe. What race has done such glorious deeds? Still it is never to be forgotten that the continental Celt deserted and betrayed the greatest of men, Napoleon, thus losing the sovereignty of the world: here the fatal blow was struck from which the continental Celt cannot hope to recover ... Celtic Ireland fell at the Boyne; this was their Waterloo. Sir Robert Peel's Encumbered Estates Bill aims at the quiet and gradual extinction of the Celtic race in Ireland: this is its sole aim, and it will prove successful. A similar bill is wanted for Caledonia, or may be required shortly: the Celtic race cannot too soon escape from under Saxon rule. As a Saxon, I abhor all dynasties, monarchies and bayonet governments, but this latter seems to be the only one suitable for the Celtic man.[56]

This is intended to be mere impartial description (though interestingly he intrudes his own, supposedly racially determined opinions towards the end of this passage), but it is difficult not to take it as justification. In the war between races Knox predicts the annihilation of the Celt through typically Saxon means of lawful process – through the Encumbered Estates Bill (the means by which, especially during and after the famine, the subdivided plots of the Irish tenant farmers were consolidated, largely through eviction) – and even ascribes the purpose of removing the Celt from the soil to the 'Orange Club of Ireland'.[59]

What we also see in Knox's view of the Celt is the integration of moral and aesthetic properties which were to become increasingly central to debates about the fitness of the Irish to rule themselves, since the Celt's 'morals, actions, feelings, greatnesses, and littlenesses, flow distinctly and surely from his physical structure; that structure which seems not to have altered since the commencement of time'.[58] Though all racial conditions possess a degree of permanence for Knox, the lack of development in the Celt's physical condition conveys his primitivism. Knox clearly felt the Celt to be an anachronistic figure, despite apparent similarities with other European races. This was a view shared by others, the Irish apparently frustrating the ontological distinction between the west and the rest on which imperial ideology largely rested.[59] Hence Kingsley's notorious observation on visiting Ireland in 1860 that 'I am haunted by the human chimpanzees I saw along that hundred miles of horrible country. I don't believe they are our fault … But to see white chimpanzees is dreadful; if they were black, one would not feel it so much, but their skins, except where tanned by exposure are as white as ours.'[60] The scientist John Beddoe suggested that Ireland was the British centre of an originally 'Africanoid' race, one characterised by prognathism, volubility and, apparently, recalcitrance, since 'the most exquisite examples of it never would submit to measurement'.[61]

The specificities of Irish physical traits are important in conveying to Knox their primeval condition:

> War is the game for which the Celt is made. Herein is the forte of his physical and moral character: in stature and weight, as a race, inferior to the Saxon; limbs muscular and vigorous; torso and arms seldom attaining any very large development – hence the extreme rarity of athletæ amongst the race; hands, broad; fingers, squared at the points; step, elastic and springy; in muscular energy and rapidity of action, surpassing all other European races.[62]

Moreover, they show a contempt for 'unremitting, steady, uniform, productive labour', which is complemented by aestheticism and imaginative capacity: they are 'warm-hearted, full of deep sympathies, dreamers on the past, uncertain'.[63] The Celt is therefore established as antithetical to the athletic Saxon who is physically fitted for global expansion. Politically, too, the Saxon is the only true democrat, and throughout his account Knox regards the remaining aristocratic influence in English culture as the residue of the Norman, and therefore Celtic, occupation (politically Knox was a radical). In this sense 1688 – whilst still leaving work to be done – was the natural expression of true Anglo-Saxon tendencies. This unfinished business would certainly be achieved, if only gradually, since change in a Saxon nation was consistent with the maintenance of order: 'to revolutionise is Celtic; to reform, Saxon'.[64]

The writings of racial scientists, though, were most influential indirectly, through the writings of Matthew Arnold. With *On the Study of Celtic Literature* Arnold attempted to provide a more positive gloss on the Celt's familiar attributes, whilst none the less confirming that these were symptomatic of an inferior, overly sensitive, and therefore feminine race who threatened to destabilise the body politic. Arnold consistently held to the Irish people's incapacity for self-government: Ireland, he argued, should be 'a nation poetically only, not politically'[65] – that is, not really. Indeed there is a connection for Arnold between Irish poeticism and the inappropriateness of political autonomy, since their imaginative condition is integral to their famous readiness 'to react against the despotism of fact'.[66] This is their central difference from the Saxon, who is characterised by scientific traits of balance and objectivity. The demonstration of this lay not least in those studies of the Celts on which Arnold's own work was substantially based: Kaspar Zeuss's analysis, for example, demonstrates that scientific 'desire to know his object, the language of the Celtic peoples, as it really is',[67] a phrase Arnold frequently repeated in defining the role of the critic (and which, in turn, prompted Wilde's Celtic inversion: 'the primary aim of the critic is to see the object as in itself it really is not').[68] This lack of a reality principle is a consequence of the Celtic nature's 'femininity', 'its nervous exaltation', determining an alertness to the secret magic of nature.[69]

In spite of the same basic tendency to attribute fundamental characteristics to race, Arnold's aim was the opposite of Knox's. Whereas Knox's attribution of complete racial alterity to the Celts ultimately reflects the failure of the Union's attempt at incorporating Ireland, Arnold's project was to resolve conflicts through the discovery of commonality. Even in science Arnold claims to discover the unifying tendency of its 'elder and diviner sister, poetry', and he demonstrates through philological examples the originary unity of the Indo-European family.[70] This is the basis of his assertion that the English constitute a 'composite' of racial characteristics – Saxon, Norman and Celtic – which makes them unsurpassed in the exercise of politics, but at the same time not so absurdly rational as the Germans, redeemed in this respect by just a hint of sentimentality. This discovery of Celtic affinities is what Arnold recommends as the basis for reconciliation: 'Let them [the Celts] consider that they are inextricably bound up with us

… we English, alien and uncongenial to our Celtic partners as we may have hitherto shown ourselves, have notwithstanding, beyond perhaps any other nation, a thousand latent springs of possible sympathy with them.'[71] David Lloyd has argued that this 'composite' quality of the English reflects the assumption of a universalist character by the imperial state which involves subsuming the various particularities of its colonial dependents,[72] though this attribution of debilitating particularities was itself the product of imperial projections which reduced the inhabitants of Ireland to the level of partial beings, incapacitated by their overwhelming subjectivity. The universality of the imperial state is consequently seen to depend on preserving the relative proportions of the whole in the interests of stability, and the dominance of Celticism as defined by Arnold would have inevitably threatened that stability. Arnold's project represented the most explicit instance of a process described by Seamus Deane: the creation of an Irish psychology 'as a form of energy that is in need of appropriation, external control, so that it can become politically sober while remaining aesthetically vivacious'.[73]

The desire to Celticise English society was aimed, not only at assimilating Ireland to the Union but also at humanising the English middle-class Philistine, whose individualism and devotion to 'machinery' Arnold felt was undermining social coherence. Ultimately Arnold's project of recovering the repressed elements of the 'composite' English character was to restore a sense of social sympathy, connecting him with the Anglican tradition represented by Burke et al. Indeed Burke was explicitly an influence on Arnold's ambition to restore a corporate, or state, sensibility[74] in order to counter the national fragmentation threatened by bourgeois individualism. Arnold's project was therefore to restore a Burkean, or Coleridgean, sense of civility, ironically by 'rediscovering' the principle of sympathy which bourgeois England had made alien, and extending that sympathy to the restive colony of Ireland from where it was supposedly derived. The metaphysical qualities Arnold attributed to this organic ideal is reflected in the fact that it represented a corporate version of the qualities Arnold claimed to have discovered in Christ in *St Paul and Protestantism*: the state should be the means of reconciling the individual to duty through the promotion of affection.

However, Arnold was clear that too much sentiment represented a political threat, and it seems that he reassessed the extent of the desirability of Celtic influences in the wake of the Paris Commune of

1871.[75] No doubt it was this which prompted Arnold's repudiation of the Renanian thesis, "'that great law by which the primitive race of an invaded country always ends by getting the upper hand, [according to which] England is becoming every day more Celtic and less Germanic'". Such unrestrained 'Hellenism' could not be countenanced by Arnold, and he held to the view that 'moral conscience, self-control, seriousness, steadfastness, are not the whole of human life certainly, but they are by far the greatest part of it; without them … nations cannot stand'.[76] Renan's thesis was one which celebrated the more poetic, civilised qualities of the Celt in contrast to the barbarism of the Teuton, reinforcing the feminisation of the Celt. The intention, of course, was to repudiate Saxon hubris, but in the English context such a strategy merely tended to bolster established perceptions of gender which had originally emerged from counter-revolutionary contexts, and which fed into imperial relations with Ireland, stressing the alignment between poeticism, hysteria and revolution. (It has been suggested that one Irish response to this feminisation was the Gaelic Athletic Association's attempts to cultivate masculine games of a distinctively Irish kind.)[77]

Arnold's later response to Celticism, conditioned by French radicalism, was reinforced by the resurgent Irish militancy of the 1880s when his support for the Liberals was severely tried. Quoting Shakespeare in the preface to his *Irish Essays*, he admonished Irish nationalists: 'Your affections / Are a sick man's appetite who desires that / Which would increase his evil?'[78] Just as his recommendations in *Culture and Anarchy* did not exclude the use of force against politically destabilising working-class protesters, he was not averse to what he saw as necessary coercion in Ireland as an element of paternal, colonial rule: 'They must be brought to order when they are disorderly; but they must be brought, also, to acquiescence in the English connection by good and just treatment.'[79] In fact his later writings on Ireland mark what Park Honan has called his 'Zenith of Conservatism',[80] confirming his ultimately reactionary temperament. The essay of Arnold's to which Honan's phrase alludes, 'The Nadir of Liberalism', sees arrangements for Irish Home Rule as the potential source of nervous tremors in the body politic. It is a consistent attack on Gladstone's record as leader of the Liberal Government, and his toleration of popular dissent on a scale which Arnold believed might result in the breakdown of the nation-state itself. Gladstone has achieved Parliamentary victories, Arnold admits, but repeatedly questions whether these have 'really satisfied vital needs and removed vital dangers of the nation?'[81] The emphasis on vitality here is clearly a deliberate, loaded metaphor, paving the way for his depiction of a possible future Irish Parliament which draws on a comparison with certain degenerate and low-brow forms of contemporary fiction – clearly not elements of 'culture' proper – which were believed literally to prey on the nerves of their largely female readership:[82] 'It will be a sensation Parliament – a Parliament of shocks and surprises.'[83]

Even those who adopted a more positive attitude towards Renan's thesis could ultimately only confirm the sexist antinomies which permeated the ideology of British rule. Oscar Wilde gave a version of the argument in his 'Celtic revival' speech to the American-Irish of San Francisco in 1882: 'the Saxon took our lands from us and left us desolate. We took their language and added new beauties to it.'[84] Another, later example was that of Grant Allen in which he accounted for the differences of 'racial tastes'. He argued that the proponents of a Celtic cultural revival in England were also political radicals – democrats, Home Rulers and socialists. Retaining the Renanian association of the Celt with aestheticism as well as the (implicit) gendering of the attributes of imperial rule and poeticism, he claimed that 'In our complex nationality the Teuton has contributed in large part the muscle, the thews, the hard-headed organisation, the law, the stability, the iron hand; but the Celt has added the lightness, airiness, imagination, wonder, the sense of beauty and of mystery, the sadness, the sweetness.'[85] In the context of such racial tastes, Allen claimed, Wilde was 'an Irishman to the core'.[86] The Anglo-Saxon's sinuous rule here associates the muscular body with the capacity to rule both itself and others, and the internalisation of such a gendered relation represented something like a Foucauldian reverse discourse:[87] revaluing certain definitive features of the dominant imperial discourse, it none the less also reproduced many of that discourse's governing assumptions. Aestheticism – certainly that of Oscar Wilde – was therefore in many ways indebted to those values which were integral to imperial hegemony, whilst it was also quite self-consciously one element within a range of forces which were unsettling to that hegemony. I will return to such questions in the final chapter. First I want to consider an English writer in whom contemplation of an imperilled imperial order precipitated apocalyptic visions.

# 5

## The wreck of an English subject:
## Gerard Manley Hopkins

Abdication of royal or imperial authority is with states no less
than with individuals the precursor of death.

A. V. Dicey[1]

GERARD Manley Hopkins admired Arnold's writings on Gladstone
and Home Rule, finding 'The Nadir of Liberalism' 'temperate but
strong'. Nevertheless he also believed Home Rule to be inevitable,
even desirable, if revolution or humiliation for Britain were to be
avoided.[2] This was a matter with which Hopkins was considerably pre-
occupied in his final years: posted to Ireland by his superiors, against
his own will and against the wishes of many in the hierarchy of the
Irish Catholic Church,[3] he was sent to serve as Professor of Greek and
Latin at the Catholic University College, Dublin. The consequence was
a greater acquaintance, though not sympathy, with Ireland and its
people. He found the job oppressive because of the sheer amount of
work that it entailed (especially in marking examinations), but he also
developed a strong sense that he was serving a cause hostile to his
own nation, since the 1880s saw a renewal of popular militancy in
relation not only to Home Rule but also the land question. There had
always been a conflict between Hopkins's national identity and his
religious affiliation, but his position in Ireland generated new levels of
self-division and, if not religious doubt, certainly religious alienation.
He once wrote that for Irish Catholics 'religion hangs suspended over
their politics as the blue sky over the earth, both in one landscape but
immeasurably remote and without contact or interference',[4] and, in
this description, religion, though ubiquitous, is the secondary, more
ephemeral term, the earth designating material considerations of possession of land and national autonomy.

The resurgence of Irish militancy in Dublin in the years of Hopkins's residence could not be ignored: the few remaining Unionists on the city council were swept from power, and the royal family was repeatedly rebuffed; whereas nationalists (including ex-Fenians) were honoured.[5] Moreover, the Catholic Church in the country at large was frequently seen as complicit with political movements, even as outrightly supportive, especially following the Land War of 1879–82 in which priests had shared platforms with 'neo-Fenians', a necessity precipitated both by the recognition that the Land League had effectively become the legitimate political authority – 'the source rather than the broker of the law'[6] – and by the Church's continual battle for hegemony with the 'godless revolutionaries'. By 1884 – after the virtual demise of the Land League – the Catholic hierarchy was sufficiently satisfied with the limited demands of the Irish National League that they endorsed the participation of the clergy.[7] With the resurgence of land agitation in the Plan of Campaign of 1886 onwards, there was disagreement within the Church, but many clergy supported it and were involved with the movement even after the British government managed to persuade the Vatican to issue a Papal Rescript condemning the Plan in April 1888.[8]

Hopkins's sense of his anomalous position was also compounded by obvious and related class distinctions, since English Catholics were not part of a popular religion at home, but derived mostly from a conservative faction within the nation's elite. In their recent biographies both Robert Martin and Norman White recognise the cultural differences between Irish and English Catholicism, and that these in many ways bore on Hopkins's desolations. Martin rightly points to those characteristics of Irish social structures which meant that Hopkins's associates were not what Oxonians would have considered gentlemen, and notes that the centre of Dublin had the air of a formerly Ascendancy-dominated city now taken over by the Catholic poor.[9] Norman White dwells in greater detail on Hopkins's strangeness amongst and estrangement from the Irish priesthood, suggesting that 'his characteristics – appearance, way of talking, Newmanite conversion, shyness and reclusiveness, educated upper-class Englishness and Oxonian mannerisms, scrupulous habits, interests in music and the visual arts, poetic composition – appeared typical facets of an English aesthete'.[10]

Hopkins's sense of alienation whilst in Ireland is explicitly a feature of at least one of the sonnets of desolation. In 'To seem the stranger', he wrote: 'I am in Ireland now; now I am at a third / Remove', referring to his estranged family, his Protestant friends and to England itself. This, he claimed elsewhere, might be offset by the mutual love between himself and God, except that the years in Ireland were characteristically ones of an absence of God, in which all of his advances 'dark heaven's baffling ban / Bars or hell's spell thwarts'.[11] At least this was Hopkins's sense of things, in which he repeatedly argued that, whatever his circumstances, his spiritual health was dependent on God's grace: 'it seems to me that I could lead this life well enough if I had bodily energy and cheerful spirits. However, these God will not give me.'[12] To accept his own view of the matter, though, is necessarily to accept that Hopkins's desolations were indeed caused by spiritual 'movements' – in the Ignatian sense that feelings of confusion or of comfort were signs of a greater or lesser separation from God – and not generated by material and ideological conditions. Unquestionably Hopkins experienced his years in Ireland in religious terms, but the religious ideas and poetics he developed during his years as a Jesuit were, despite their idiosyncrasy, related to more mainstream aspects of his home culture. His sense of the absence of God was not coincidental with his final years in Ireland; rather, his first-hand experience of what he perceived as the impending disintegration of the British empire determined his sense of loss, and this crisis of faith was also integrally bound up with the manly identifications which I have argued became so central to imperial ideology in the latter half of the nineteenth century.

### State and body

Hopkins's political sensibilities are revealed in two poems written whilst in Ireland: 'Harry Ploughman' and 'Tom's Garland' were written more or less at the same time (1887–8), a fact which in itself should alert us to possible thematic connections. Both concern the male body. Harry Ploughman is the name given to the idealised figure of the farm labourer at work on his field, and Hopkins's intention is to present as striking a picture as possible – it is, he wrote to Robert Bridges, 'a direct picture of a ploughman, without afterthought';[13] and again, 'I want Harry Ploughman to be a vivid figure before the mind's eye; if he is not that the sonnet fails':[14]

Hard as hurdle arms, with a broth of goldish flue
Breathed round; the rack of ribs; the scooped flank; lank
Rope-over thigh; knee-knave; and barrelled shank –
    Head and foot, shouldér and shank –
By a grey eye's heed steered well, one crew, fall to;
Stand at stress. Each limb's barrowy brawn, his thew
That onewhere curded, onewhere sucked or sank –
    Soared ór sank –,
Though as a beechbole firm, finds his, as at a rollcall, rank
And features, in flesh, what deed he each must do –
    His sinew-service where do.
He leans to it, Harry bends, look. Back, elbow, and liquid waist
In him, all quáil to the wallowing o' the plough. 'S cheek
  crímsons; curls
Wag or crossbridle, in a wind lifted, windlaced –
    Wind-lilylocks-laced;
Churlsgrace too, chíld of Amansstrength, how it hángs or hurls
Them – broad in bluff hide his frowning feet lashed! raced
With, along them, cragiron under and cold furls –
    With-a-fountain's shining-shot furls.[15]

The language here is characteristically concrete, but the vividness is constantly that yielded by metaphor: Harry Ploughman is never immediately himself. Initially the ploughman's body is presented through analogies with both wood – 'hurdle', 'rack', 'barrel' – and rope, amongst others, to detail its bone structure and sinews, until the whole body is transformed into the disciplined crew of a ship in lines 5 and 6 – 'By a grey eye's heed steered well, one crew, fall to; / Stand at stress'. Harry's body becomes a manned ship imbued with the singleness of purpose which its crew must have. Moreover, each limb is ranked and doing its 'sinew-service', and each of these imagined figures-within-a-figure is also ship-like, down to his 'beechbole firm' (his mast-like rigidity). Harry's body bends to the purpose of directing the plough in the same way as a ship steers its course, not without difficulty. His hair – 'curls' – has some of the connotations of the rigging of the topmasts being blown by the wind (though it is also, in another metaphor, a 'fountain's shining-shot furls').

In 'Tom's Garland', though, the body is avowedly metaphorical, the metaphor being that of the body politic. Writing to a Bridges perplexed by the poem's difficulties, Hopkins claimed that the body metaphor is deployed in the same way as it is in Plato, St Paul, Hobbes and elsewhere as an image of the well-ordered society:

The head is the sovereign, who has no superior but God and from heaven receives his or her authority ... covered, so to say, only with the sun and the stars, of which the crown is a symbol, which is an ornament but not a covering; it has an enormous hat or skull cap, the vault of heaven. The foot is the daylabourer, and this is armed with hobnail boots, because it has to wear and be worn by the ground; which again is symbolical, for it is navvies or daylabourers who, on the great scale or in gangs and millions, mainly trench, tunnel, blast, and in other ways disfigure, 'mammock' the earth and, on a small scale, singly, and superficially stamp it with their footprints ... But this place still shares the common honour, and if it wants another advantage, glory or public fame, makes up for it by another, ease of mind, absence of care.[16]

The striking thing about this description – and about the poem itself – is the pervasive confusion of metaphor and metonymy: the sovereign is both head and has no other head besides God, hence his actual head must be bare in order to symbolise precisely this sovereignty; the foot is the labourer, just as his actual foot is in turn symbolic of the work labourers do. This hierarchical conception of society, and the sense that all share the honour of being a part of the commonwealth, is compressed into one image in particular in the poem, one which further emphasises the slippage between metaphor and those physical attributes which represent the individual's position:

> Country is honour enough in all us – lordly head,
> With heaven's lights high hung round, or, mother-ground
> That mammocks, mighty foot.[17]

The picture is completed by the unemployed: the dangerous malcontents of society who have neither comfort nor status, and consequently threaten its integrity, the 'Loafers, Tramps, Cornerboys, Roughs, Socialists and other pests of society',[18] whose 'packs infest the age'.

The body in each of these poems is more than simply itself, then. In 'Tom's Garland' it is invested with the hopes of a united and healthily functioning society; in 'Harry Ploughman' it is almost subliminally ship-like. But, of course, this trope of the ship is itself another ancient metaphor for the state, and in the later nineteenth century in particular the rural labourer was a nostalgic symbol of a past order, a pre-industrial commonwealth in which the 'packs' of malcontents were imagined to be absent. The 'direct picture without afterthought' that Hopkins wanted to evoke therefore demonstrates the way in which the male body was for him compulsively invested with ideals about the state of the nation. The metaphorical relationship between the two in 'Tom's Garland' is only an explicit version of what is already there as soon as the body is invoked by Hopkins. Moreover, this actualisation of the ideals of a healthy state in the body is present in 'Tom's Garland' also in that slippage between metaphor and metonymy.

This symbolism of the body in a reciprocal relationship with the condition of the nation is not merely an acceptance of Plato *et al.*, however. The tradition of Christian manliness crystallised many aspects of a Protestant culture in a valorisation of the body based on unity, maturity, work, discipline and purpose, and this ideology was so pervasive that it was virtually inseparable from a sense of what English manhood must be. Harry Ploughman's is only one of the bodies in Hopkins's writings which evinces such convictions. It is true that there is little biographical evidence of Hopkins's indoctrination with manly ideals – his school, for instance, was not especially sporty[19] – but there are indications of an interest in athleticism: on arriving at Oxford he lamented his nurse's omission of his dumb-bells in packing his things;[20] Alison Sulloway notes that he was not immune from the Oxford fascination with boating;[21] and swimming was his favourite pastime. However, it is his writings which evince the influence of Christian manliness most clearly [22] in the repeated emphasis on the male form and its relations to both the deity and the nation. By Hopkins's time the tenets of Christian manliness had been integrated into racial perceptions of the Anglo-Saxon, but inevitably Hopkins's acceptance of what was, in provenance, Protestant thinking was to create irreconcilable contradictions and religious dilemmas which became most clearly manifest when he was confronted with popular Irish hostility to English rule.

Irish rebelliousness, and the perceived sense of English irresolution in the face of it, deeply affected Hopkins; it represented for him the culmination of a number of years' fears that the empire was disintegrating. Another letter to Bridges, written from Ireland in 1887, sums up so many of his feelings. The English, he claims, had never before cared about Ireland, but

> now, as fast as these people wake up and hear what wrong Eng-
> land has done (and has long ceased doing) to Ireland, they, like
> that woman in Mark Twain, 'burst into tears and rushing

upstairs send a pink silk parasol and a box of hairpins to the seat of the war' … with an unwavering will, or at least a flood of passion, on one, the Irish, side and a wavering one or indifference on the other, the English, and the Grand Old Mischiefmaker [Gladstone] loose, like the Devil, for a little while and meddling and marring all the fiercer for his hurry, Home Rule is in fact likely to come and … may perhaps in itself be a measure of a sort of equity.[23]

Will is here counterposed with feminine vacillation, presided over by the devilish Gladstone. Will in its proper sense may be seen in the severe imperial rule apparently lacking in Ireland,[24] whereas Hopkins significantly checks himself when talking of the 'will' of the Irish – the less disciplined, more Romantic and therefore, to Victorian notions, effeminate term 'passion' is substituted. British imperialism, in strictly conventional ideological terms, figures implicitly as a masculine imposition of order. Norman White is surely guilty of the biographer's sin of over-generosity towards his subject in his assessment of Hopkins's support for Home Rule when he claims that 'from his experience and knowledge he supports the main ideal of the Home-Rulers, though he is outraged by the widespread civil disobedience, momentarily subscribing to *Punch's* caricature of the Irish as ungovernable, wild people'.[25] It was precisely *because* Hopkins believed the Irish to be ungovernable that he advocated Home Rule; indeed he considered it inevitable. The 'equity' referred to above was more a reflection of England's decline than of Ireland's right.

### The body of Christ

'The great aid to belief and object of belief', Hopkins claimed to his friend E. H. Coleridge in 1864, before his formal conversion, 'is the doctrine of the Real Presence in the Blessed Sacrament of the Altar. Religion without that is sombre, dangerous, illogical, with that it is – not to speak of its grand consistency and certainty – *loveable*'.[26] Hopkins's intimation of Christ's presence was at the heart of his religious convictions. In a couple of sermons preached whilst he was on supply at Bedford Leigh in 1879, he reaffirmed the emotional importance, for him, of the human form taken on by Christ. Hopkins contrasted the love for God – 'a cold sort of love', that of 'a subject for his ruler' – with that for Christ, which was 'enthusiasm for a leader, a hero, love for a bosom friend, love for a lover'.[27] In physique, mind and character

Christ was beautiful: 'picture him', he instructed his congregation,

> in whom the fulness of the godhead dwelt bodily, in his bearing
> how majestic, how strong and yet how lovely and lissome in his
> limbs, in his look how earnest, grave but kind. In his Passion all
> this strength was spent, this lissomness crippled, the beauty
> wrecked, the majesty beaten down. But now it is restored, and
> for myself I make no secret I look forward with eager desire to
> seeing the matchless beauty of Christ's body in the heavenly
> light.[28]

This classical synthesis of body, mind and character – prized above all
in the English public schools and universities – was something Hopkins also appreciated in his friends. In a now famous – to some regret-
table – letter to Bridges, written at the same time as these sermons, he
acknowledged that 'no-one can admire the beauty of the body more
than I do ... But this kind of beauty is dangerous. Then comes beauty
of the mind, such as genius, and this is greater than the beauty of the
body and not to call dangerous. And more beautiful than the beauty
of the mind is beauty of the character'.[29] Bridges, then, shared the
finest qualities of Christ, and indeed this idea of beauty as being
derived in form from Christ lay behind Hopkins's conviction that

> Christ plays in ten thousand places,
> Lovely in limbs, and lovely in eyes not his
> To the Father through the features of men's faces.[30]

Hopkins is here observing the imitation of Christ in the bodies of those
acting in ways which seem compatible with God's gift of grace. However, those figures whom Hopkins explicitly compared to Christ betray
what kind of activity he considered most in keeping with that
example. They included not only friends such as Bridges but more
generally the English gentleman, who possessed 'that chastity of mind'
which Hopkins regarded as being typical of Christ in his self-sacrifice.[31] More revealing was the imitation of Christ to be seen in the
short lives of great conquerors such as Alexander and Caesar, since
success through failure – through sacrifice – was Christ's example.[32]
Later, in correspondence with the arch-Tory Coventry Patmore, he
added Thomas More and General Gordon to the list,[33] and, as I have
already demonstrated, the manhood of soldiers in general reminded
Hopkins of Christ.

Just as Hopkins's particular image of Christ was clearly derived
from an imperial culture which celebrated the male physique as the

potential embodiment of Christian virtue, Hopkins's emotional attachment to Christ was an alienated form of love for such men. I pursue this in the discussion of Hopkins's sexuality in the following chapter. Here, though, I want to establish the way in which this same culturally-determined figure of Christ was crucial to Hopkins's experience of the world as unified, since he also perceived Christ as immanent within the disparate phenomena of creation, the force which licensed his celebration of the diversity of nature by reminding him of the creative power behind it.

This principle of unity took the form of his concept of 'inscape'. I do not intend to attempt a precise definition of this term here, but it is generally accepted that inscape refers in some sense to the material form generated by the divine creative energy which binds phenomena together, the energy itself being instress (though instress is also the means of intuiting inscape). It is this creative power which Hopkins imagines, for example, 'hast bound bones and veins in me, fastened me flesh' in the first stanza of 'The Wreck of the Deutschland', and this personal apprehension of creative power as the binding force of his body should come as no surprise, since the concept of stress as the force which generates inscape seems to derive at least partly from an analogy with the male body. Take, for example, Hopkins's description of Frederic Walker's painting 'The Harbour of Refuge' written in 1873. Here he particularly admires the figure of a young man mowing: 'a great stroke, a figure quite made up of the scythe and swing and sway of the whole body even to the rising of the one foot on tiptoe while the other was flung forward was as if such a thing had never been painted before, so fresh and so very strong'.[34] Written two years before Hopkins resumed writing poetry with 'The Wreck of the Deutschland' after a lengthy silence, the diction and rhythmic stress here pre-empt that of the later poetry with its sprung rhythm and the heavy alliteration which further emphasises that rhythm. In anticipation of Harry Ploughman, it could be said that this is a body 'at stress' – something suggested by the language – and in its freshness and originality it appears to capture precisely that quality which Hopkins designated inscape.

Although Hopkins's use of the term inscape precedes his discovery of his favourite philosopher, John Duns Scotus, it was almost certainly in him that Hopkins found validation of his theories. Accounts of this influence are not uncommon, but, since Scotus's theories are important to my argument at this point, I will briefly recount them.[35]

Scotus proposed a distinction between two modes of consciousness: that of innate memory which is received from the creative mind of God, but which only allows us to understand the world confusedly; and that of abstraction, of imposing distinct categories on the objects of our knowledge, yet at the same time imposing something of ourselves, our *haecceitas*, or 'thisness', on them. Insight would therefore be the possibility of discerning the universal – God's being – in the particular, made possible in Scotian philosophy through the univocity of being, the belief that being is the primary philosophical category in some sense common to both created nature and God. In this Hopkins found a reconciliation of the universal with his love for the specific in nature; it permitted a celebration of the concrete rather than the Platonic denigration of it in which many of his class were steeped. As Efrem Bettoni comments, 'individuality, in Scotus's system, is the ultimate perfection of things: it enables them to receive in themselves the act of existence. Only thus they become *real* in the full sense of the term.'[36] Hopkins's poetry repeatedly enacts this apprehension of the particular in its relation to the universal, though it is mostly the specific figure of Christ whose presence he discovers in the created world.

Hopkins also claimed that his poems were organised in terms of the principles of inscape – 'Poetry is in fact speech only employed to carry the inscape of speech for the inscape's sake'[37] – and in this once again the most immediately obvious analogy is with the male body. For example Hopkins saw Dryden as 'the most masculine of our poets; his style and his rhythms lay the strongest stress of all our literature on the naked thew and sinew of the English language'.[38] This ideal of poetic language as analogous to the body is taken up and extended in an account of inscape in Hopkins's poetry by J. Hillis Miller:

> There must be no flaccid or lax, no blurring or smudging of the pattern, but each part of the poem must be wound up to an intense stress or pitch of distinctiveness … all the special characteristics of Hopkins's verse … are there to achieve the highest possible degree of what he called 'brilliancy, starriness, quain, margaretting'. These techniques of patterning work together to produce the extraordinarily sinewy and burly texture of Hopkins' poetry, its heavy substance and strongly marked inner structure, as of bones, veins, and tendons binding together a body and making it one. His description of 'Harry Ploughman' might be taken as a description (and example) of the texture of his own poetry.[39]

Inscape therefore appears to have a direct analogy with the male body, its stress being comparable with the energy displayed in the body in action (though perhaps arrested, as in Walker's painting). The binding force of a Hopkins poem lies not in the regularity of stress and slack, as in ordinary metre, but precisely and only in moments of stress.

It was precisely this internal order that the poetry of the Irish lacked. Writing of the Anglo-Irish poet Samuel Ferguson, Hopkins argued, 'he was a poet as the Irish are ... full of feeling, high thoughts, flow of verse, point, often fine imagery and other virtues, but the essential and only lasting thing left out – what I call *inscape*, that is species or individually-distinctive beauty of style'.[40] Assimilating Ferguson – actually a defender of Protestant privilege and imperial rule – to the anarchic condition he perceived more generally in Irish culture and society, Hopkins here stigmatises Irish poetry as Romantic in the worst sense – as lacking in distinctness; that is, lacking the particular, individual ordering of its matter which also intimates a universal order. Paradoxically – but consistently – in this lack of individuality, Hopkins senses not a blanket order-in-sameness but an indication of the disordered lack of individual control. In the espousal of vague national sentiments there is only evidence of the need for greater subjection, and this is further indicated by the claim he made to be able to 'instress' the nature of crowds, though he succeeded in doing so only where those crowds – especially workers – had 'a common line of force and positive energy'. Tellingly, in the crowds of Home Rulers in Ireland he saw merely anarchic disorder.[41]

In this way, and to this extent, poetry and all other forms of beauty partake of the nature of Christ, of the disciplined manliness which was the ideal form of physical beauty. In this world this manliness was present for Hopkins at its most perfect in its sacrificial form (hence the veneration for General Gordon *et al*). Hopkins's real distinction from the mainstream tradition of Christian manliness lay in his recognition that the admiration of the body was 'dangerous' and therefore had to be tempered with a proper asceticism. This was epitomised in the body's most selfless act.

### Body and wreckage

According to Hopkins's idiosyncratic theology, Christ's sacrifice – in which 'all this strength was spent, this lissomness crippled, this beauty

wrecked, this majesty beaten down' – was implicit in the very reduction of God to man, itself the prototypical act of sacrifice: 'It is as if the
blissful agony or stress of selving in God had forced out drops of sweat
or blood, which drops were the world'.[42] The image clearly prefigures
the crucifixion, and is a revealing one, indicating also how Hopkins
perceived the world, in Hilary Fraser's phrase, in terms of 'a kind of
moral counterpoint':[43] it is, wrote Hopkins, as if 'God shewed us in a
vision the whole world enclosed in a drop of water, allowing everything to be seen in its native colours; then the same in a drop of
Christ's blood, by which everything whatever was turned scarlet,
keeping nevertheless mounted in the scarlet its own colour too'.[44]
Nature, properly instressed not only reveals its created form, but is
tempered by the intimation of sacrifice.

Hopkins's image of God's reduction of himself to man anticipates
Christ's 'wrecking': it is a prefiguration of the blood and sweat of the
crucifixion. The term 'wreck' itself is important, part of a nexus of onomatopoetic associations made by Hopkins in his poetry, though never
anywhere stated explicitly by him. In the early diaries there are long
lists of words related by some phonetic root, with elaborate attempts
to make semantic connections between them in order to suggest a
common etymology. The word 'wreck' has a number of etymologically
related and/or phonetically similar connections which also have a
semantic link. These include *reck, reckon, rack* and *wrack*, and Hopkins's use of them in the poetry and elsewhere strongly suggests that
he believed they were related onomatopoetically (he uses some of
them interchangeably). Their relationship derives from this sense of
the omnipresence of the sacrificed Christ. *Wreck* clearly refers to shipwreck, a meaning it shares with both *wrack* and *rack*, but these last
two are also related in their reference to 'a mass of cloud, driven
before the wind in the upper air' (*OED*). The imagistic unity of the
three words is demonstrated in an important, if deceptively brief, 1871
entry in Hopkins's *Journal* in which he instresses a cloud formation: 'it
was vaulted in very regular ribs with fretting between: but these are
not really ribs; they are a "wracking" install made of these two
realities – the frets are scarves of rotten cloud bellying upwards and
drooping at their ends'.[45] The vaulted ribs which give way to the
impression of 'wracking' imply the broken structure of a ship, an
image of wreck emphasised also in the sense of the clouds 'bellying
upwards', capsized. Mention of 'ribs' makes an obvious connection
with the body, here necessarily an allusion to a wrecked body; but

'vaulted' ribs also make reference to ecclesiastical architecture, suggesting that Hopkins had in mind the ruins of the monasteries, symbolic of English schism and the moment at which the English people became formally separated from God. *Rack* is, of course, a familiar instrument of torture – one used on Catholics in Elizabethan times – but it is also the process of drawing off wine from the lees of grapes, an image directly appropriated from Herbert to refer to the crucifixion in the early poem 'Barnfloor and Winepress': 'For us by Calvary's distress / The wine was rackèd from the press.'[46] Remembering Harry Ploughman's 'rack of ribs' therefore completes the imagistic unity I have been describing. The structure of a ship and the structure of certain cloud formations resemble the body which in death, most notably in sacrifice, is wrecked. *Reck* means simply 'to have a care', but is related to *reckon*, judgement. Every death, then – every wrecking of the physical body – calls to mind associations of (self-) sacrifice and judgement, and, in the English context, necessarily introduces consideration of the heretical position of the nation.

I would argue that this nexus of associations and wordplay permeates the poetry to the extent of being the single most important and consistent source of its imagery, and is there in incipient form even in the earliest extant poem of Hopkins, in the lines about the martyrdom of St Laurence:

> For that staunch saint still prais'd his Master's name
> While his crack'd flesh lay hissing on the grate;
> Then fail'd the tongue; the poor collapsing frame,
> Hung like a wreck that flames not billows beat[47]

The linkage of ribcage, the hull of a ship, torture and sacrifice are all present here, long before Hopkins's thoughts had turned to conversion. They are perhaps indicative of his ascetic predisposition to Catholicism at the same time as they evince an early admiration for heroic self-sacrifice as a Christian duty.

The very title of 'The Wreck of the Deutschland'[48] therefore invokes this onomatopoetic linkage, and indeed its diverse features are to be found in the poem. The first part is explicitly concerned with the fear of death and with redemption, in which the process of dying well is crucial, as to die in mortal sin is to be damned; the aim must be to die filled with God's grace, and this is compared to the way in which

> a lush-kept plush-capped sloe
> Will, mouthed to flesh burst,
> Gush! – flush the man, the being with it, sour or sweet,
> Brim, in a flash, full!

(st. 8)

Of course this is a variant of the image of the racking of grapes I have already referred to, and therefore implies that the crucifixion – through which all grace is communicated – must always inform our consciousness. It is this condition which the central figure of the nun achieves in her final moments.

However, the nun is not the only figure to evoke Hopkins's admiration in the poem; there is also that of a German sailor. Still, his experience of the storm is tragically different from hers:

> One stirred from the rigging to save
> The wild woman-kind below,
> With a rope's end round the man, handy and brave –
> He was pitched to his death at a blow,
> For all his dreadnought breast and braids of thew:
> They could tell him for hours, dandled the to and fro
> Through the cobbled foam-fleece. What could he do
> With the burl of the fountains of air, buck and the flood of the
>   wave?

(st. 16)

The sailor's manliness is in opposition to the hysterical 'woman-kind' below, and is demonstrated by his moral act. In the sense that he was 'pitched' to his death, he died through an act of duty, but his death 'at a blow' suggests the force of the power behind the wreck. That this force is God cannot be doubted, given Hopkins's initial demand in the poem that He 'Wring thy rebel ... / ... with wrecking and storm' (st. 9), and the very image of flooding and battering waves recalls that used of the passion referred to in the first part as being 'in high flood yet' (st. 7) (that is, Christ's sacrifice has an eternal relevance). Despite the sailor's manliness being outwardly manifest in his physical condition, then, it is not enough to save him – he is powerless against a storm which is God-sent – even though his physique is itself that of a 'dreadnought'[49] with braided sinews (muscles like ropes). In this very description, comparing him to a ship, he becomes a symbol of the broader tragedy of the wreck, a wreck which has a dual significance ('O Deutschland, double a desperate name!' (st. 20)). In addition to being this specific ship, it is also symbol of a Protestant nation; it is both literal ship and ship of state. Just as the sailor's body is related to the fate of the ship, then, it is also related to the fate of his nation in the sense that Protestantism, though distinguished by its high sense of moral duty, is formally outside the Catholic Church. The sailor's action, therefore, cannot save him, and the implication is that his nation is also doomed; hence the bleak, comfortlessness of his representation in the poem, his powerlessness to be saved through an act of pure moral will.

All of this also establishes the significance of this particular tragedy for Hopkins: he appeals to the nun to become intercessor on England's part and the poem becomes a prayer for the return of England to the Roman Catholic Church in order to save it from the hopeless wreckage of a *Deutschland*, as well as to save the individuals who comprise his nation. Christ is praised as king, hero and high priest, rightfully the crowning figure of a nation – England – unsurpassed in mind, character and body ('our thoughts' chivalry's throng's Lord' (st. 35)).

The thematic similarities between this poem and 'The Loss of the Eurydice'[50] are obvious: both take the events of a shipwreck as the basis of a meditation on judgement. 'Eurydice' also ends with a prayer – that the ship's English sailors will not be damned – and it is in the body of a drowned sailor that Hopkins finds the symbol for his grief over the fall of England from divine grace. The sailor is 'all of lovely manly mould' (l. 74), and in being 'strung by duty ... strained to beauty' (l. 78), there is precisely that sense of the body's activity under the moral imperative of work which informed the concept of inscape. In this he is a type of the national character – 'He was but one like thousands more' (l. 85) – and the connections between this body's instressed form and ship imagery ('*strung* by duty') again represents the condition of the nation-state as manifest in its people.

However, this passage is immediately followed by a sense of the degeneration of the race, of the poet's 'Fast foundering own generation' (l. 88). Hopkins cannot suppress the conviction that the nation's people are becoming less manly, and his other writings make clear that this is largely as a consequence of industrialisation.[51] In a letter to Bridges whilst serving in Liverpool, he related his sense of this physical degeneration and its imperial implications during the annual procession of the horses:

I remarked for the thousandth time with sorrow and loathing the base and bespotted figures and features of the Liverpool crowd. When I see the fine and manly Norwegians that flock hither to embark for America walk our streets and look about them it fills me with shame and wretchedness. I am told Sheffield is worse though. We have been shamefully beaten by the Boers (at Majuba it was simply that our troops funked and ran), but this is not the worse that is to be.[52]

The shame felt at the physically 'base and bespotted figures' immediately leads into a consideration of empire, of its disintegration. The worse that is to be, though, came for Hopkins in a nearer part of the empire.

### Dismemberment

If Ireland rarely figures positively in Hopkins's later poems, its negative presence is pervasive. Even in his final poem, 'To R.B.'[53] the reference to 'My winter world' is prefigured in a letter to his mother from Dublin in which he states that 'the weather is wintry. It is steadily snowing. But the political weather is beyond measure severer to me'.[54] The anxiety about England's demise as an imperial power is also clearly the subtext of his chauvinistic attempt at optimism, the embarrassingly patriotic 'What shall I do for the land that bred me', suggested to him as a result of a walk in Phoenix Park (a somewhat ironic source of inspiration, given that this was the site of the political assassinations of the Chief Secretary Lord Curzon and his Under-Secretary in 1882).

The ultimate expression of his alienation from all that he had previously celebrated – one of the two poems which mark out Hopkins's realisation of his lot after which 'the rest of his life was a playing out of the role described'[55] – is the vision of 'Spelt from Sibyl's Leaves'. The language of this poem, as in the sonnets of desolation, loses its capacity to mediate between the concrete and the transcendent, instead taking on an apocalyptic symbolism in its evocation of ultimate negation. Here we find the characteristic Scotian celebration of the difference of the world united in God through the immanence of Christ in nature instead overwhelmed by darkness and (un)resolved into a severe binarism:

Earnest, earthless, equal, attuneable, | vaulty, voluminous, …
    stupendous
Evening strains to be tíme's vást | womb-of-all, home-of-all,
    hearse-of-all night.
Her fond yellow hornlight wound to the west, | her wild hollow
    hoarlight hung to the height
Waste; her earliest stars, earlstars, | stars principal, overbend us,
Fíre-féaturing héaven. For éarth | her béing has unbóund; her
    dápple is at énd, as-
Tray or aswarm, all throughther, in throngs; | self ín self stéepèd
    and páshed – qúite
Disremembering, dismembering | all now. Heart, you round me
    right
With: Óur évening is óver us; óur night | whélms, whélms, ánd
    will énd us.
Only the beakleaved boughs dragonish | damask the tool-smooth
    bleak light; black,
Ever so black on it. Óur tale, O óur oracle! | Lét life, wáned, ah lét
    life wínd
Off hér once skéined stained véined varíety | upon, áll on twó
    spools; párt, pen, páck
Now her áll in twó flocks, twó folds – bláck, white; | ríght, wrong;
    réckon but, réck but, mínd
But thése two; wáre of a wórld where bút these | twó tell, éach off
    the óther; of a ráck
Where, selfwrung, selfstrung, sheathe- and shelterless, | thoúghts
    agáinst thoughts ín groans grínd.[56]

That binarism of 'two flocks' is a reference to the second coming – 'And before him shall be gathered all nations: and he shall separate them one from another, as a shepherd divideth his sheep from the goats' (Matthew 25: 32) – but that very reference to the division of nations perhaps belies the real determining force behind Hopkins's desolation. It is in Ireland that, for the first time, Hopkins writes in terms of an absolute division of subjectivity, between a country predominantly devoted to his faith and the country of his birth which governs it, with no means of reconciling that division since the one true arbiter of such decisions is absent from him.

    The following is taken from his retreat notes, written a few years after 'Sibyl's Leaves' was completed. It shows the contradictory position he considered himself to be in throughout his stay in Ireland:

All moral good, all man's being good, lies in two things – in being right, being in the right, and in doing right … Neither of these will do by itself ….

… The Irish think it enough to be Catholics or on the right side and that it is no matter what they say and do to advance it; practically so, but what they think is that all they and their leaders do to advance the right side is and must be right. The English think, as Pope says for them, he can't be wrong whose life is in the right ….

…. the Catholic Church in Ireland and the Irish Province in it and our College in that are greatly given over to a partly unlawful cause, promoted by unlawful means, and against my will my pains, laborious and distasteful, like prisoners made to serve the enemies' gunners, go to help on this cause.

Later the same day, he added:

All my undertakings miscarry: I am like a straining eunuch. I wish then for death: yet if I died now I should die imperfect, no master of myself, and that is the worst failure of all. O my God, look down on me.[57]

Ireland is in rebellion against English rule, the rule – as Hopkins sees it – of a virtuous and manly people, and yet England is the heretical nation. Ireland is unruly, anarchic, a country which threatens to tear that virtuous empire apart, and Hopkins cannot help but feel that he is acting in its service. The result is a feeling of impotence, of his own creative unmanning – 'straining eunuch' – which proceeds from his enervating physical as well as mental condition unrelieved by grace (Hopkins complained of his persistent lack of energy and general ill-health in Ireland, symptoms which elsewhere had been at worst intermittent.)

The darkness of the opening of 'Sibyl's Leaves', then, represents Hopkins's own sense of desolation as well as an intimation of the last judgement. In Daniel Harris's words, Hopkins's 'perturbations and ambivalences [at this time] seemed so hopelessly complicated that only the Apocalypse might resolve them'.[58] The specific location of Hopkins's confusions is indicated in the poem by one seemingly insignificant word: 'Disremembering' is not simply a convenient invented homophone to place next to 'dismembering', but is also a parody of Irish speech – Hopkins used the word in a letter home to his sister mimicking the Irish tongue[59] – and as such it locates Ireland precisely as the place of his alienation from the variety of the natural world. Worse, this world is dismembered, its unity – like that of the poet – 'pashed', and the creative force is no longer present in him.

The rack depicted in *this* poem, then, is no sacrifice of self in imitation of Christ, since Christ is absent from Hopkins; it is a *self*-racking, a scrupulous inability to perceive any possible good in his present position, leaving only 'thoughts against thoughts' grinding on each other in an undecidable moral relation rooted in the poet's own deeply divided identity in Ireland as both English and Catholic. The absence of Christ is the absence of that imaginary body – derived, as I have argued, from imperial ideology – through which Hopkins had experienced the world at its most beautiful as ordered, disciplined and unified. The obliteration of this body was the source of his intense psychological suffering, consciously experienced as the absence of God.

# 6

## Hopkins, body and sexuality

THE conceptualisation of the body in Hopkins is never separable from his grasp of the social, of the unity and virtuous nature of the commonwealth, at the same time as it is imbued with profoundly religious feelings of awe. However, since Hopkins was also conscious of the potentially erotic attractions of the male form, there is an obvious sense in which the virtuous nature of this bodily conception of nation could be compromised: if the body was admirable for its symbolic qualities this admiration could always risk the possibility of developing into desire. In my discussion of Hopkins's imperialist fixation on the male body I have only touched on this aspect of its appeal. Here I want to pursue in more detail the problem (for Hopkins) of human sexuality. I have chosen to keep these two arguments separate – though the separation is no doubt artificial – in order to preserve the clarity of each.

Hopkins's ambivalence towards the male form was most notably demonstrated by his recognition of his poetic similarities to Whitman, whose own sensuous depictions of the body simultaneously encompassed an American liberal, democratic political ideal at odds with Hopkins's rigidly hierarchical one as expressed in 'Tom's Garland'. The few poems of Whitman that Hopkins had read would have been enough to convince him of this dangerously democratic and, at the same time, sexually charged nature of the American's work. Writing to Bridges he made his ambivalence explicit: 'I always knew in my heart Walt Whitman's mind to be more like my own than any other man's living. As he is a very great scoundrel this is not a pleasant confession. And this makes me the more desirous to read him and the more determined that I will not.'[1] The affinity with Whitman is remarked on in terms of both self-realisation and conscious denial – the *desire* to read him and the disciplined necessity of suppressing this desire. It is, above all, an indication of Hopkins's simultaneous sexual self-awareness and self-regulation,[2] two facets of his character which could only have been accentuated by the Ignatian discipline of his order. Consequently I will be suggesting here – in contrast to other accounts – that, though Hopkins's sexual censoriousness was socially determined, his rigour in this respect was governed by a partly conscious rationalisation of his longings.

As we have seen, Hopkins shared a more pervasive social concern for the physical degeneracy of the urban working class and the way in which this might lead to imperial decline. In his case this was also underpinned by other anxieties. Peter Stallybrass and Allon White have discussed the Victorian middle class's simultaneous disgust and fascination with the dirt, disease and vice of the urban poor. The early Victorian reformers' obsession with these, for example, was related to pervasive forms of self-denial: 'As the bourgeoisie produced new forms of regulation and prohibition governing their own bodies, they wrote ever more loquaciously of the body of the Other – the city's "scum".'[3] This obsession with the poor was a means of class differentiation through moral differentiation: all the 'low' morals of the poor came to be associated both metonymically and metaphorically with their filthy condition, and this process of differentiation entailed the renunciation of many 'sinful' pleasures, not least sexual ones, in the process of middle-class self-definition. As the child

> grows up/is cleaned up, the lower bodily stratum is regulated or denied, as far as possible, by the correct posture ('stand up straight', 'don't squat', 'don't kneel on all fours' – the posture of the servants and savages [i.e. those who mediate between the purity of the home and the filthy world outside]), and by the censoring of lower 'bodily' references along with the bodily wastes.

As the body's 'low' is 'forgotten', the city's 'low' becomes the site of concern, 'a preoccupation which is itself intimately conceptualised in terms of discourses of the body'.[4] Consequently the characteristic responses of the middle classes towards the urban working class mingled fear and desire, disgust and fascination. Such an ambivalence was certainly characteristic of Hopkins, in whom it became bound up with traditionalist and imperialist sensibilities.

From an early age his poetry demonstrates an extraordinary degree of asceticism. This is the opening of his unfinished poem 'Il

Mystico' written in 1862:

> Hence sensual gross desires,
> Right offspring of your grimy mother Earth!
> My spirit hath a birth
> Alien from yours as heaven from Nadir-fires:
> You rank and reeking things,
> Scoop you from teeming filth some sickly hovel,
> And there for ever grovel
> 'Mid fever'd fumes and slime and cakèd clot:
> But foul and cumber not
> The shaken plumage of my Spirit's wings.[5]

The association of sensuality with earth, dirt, 'sickly hovel', grovel (with its simultaneous associations of poverty and a lack of bodily uprightness), fumes and 'slime' correspond with the paradigm outlined by Stallybrass and White: the topos of the body is purged of sin through an imagined expulsion of filth to some geographical other place of primitivism; but this is an act of self-will which, through its attempts at exclusion and distantiation, simultaneously – and necessarily – recognises the proximity of that other place.

Mention of the word 'slime' in this passage brings me to a consideration of another of Hopkins's onomatopoetic associations, and one which connects this savage other place – distinctly unurban and feminine in 'Il Mystico' – with the topos of the city, at the same time as it introduces a consideration of the foul practices of the workers. '*Slum* is probably connected with *slime*', Hopkins wrote in his early diaries,[6] and this general connection of fluid filth with the inner cities is repeated in more particular forms at other points in these notes: '*Hawk* is sell about the streets. I had imagined this to be derived from the brawling or screeching the hawkers made in proclaiming their wares, to *hawk* meaning to make a noise in the throat, as before spitting'[7] (Hopkins considers other possibilities, but this one suggests itself to him most naturally). A few entries later, his interest in spitting continues with the following lists:

> *Spuere, spit, spuma, spume, spoom, spawn, spittle, spatter, spot, sputter.*
>
> ———
>
> *Mucus, muck.*[8]

Of course there is one word missing from the first of these lists. Given the inclusion of *spume* – froth – and especially *spawn* – indicating that

Hopkins was thinking in part about reproduction – it is reasonable to suppose that he was finding connections for *sperm* (though he clearly chose to censor the word). Indeed the association between bodily fluids, filth and working-class communities is a pervasive one which extends beyond these references into Hopkins's letters and even his poetry. Frequently it provokes a sense of shame. There is the instance of the letter to Bridges quoted above in which the 'base and be*spotted*' (my emphasis) Liverpudlians fill Hopkins with 'shame and loathing' in comparison to the manly Norwegians. On another occasion, having experienced life in the industrial north of England and in Glasgow, Hopkins attacks the filth of contemporary English civilisation as a means of defending Catholic countries from Bridges's accusation of squalor:

> spitting in the North of England is very, very common with the lower classes: as I went up Brunswick Road (or any street) at Liverpool on a frost morning it used to disgust me to see the pavement regularly starred with the spit of the workmen going to their work; and they do not turn aside, but spit straight before them as you approach, as a Frenchman remarked to me with abhorrence and I cd. only blush … And our whole civilisation is dirty, yea, filthy, and especially in the north; for is it not dirty, yea filthy, to pollute the air as Blackburn and Widnes and St. Helen's are polluted and the water as the Thames and the Clyde and the Irwell are polluted? The ancients with their immense public baths would have thought even our cleanest towns dirty.[9]

The filth of his nation was therefore a subject which compelled feelings of shame when compared with the conditions of other European nations and with classical civilisations, and the most recurrent metonymic representative of this filthy condition was spit, a bodily fluid whose mucus/muck imagistically suggested to Hopkins the slime/slum which epitomised for him the repulsive fascination of the city. 'The Sea and the Skylark' (1877) gives this nexus of ideas a further religious significance: 'Our make and making break, are breaking, down / To man's last dust, drain fast towards man's first slime.'[10] The disgust that Hopkins demonstrates towards the city's physically degenerate workers, the shame he feels for them, results from embarrassment about and fears of their potency: he seems to perceive the degeneration of his own race in sexual terms as a fall from the virtuous, upright condition of the ideal male body.

The imagined dissolution of the rigidity of the disciplined body into a repulsive and viscous fluidity, into 'man's first slime' – and, by extension, the dissolution of the social body – inevitably provokes other associations with another kind of fluid dissolution discussed in the previous chapter, that of 'wrecking'. As I have argued, 'wrecking' was primarily associated with Christ's self-sacrifice in Hopkins's religious thought, and with the individual's imitation of Christ and the need for bodily denial, the standard by which that individual would be judged. Wrecking, though, was itself a form of dissolution into fluidity, one present in Hopkins's image of God's selving as Christ, and again in the depiction of the scene of the crucifixion in 'The Wreck of the Deutschland'. Here, at greater length, is the passage from Part One in which the crucifixion is related to individual redemption:

> It dates from day
> Of his going in Galilee;
> Warm-laid grave of a womb-life grey;
> Manger, maiden's knee;
> The dense and the driven Passion, and frightful sweat;
> Thence the discharge of it, there its swelling to be,
> Though felt before, though in high flood yet –
> What none would have known of it, only the heart, being hard
> at bay,
>
> Is out with it! Oh,
> We lash with the best or worst
> Word last! How a lush-kept plush-capped sloe
> Will, mouthed to flesh-burst,
> Gush! – flush the man, the being with it, sour or sweet,
> Brim, in a flash, full! – Hither then, last or first,
> To hero of Calvary, Christ,'s feet –
> Never ask if meaning it, wanting it, warned of it – men go.[11]

The crushed sloe, releasing its sour or sweet juices, as a metaphor for the individual's sinful or redemptive last thoughts relates to the crucifixion not only through being a variant on the image of the racked grapes in 'Barnfloor and Winepress' but through its relationship to the previous stanza's depiction of the scene of the crucifixion and its emphasis on 'swelling' and 'discharge'. The sensuality of both images is remarkable, and the reference to 'fleshburst' in particular invites an erotic reading. Moreover, such a reading is legitimised by the connections Hopkins establishes between this and the rest of the poem, since the meditation on death and judgement at this point relates directly to the treatment of the central figure of the nun whose relationship to

Christ is also sexualised (and famously so). Following the nun's cry 'O Christ, Christ come quickly' in the midst of the storm, Hopkins asks: 'Is it lóve in her of the béing as her lóver had béen?' ('Wreck', st. 24–5). This prompts Robert Martin to remark that 'it is almost impossible to believe that Hopkins would intentionally have evoked the sexual ambiguity of her call to Christ … but it is difficult to ignore the erotic overtone in [this] context'. His resolution of this apparent blasphemy, though, seems rhetorical rather than genuinely convincing: Martin suggests that Hopkins's repressed sexual feelings 'naturally seeped into his imagery with unconscious strength'.[12] To the contrary, it seems to me there is nothing unconscious about this imagery, nor could there have been in a writer so morally and verbally scrupulous as Hopkins. One clue to Hopkins's real thinking is perhaps provided in another tacit reference to sexual emissions in the poem. The description of Luther as 'beast of the waste wood' clearly expresses contempt for Luther's vindication of the sexual act,[13] and thus establishes a division in the poem between a divine love which is figuratively presented as sexual and the corporeal sexuality which Hopkins maintained was sinful.

It is perhaps worth noting at this point that Hopkins's description of the supreme act of divine love in terms of the definitive act of male sexuality does not make him altogether unique amongst his contemporaries. Christ's mysterious status as human and divine enabled a number of other Anglo-Catholics and converts to Catholicism to celebrate the deity's erotic potential. This was the case with Digby Mackworth Dolben, with whom Hopkins seems to have fallen in love after only one meeting in 1865. Dolben's verse is full of imagery of a bloody consummation between himself and his beloved (Christ). The following, from 'The Prodigal's Benediction', gives some indication of the tenor of his writing:

> O Thou only beautiful,
> Thou only wise, I thank Thee that at length,
> Seeing all else was vain, I turned to Thee,
> And laid my weary load of sin and shame
> Upon Thy bleeding back, to bear away
> Into the wilderness of that last cry,
> 'My God, my God, Thou hast forsaken Me.'
> I cannot thank Thee, I can only say,
> 'Take, dearest Lord, this crushed and bleeding heart,
> And lay it in Thy hand, Thy piercéd hand,

That Thine atoning blood may mix with mine,
Till I and my Belovéd are all one.'[14]

As both Robert Martin and Norman White point out, Robert Bridges later suggested that 'the reading of [Dolben's] poems makes one see why schoolmasters wish their boys to play games'.[15]

We can verify Hopkins's erotic response to the scene of the crucifixion through his own records. Prior to his conversion, in 1865, he practised confession with Henry Parry Liddon. His confessional notes are included in his early notebooks and manuscripts, though they were, until recently, censored by his editors. Finally published in 1989, they record the extent of his anxiety about sins of temptation. Many of these involve the attractions of other men, but there are also numerous instances of sexual temptation possessing him in relationship to the crucifixion: 'The evil thought in writing on our Lord's passion'; 'The evil thought slightly in drawing made worse by drawing a crucified arm on same page'; 'I had also a horrible thought but I doubt if it was a temptation. It was about personal love of Ch.' (the status of this is clearly not as certain as the others); 'Having an evil thought in looking on a beautiful crucifix of Aunt Kate's'; 'Weak scrupulosity in looking at Bramley's picture and in thinking of our Lord on the cross'.[16] Christ's crucifixion was therefore the scene which acutely condensed Hopkins's dilemmas about male beauty: it represented the most affective reproof to his sinful condition but simultaneously provoked in him the sin which he most insistently attempted to subdue. The result seems to have been a resolution of his dilemma by projecting satisfaction of his sexual urges on to an anticipated ecstatic release from the human condition. Hopkins therefore anticipated the moment of death as potentially a moment of blissful release only imaginable by him in sexual terms.

This simultaneous polarisation of and comparison between sexual and divine love is presented most starkly in the octet of the sonnet 'God's Grandeur'. Again it is the urban worker who secretes repulsive fluids:

The world is charged with the grandeur of God.
    It will flame out, like shining from shook foil;
    It gathers to a greatness, like the ooze of oil
Crushed. Why do men then now not reck his rod?
Generations have trod, have trod, have trod;
    And all is seared with trade; bleared, smeared with toil;
    And wears man's smudge and shares man's smell: the soil
Is bare now, nor can foot feel, being shod.[17]

The ejaculation of oil which brings the first quatrain to its climax is clearly another variant on the racking image. The suggestion is that Christ's sacrifice is integral to God's grandeur, the benign counterpart to 'his rod'. But this climax contrasts pointedly with 'men's smudge' and 'men's smell' in line 7. As Richard Dellamora points out, then, the poem 'has analogues with bodily processes, in particular seminal emissions, regarded positively in the first four lines and negatively in the next four'.[18] The word used to describe the racking of the oil – 'Crushed' – is given strong emphasis by its position at the opening of a line. Significantly, it also crops up in the confessional notes: 'Not crushing enough evil thoughts'.[19] This might be a coincidence, but it is certainly a striking one given the synonymity between *crush* and *wreck*, both in ordinary usage and in Hopkins's particular one, and again suggests that the temptation which Hopkins obsessively suppressed returned, redeemed of its sin, as the image of ultimate renunciation and justification.

In a neat reinversion of Feuerbachian logic, Hopkins once acknowledged that 'we are obliged to think of God by human thoughts'.[20] His erotic response to the scene of the crucifixion was one determined by the desires prompted in him by a pervasive deification of the male body within his own homosocial culture. The imperial ideal of manliness was an idealising one which, though it valorised the body, did so only as an indication of some putative inner moral value which itself entailed the containment of sexuality. In Hopkins's case this sexual denial was clearly enhanced and structured in distinctive ways by the beliefs of his order. Consequently Hopkins's sexual response to the male body generated a complex self-division which involved the deferral of an imagined satisfaction until the moment of death and redemption, and, simultaneously, a projection of sinfulness on to the repellent and degenerate working class who, he believed, were themselves the principal threat to upright imperial manliness.

# 7

## Buggering Gerald:
## Wilde and English virtue

I<small>N</small> 1914 Rupert Brooke invoked the resilience and resoluteness of the athlete in his picture of soldiers entering battle. They were, he imagined, 'as swimmers into cleanness leaping'.[1] Such sentiments were prevalent amongst England's officer class on the outbreak of a war that was popularly considered the means by which English manliness might prove itself, the very event for which public school training had been an ideal preparation.[2] Not least amongst the effects of such a renewal of manliness would be the virilisation of art: Brooke's heroes contrast with the 'half-men' of peacetime. Another soldier-poet, Ivor Gurney, hoped to 'make / The name of poet terrible in just war, / And like a crown of honour upon the fight',[3] whilst the lesser-known – and, given the context, rather inappropriately named – Joyce Kilmer attacked those who had made poetry the object of 'the merchant's sneer, the clerk's disdain', depicting such people as 'little poets mincing there / With women's hearts and women's hair': they should 'leave the poet's craft to men!'[4] The association between art and femininity was well established, but it seems clear that these attempts to purge poetry of feminine – or rather, effeminate – associations was a consequence of the ascendancy of the aesthete who had come to personify the artist in the popular English imagination.

The bathing scene which Brooke invokes was a traditional one, and it was also an integral part of the public school's disciplinary regime.[5] But such scenes could also provoke ambivalent responses, and Brooke himself was not immune to the body's erotic appeal. Whilst in training he wrote to Lady Eileen Wellesley: 'Occasionally I'm faintly shaken by a suspicion that I might find incredible beauty in the washing place, with rows of naked, superb men bathing in a September sun … if only I were sensitive. But I'm not. I'm a warrior. So I think of nothing.'[6] 'Sensitivity' was by this time itself a by-word for the artistic temperament, denoting a feminine, over-responsive nervous temperament,[7] but here it also connotes a vulnerability to same-sex desire which, by now, was virtually synonymous with effeminacy: Brooke must suppress his consciously erotic thoughts in order to be a warrior, a suitably heroic participant in the conflict. Presumably such determination was symptomatic of his break with the Bloomsbury group, the artistic crowd with which he was once associated.

No one was more responsible for the notoriety of the artist in this sense than Oscar Wilde. He also seems to have enjoyed the pleasures of bathing and the sights it afforded, but the male body did not necessarily carry the same connotations for him as it did later for Brooke. On vacation from Oxford in 1876 he wrote to his friend William Ward from Ireland: 'I ride sometimes after six, but don't do much but bathe, and although always feeling slightly immortal when in the sea, feel sometimes slightly heretical when good Roman Catholic boys enter the water with little amulets and crosses round their necks and arms that the good S. Christopher may hold them up.'[8] It is doubtful that Wilde had in mind the English bathing tradition when he wrote this, but a comparison with that tradition is none the less instructive. Wilde – clearly punning on the word 'immortal' – acknowledges the eroticism of the scene without demonstrating any accompanying anxiety. His relationship to these Catholic Irish boys, though, is mediated by distance, since Wilde was of Anglo-Irish provenance and, whilst at Oxford, suppressed the signs of his Irishness by cultivating an impeccable English accent. The attraction he feels here is therefore one of desire rather than identification, finding the boys' alterior appeal in their apparent freedom and naive faith (the only role attributed to their religion is one of protection, not repression). Moreover, the religion and the desire are conflated – Wilde feels 'sometimes slightly heretical' in the boys' presence – so that the temptations of sexual and religious perversion are collapsed. The boys represent an unselfconscious liberty, rather than self-restraint, and their nationality and religion are both bound up with this.

At this stage of his life Wilde was flirting with the idea of conversion, like so many Oxonians before and after. The Catholicism which appealed to him appears to have been a distinctly English version,[9] one as alien to the Irish boys of his desires as the Protestantism integrally bound up with the imperial centre of Britain. Yet Catholicism's attraction lay not in the kind of consistency which those such as Hopkins had claimed for it. As some testimony to Wilde's seriousness about the faith, it is true that he believed that the Incarnation helped him 'grasp at the skirts of the Infinite', but typically went on to add that grasping the atonement was more difficult.[10] Equally demonstrative of Catholicism's real appeal, in this respect, was his flight from it. In 1878 the Reverend Sebastien Bowden wrote earnestly to Wilde from the Brompton Oratory exhorting him to confess his sins and enter the Catholic faith: 'you would put from you all that is affected and unreal and a thing unworthy of your better self and live full of the deepest interests as a man who feels he has a soul to save and but a few fleeting hours in which to save it'. Those emphases on the renunciation of the frivolous and the moral imperative contained in the passing of time decided him; his reply took the form of a bunch of lilies.[11] Wilde was attracted to Catholicism only for so long as it seemed to offer the possibility of a retreat from the supposedly rational and aesthetically unappealing, deeply conscientious world of Protestantism. Catholicism and, by extension, Catholic subjects were symbolically opposed to the constraining world of English moralism[12] (however wide of the mark this might seem to us). The attractions of the Catholic Irish boys lay, then, in perceptions Wilde derived from an environment rather different from the one which they inhabited. Indeed it might be argued that Wilde was confirming, if revaluing, the popular English sense of Catholicism as sanctioning moral depravity.

Bowden's moralism finally deterred Wilde from becoming these boys' co-religionist at this time, but Wilde did lay claim to the same racial provenance, and this too he made a sign of his distance from English culture. Wilde, as we have already seen, subscribed to the Renanian association of Celticism with aestheticism, but without Arnold's reservations. From his speech in San Francisco to his later plays, Wilde constantly draws on the Celt/Saxon opposition, equating it with the forces of aestheticism/moralism, even if the opposition typically manifests itself in apparently trivial comments. In discussing the music arrangements for her reception with Algernon in *The Importance of Being Earnest*, Lady Bracknell – the elderly figure of authority – excludes Celtic in favour of Teutonic entertainment: 'French songs I cannot possibly allow. People always seem to think that they are improper, and either look shocked, which is vulgar, or laugh, which is worse. But German sounds a thoroughly respectable language, and, indeed I believe is so.'[13] The second act opens with Miss Prism – along with Chasuble, the representative of religious morality – attempting to teach Cecily her German grammar. Cecily resists: 'I don't like German. It isn't at all a becoming language. I know perfectly well that I look quite plain after my German lesson.'[14]

Wilde's wholehearted acceptance of the Renanian association of Celticism and poeticism also complemented his political support for Home Rule. His mother was a well-known Irish republican poet, and he retained some of her commitments, if not her earnestness. In 1888 he wrote to Gladstone, sending him a copy of *The Happy Prince* with a note explaining that 'I should like to have the pleasure of presenting it, such as it is, to one whom I, and all who have Celtic blood in their veins, must ever honour and revere, and to whom my country is so deeply indebted'.[15] Later, reviewing Froude's predictably bigoted recommendations for 'resolving' the Irish question, he claimed that in Blue Books on Ireland 'England has written down her indictment against herself, and has given the world the history of her shame'.[16]

On the other hand Wilde was not uncritical of the form that his mother's political commitments took, and he distanced himself from the nationalist sentiments she had expressed in the language of blood-sacrifice. In his early 'Sonnet On Liberty', for example, he claims that revolutionary activities appeal to him only in so far as they give form to his own feelings (they 'mirror my wildest passions like the sea'), though he also betrays 'some' sympathy with these 'Christs that die upon the barricades'.[17] This valorisation of individual experience over self-sacrifice is typical of Wilde and demonstrates clearly enough that it was not simply a response to what he considered the Teutonic moralism of English culture, though it was mostly expressed in relation to this. Wilde's antipathy to self-sacrifice actually lay in a philosophical rejection of practical interventions in the course of history and his belief in a different form of freedom, and these are persistent themes in his work.

The denigration of the purposiveness of both the English gentleman and the revolutionary is evident in one of Wilde's wittiest and least sentimental short stories, 'Lord Arthur Savile's Crime'. The prime object of Wilde's satire is Savile's devotion to duty and his simultaneous lack of philosophical sophistication. Savile is told by a cheiromantist, Mr Podgers, that he is destined to commit a murder, and reflects on the necessity of getting this out of the way prior to his imminent marriage:

Many men in his position would have preferred the primrose

paths of dalliance to the steep heights of duty; but Lord Arthur was too conscientious to set pleasure above principle. There was more than mere passion in his love; and Sibyl was to him a symbol of all that is good and noble. For a moment he had a natural repugnance against what he was asked to do, but it soon passed away. His heart told him that it was not a sin, but a sacrifice; his reason reminded him that there was no other course open. He had to choose between living for himself and living for others, and terrible though the task laid before him undoubtedly was, yet he knew that he must not suffer selfishness to triumph over love. Sooner or later we are all called upon to decide the same issue – of us all, the same question is asked. To Lord Arthur it came early in life – before his nature had been spoiled by the calculating cynicism of middle-age, or his heart corroded by the shallow, fashionable egotism of our day, and he felt no hesitation about doing his duty. Fortunately also, for him, he was no mere dreamer, or idle dilettante. Had he been so, he would have hesitated, like Hamlet, and let irresolution mar his purpose. But he was essentially practical. Life to him meant action, rather than thought. He had that rarest of all things, common sense.[18]

Seeing the act of murder as his duty, Savile commits a philosophical mistake in the belief that the fates can be propitiated by an act of will (a mistake emphasised at the end of the story by Lady Windermere's final scepticism towards cheiromancy). It is to this that his dedication to action and 'common sense' leads him. Indeed at other times he considers himself 'predestined' or even guided by the fates to carry out the murder. In this his reason is defective, and his heart – in regarding this as a sacrifice rather than a sin – is dictating pagan terms. 'Living for others' – the morality Wilde later denigrated in *The Soul of Man Under Socialism* – is therefore represented as the sacrifice of others for the sake of marriage, the institution on which the absurd and contradictory morality of Savile is centred. Ultimately, though, marriage becomes the reward for Savile's 'virtuous' disdain for egotism and cynicism, as the narrative parodies conventional Victorian fictional endings. But this comedic ending is also unsettling – it rests on an undiscovered murder (Podger's) – and any perception of marriage as the outcome of some ineluctable process of justice is undermined: Savile's crime remains not only undiscovered but also unpunished, and, if providence is at work, crime has been rewarded in the way virtue normally would be.

Savile's attempts to pre-empt his destiny at one point lead him to seek the services of a Nihilist bomb-maker in order to blow up his uncle, the Dean of Chichester, and this leads to Wilde's complementary satire on revolutionaries. The Dean collects clocks, so Savile chooses as the machinery of his assassination an explosive device in the form of 'a pretty little French clock, surmounted by an ormolu figure of Liberty trampling on the hydra of Despotism'.[19] The clock fails to go off, and Herr Winckelkopf (the enlisted bomb-maker) has to admit that 'dynamite, as a destructive force, was, when under the control of machinery, a powerful, though a somewhat unpunctual agent'.[20] The actual fate of the clock is related in a letter to Savile's mother from the Dean's daughter:

> We have had great fun over a clock that an unknown admirer sent papa last Thursday ... Parker unpacked it, and papa put it on the mantelpiece in the library, and we were all sitting there on Friday morning, when just as the clock struck twelve, we heard a whirring noise, a little puff of smoke came from the pedestal of the figure, and the goddess of Liberty fell off, and broke her nose on the fender! Maria was quite alarmed, but it all looked so ridiculous, that James and I went off into fits of laughter, and even papa was amused. When we examined it, we found it was a sort of alarum clock, and that, if you set it to a particular hour, and put some gunpowder and a cap under a little hammer, it went off whenever you wanted ... Do you think Arthur would like it as a wedding present? I suppose they are quite fashionable in London. Papa says they should do a great deal of good, as they show that Liberty can't last, but must fall down. Papa says Liberty was invented at the time of the French Revolution. How awful it seems!
>      .... Reggie has just had another explosion, and papa has ordered the clock to the stables. I don't think papa likes it so much as he did at first, though he is very flattered at being sent such an ingenious toy. It shows that people read his sermons, and profit by them.[21]

Even though Savile's purpose in killing his uncle is a 'family affair', a 'private matter', the parody of revolutionary gestures is clear. Not only does the clock fail to work, but its symbolism is inverted as anti-libertarian – a denial of revolution's attempts to triumph over the course of time, and ultimately a proof to the Dean of the efficacy of Tory religious preaching. The irony is that it is proposed as a wedding present for Savile, an irony whose focus is directed against intentionality, since the clock's *intended* destructive purpose in killing the Dean is, of course, to facilitate the wedding. This satire on action is completed by Savile's eventual – and unplanned – choice of victim, the cheiroman-tist himself: Savile happens across him *by chance* and throws him into the Thames. Podgers thus becomes the unforeseen victim of his own prophecy.[22]

### History, art and freedom

Wilde's scepticism about the effectiveness of practical action was an attitude he developed as a result of his private study as a student. In his Oxford commonplace book, following a quotation from Walter Pater, he wrote: 'We are indeed compassed by the high unver [never?] leaped mountains of necessity, but for him who knows his limitations this dark horizon *becomes the sunlit circle of duty*[.] The cross of Christ will cast no shadow when the sun of Truth is high in the heaven.'[23] The determinism here is consistent with other jottings in this manuscript, but the importance of this passage lies in its demonstration that Wilde early on believed that the realm of freedom was severely circum-scribed and that the (Christian) culture of self-sacrifice – discernible in both English morality and his mother's brand of Irish republicanism – was both deluded and ineffective in terms of its purchase on the future. Though his reading of his aetheticist mentor Pater encouraged such views in Wilde, the principal influence on his determinist view seems rather to have been philosophical and Wilde demonstrates an acceptance in these notebooks of the main features of the work of the late nineteenth-century thinker Herbert Spencer.

Spencer's sociology – based on his 'synthetic philosophy' – is interesting primarily as an elaborate reworking of established means of understanding society and historical process. Profoundly influ-enced by evolutionary theory, he conceptualised society as a develop-ing and increasingly complex division of parts which is none the less organic. Amongst his Spencerian jottings Wilde records that the science of society 'rests on the science of life: sociology on Biology • the state as Plato saw is "man writ large": now in spite of his imper-fect psychology, and ignorance of biology Plato saw the real analogy between the individual and the social organism.'[24] There are distinc-tive features of Spencer's thought, but it also built on the dominant English understanding of nation-state development. In Spencer's case organic development is not simply a gradual evolution but one which proceeds from a state of simplicity to one of complexity. Just as the organism increasingly evolves its own 'physiological division of labour', so human societies – comprised of individuals – advance by a dual movement towards differentiation (or specialisation) and integration (or mutual dependence). In this way Spencer apparently resolves two of the dominant influences on his thinking – economic liberalism and evolutionary thought – and simultaneously reconciles the claims of individualism with those of social coherence.[25] The resolution is only apparent, though, since the principle of individualism, if pressed to its logical conclusion, could clearly contradict that of mutual dependence, and logically speaking the effect of too much individualism – of too great a departure from conformity to the demands of the whole organism – would be some form of degeneracy of the organism itself, a disintegration of its structure. Wilde was influenced by Spencerian positivism in his years as a student – especially in his essay 'The Rise of Historical Criticism' – and adhered to its overall deterministic features in his later work.[26] His subversive strategies in later life were also predicated on organicist ideology, since his radical individualism involved the sense that it was ultimately inimical to the overall health of the social organism, a degenerative influence.

According to this kind of strongly determinist thought, then, mere voluntarism was ineffective, and therefore social and cultural change – which Wilde certainly desired – would have to be brought about by other means. But in such a determinist world, in what possible sense might the individual be free to bring about such changes? It was not until 'The Critic as Artist' that Wilde fully and explicitly expounded his understanding of freedom in a discussion of history, art and the importance of the sinner. In this piece Wilde invokes an utterly determinist view of history at the same time as he represents art as the means by which we can exert some freedom from the laws of necessity. The assertion made by Gilbert – Wilde's spokesperson in the essay – that talking is superior to action introduces this issue, since action is impotent, unable to affect the future in determinate ways. It is necessarily juxtaposed to the imagination which requires inactivity. Hence it is more difficult to write history than to make it, and 'The one duty we owe to history is to re-write it ... When we have fully discovered the scientific laws that govern life, we shall realise that the one person who has more illusions than the dreamer is the man of action. He, indeed, knows neither the origin of his deeds nor their results.'[27] The crucial word of the first sentence is not, as is it is often taken to be, 're-write', but 'duty', since this is a denial of the view that we should draw moral lessons about conduct from the past, or that we can know how our actions will affect the future; it is essentially a denial of that commonsense commitment to purposive action so integral to English manliness. As Philip E. Smith and Micheal S. Helfand demonstrate in their introduction to the *Oxford Notebooks*, 'The Critic as Artist' rejects the emphasis on action in favour of an individualism which is itself racially determined. Against the conformism demanded by society, Wilde argues that individuals should become conscious of their souls, which are the culmination of racial development and which consequently permit us access to the diverse experiences of previous ages. The exploration of this racial legacy would generate a diversity subversive of mere conscientious obedience, thereby generating progress by encouraging heterogeneity within the race.[28] It is through this racial inheritance that the temptation to evil is to be found, not least through art, which is the record of the soul in other ages. The scientific principle of heredity may have denied the possibility of freedom in the practical sphere, but, argues Wilde,

> in the subjective sphere, where the soul is at work, it comes to us, this terrible shadow, with many gifts in its hands, gifts of strange temperaments and subtle susceptibilities, gifts of wild ardours and chill moods of indifference, complex multiform gifts of thoughts that are at variance with each other, and passions that war against themselves. And so it is not our own life that we live, but the lives of the dead, and the soul that dwells within us is no single spiritual entity, making us personal and individual, created for our own service, and entering in us for joy. It is something that has dwelt in fearful places … It fills us with impossible desires, and makes us follow what we know we cannot gain.[29]

Temptation is the legacy of racial development, and art comes to represent the realm of freedom, the means by which this temptation can be given purely formal expression. The critical spirit – one of judicious selection – permits the perfection of that culture made available through the soul's inheritance; hence Wilde's emphasis on self-culture, the rejection of sincerity, the adoption of masks and the multiplication of personalities. These are the not product of some proleptic postmodernist theory of the self but of Wilde's conviction that the self is racially determined,[30] and the individual's realisation of potential in this respect is precisely what makes him or her modern.

This insistence on a racial, and thereby cultural, connection with past ages also connects him with a strand of thought in aestheticism present, for instance, in Pater's important essay on the German art critic Winckelmann. It is a strand indebted to the Oxford Greats tradition of Greek studies inaugurated by Benjamin Jowett and recently analysed by Linda Dowling. Dowling claims that, up until Wilde's conviction, Oxford Hellenism served 'as a legitimating discourse for male love, one capable of enlisting within its discursive structures even conscious opponents of homoeroticism'.[31] Dowling's evidence for this seems mainly confined to the applause which greeted Wilde's famous speech in the dock about the love that dare not speak its name. This is a rather tenuous basis for the argument, given that there are obvious grounds for assuming that many of Wilde's supporters were present in the gallery. Moreover, Hyde's account suggests that the acclaim was not exactly universal, since the applause was 'mingled with some hisses'.[32] None the less, in certain circles Greek culture was juxtaposed with the Christian proscription on same-sex love as a means of historicising the present and thereby anticipating a changed future. Pater's essay on Winckelmann hints at this project, arguing that Greek culture was of an aesthetic nature, preceding the influence of the Christian myth of the fall and the sense of guilt which accompanied it.[33] Possibly more significant to Wilde is John Addington Symonds's version of this thesis, since Symonds's work on the Greeks developed into an explicit apologia for male same-sex desire.[34] This is his depiction of the appeal of Greece in *Studies of the Greek Poets*: 'Like a young man newly come from the wrestling-ground, anointed, chapleted, and very calm, the Genius of the Greeks appears before us. Upon his soul there is no burden of the world's pain; the creation that groaneth and travaileth together has touched him with no sense of anguish; nor has he yet felt sin.'[35] Such a culture preceded any division between body and spirit and consequently based its ethics on the harmony of the body. It was the Greeks' sense of beauty which guided them rather than an abstracted 'Mosaic' conscience, but the triumph of the Romans led to a degeneration of this Greek ideal in moral matters, and the result was the intrusion of a reproachful spiritual regime in the form of Christianity which counterposed flesh and spirit. Significantly Symonds places his faith in science as 'our redeemer',[36] having the capacity dialectically to reconcile the body/spirit duality by somehow uniting conscience with the physical laws which govern existence. Evolution, for Symonds as well as for Wilde, was the source of hope for the future.

Here, then, we have the artist personified by Greek culture, insensible of the dictates of conscience and guided by the pursuit of beauty. Symonds is more explicit about precisely what he is defending in *A Problem in Greek Ethics*. Written in 1873, but not published until ten years later – and then privately – the book seems principally an apologia for Greek pederasty as being manly, possibly even originating in the military camaraderie the Dorians introduced into Greek society after the Homeric era.[37] That the real ethical issue of *Greek Poets* is that of male same-sex love is made clear by analogous passages in *Greek Ethics* which describe the transition from pagan to Christian ethics through the degeneration of the original aesthetic morality of the Greeks once the Roman empire had overtaken them: 'While the paiderastia of the Greeks was sinking into grossness, effeminacy, and aesthetic prettiness, the moral instincts of humanity began to assert themselves in earnest. It became part of the higher doctrine of the Roman Stoics to suppress this form of passion. The Christians, from St. Paul onwards, instituted an uncompromising crusade against it.'[38] Symonds's work is crucial to an understanding of the cultural connections between male same-sex desire and aestheticism. In attempting to aestheticise English culture, Wilde must have been conscious all along of the connections Symonds had drawn with such desires – most obviously, *Dorian Gray* in its very title invokes Symonds's theory about the origins of pederasty in Greek culture, at the same time as it suggests that the eponymous central character only imperfectly embodies Greek values. However, Wilde was also less anxious than Symonds about the correlation between aestheticism, same-sex desire and effeminacy, seeing himself as an unregenerate – even degenerate – Hellenist, and this is also a measure of the distance between Wilde's coded legitimations of same-sex desire and the anxieties to be found in the work of those Uranians of the time who maintained their indebtedness to Christian manliness by disavowing, or at least denigrating, sexual desire.

Whilst constantly looking back to the Hellenic ideal, Wilde was insistent throughout his work that the route to a new aestheticism was to be found through the influence of the Celt (indeed, the racial connection between Hellenism and Celticism had already been made by Arnold). In 'The Critic as Artist' Wilde emphasises that 'it is the Celt who leads in art'.[39] More significantly, 'Pen, Pencil and Poison' is subtitled 'A study in green', and, to demonstrate that this is not simply a parody of Whistler, Wilde claims that Wainewright had that curious love of green, which in individuals is always the sign of a subtle artistic temperament, and in nations is said to denote a laxity, if not a decadence of morals. Like Baudelaire he was extremely fond of cats, and with Gautier, he was fascinated by that 'sweet marble monster' of both sexes that we can still see at Florence and in the Louvre.[40]

Aestheticism, race, amorality and an ambiguous sexuality here dove-tail with each other in Wilde's defence of the artist-criminal, the figure of progress. Clearly Wilde regarded the Celt as the potent agent of subversion within moralistic English society, and, again, the estab-lished Celtic character is confirmed, yet valorised.

Wilde's theorisation of subversion entailed appropriating ele-ments of dominant racial and positivist thinking for his own ends, and in this he was not exceptional. Many defenders of same-sex desire at the time placed their hopes in an evolutionary historical progress which would annul Christian moralism. Wilde even alluded to this in the dock. Carson asked him if he believed his claim that 'Religions die when they are proved to be true', to which Wilde replied, 'It is a sug-gestion towards a philosophy of the absorption of religions by science.'[41] On Wilde's death George Ives, a 'Uranian' acquaintance, wrote in his diary that 'we must leave to time and evolution and then our day will come.'[42] No doubt Ives's fatalism at this time was in part determined by the defeat sustained by Wilde and the example that had been made of him, but it also expresses convictions which pre-dated the trials, convictions which perhaps reflect the relative power-lessness and isolation of these would-be reformers in relation to the dominant sexual morality of the time.

Simultaneously, however, science – never above ideology – was also the means by which conventional moral wisdom was being rein-forced, discovering in the body itself the inexorability of moral laws. If science absorbed religion, it none the less perpetuated many of reli-ogion's teachings. In this respect the dire apocalypticism of Max Nordau was more in keeping with the times than the relative liberal-ism of a handful of sexologists. Nordau – drawing widely on European scientific thought, including that of the influential English psycholo-gist Henry Maudsley[43] – warned of the pervasive dangers to the advanced white races epitomised by a range of individuals. The *fin de siècle* artist, he claimed, was a product of the cumulative effects of the nineteenth-century pace of living, a condition exacerbated in France by the fact that modernity had superseded the massive loss of blood and 'violent moral upheavals' of the Revolutionary period[44] (hence France's pre-eminence as a nation of degenerates). For Nordau 'Morality – not that learnt mechanically, but that which we feel as an internal necessity – has become, in the course of thousands of generations, an organised instinct',[45] and was threatened by the nervous hyper-sensitivity of the artist who thrived on and encouraged various forms of perversion of the instincts, including sexual perversion. When we find Wilde petitioning the Home Secretary from prison, pleading for clemency on the grounds that his offences were 'forms of sexual madness', and citing his own inclusion in Nordau's book as a scientific demonstration of 'the intimate connection between madness and the literary and artistic temperament',[46] it is tempting to see in this some form of Foucauldian confession. Rather, it was expediency, as Wilde the artist-criminal in exile demonstrated by becoming a shameless recidivist.[47] None the less, this tactical invocation of *Degeneration* - though it failed to persuade the Home Secretary – is testimony to Nordau's compatibility with established moral values, values which continued to be shaped by religious forces.

## Momentary pleasures

The juxtaposition between the 'modern', progressive sensibility, as outlined in 'The Critic as Artist', and the conventional view of duty is represented in Wilde's work as that between the dandy and the puritan, the most extreme representative of Protestant repressiveness. In at least one of his plays it is the puritan who wins: Mrs Arbuthnot triumphs over the machinations of Lord Illingworth in *A Woman of No Importance*, but this play is none the less a useful one for considering the various elements of Wilde's sense of his own dissidence. The play's debates about morality and marriage have as their context the moral purity debates of the 1880s and 1890s in which women moral purity campaigners attempted to establish themselves, with a large degree of success, in the role of the country's moral guardians, using rhetoric clearly indebted to Evangelical Christianity. According to Kerry Powell, purity campaigners aimed to reform public and private life by an extension of women's influence, attempting to abolish the double standard in order to produce an improvement in the morality of public servants. Their intention was to influence public life by the extension of domestic standards, making the family the touchstone of morality, public and private, and setting up the woman as symbol of pristine virtue tainted only by the depravity of men.[48] As the MP Kelvil comments in Wilde's play, 'Woman is the intellectual helpmeet of man in public as in private life. Without her we should forget the true ideals.'[49] In this context it should also be noted that purity movements played an important role in the successful passage of the 1885 Criminal Law Amendment Act which encouraged legislative moral reform and into which Labouchere inserted his own Amendment outlawing sexual acts between men.[50] The tone of this movement was distinctly indebted to Old Testament morality, and its class composition was also significant, drawing on old antagonisms: Frank Mort records that 'purity usually worked by forging allegiances between sections of the Evangelical middle class, the petty-bourgeoisie and the respectable working class against the aristocracy'.[51] Wilde's adoption of the persona of the aristocratic libertine, along with his deliberate alignment with French culture, must be seen in this light as calculated to provoke the most zealous promoters of middle-class morality, and it also marks a distinction between his attitude to purity movements and that of nineteenth-century liberalism. Wilde seems to have been impressed by John Stuart Mill's attacks on the influence of philanthropic, religious and moral currents, but most of all of 'the ascendancy of public opinion in the state' in shaping English society. 'If resistance [to these developments] waits till life is reduced *nearly* to one uniform type', Mill wrote, 'all deviations from that type will come to be considered impious, even monstrous and contrary to nature. Mankind will speedily become unable to conceive diversity, when they have been for some time unaccustomed to see it.'[52] This fairly accurately describes how Wilde himself came to be seen, of course, and the language of 'types' here would no doubt have appealed to Wilde's evolutionary perspective. None the less, Wilde did not promote himself as a liberal defender of rights, but posed as an aristocrat disdainful of common morality, making him vulnerable to the old class-based discourse – still powerful in terms of the moral policing of the nation – of effeminacy and corruption, which was duly mobilised against him.

The thematic concerns of *A Woman of No Importance* are closely related to those questions of the moralisation of time and racial determinism that I have been pursuing here. Mrs Arbuthnot is the woman with a past who initially accepts – and has lived her life accepting – the absolutist judgement (articulated by Hester Worsley) that 'if a man and woman have sinned, let them both go forth into the desert to love or loathe each other there ... but don't punish the one and let the other go free. Don't have one law for men and another for women.'[53] This plea for equal contempt is essentially the crux of the play's concerns, since Mrs Arbuthnot has abjectly accepted the consequences of her sinful past whilst that of Lord Illingworth has yet to catch up with him. The reason for this is partly that Illingworth philosophically rejects the claims of puritanism in his repudiation of the moral lessons of the past. The central battle becomes one over the possession of their son Gerald, his future and, implicitly therefore, that of the race:

> MRS ARBUTHNOT: ... You don't realise what my past has been in suffering and shame.
>
> LORD ILLINGWORTH: My dear Rachel, I must candidly say that I think Gerald's future considerably more important than your past.
>
> MRS ARBUTHNOT: Gerald cannot separate his future from my past.
>
> LORD ILLINGWORTH: That is exactly what he should do. That is exactly what you should help him to do. What a typical woman you are! You talk sentimentally, and you are thoroughly selfish the whole time....
>
> MRS ARBUTHNOT: He was not discontented until he met you. You have made him so.
>
> LORD ILLINGWORTH: Of course, I made him so. Discontent is the first step in the progress of a man or a nation. But I did not leave him with a mere longing for things he could not get. No, I made him a charming offer. He jumped at it, I need hardly say. Any young man would. And now, simply because it turns out that I am the boy's own father and he my own son, you propose practically to ruin his career.[54]

Illingworth's position here is the opposite of Old Testament morality which dictates that the sins of the parents be visited on the children. He refuses such hereditary principles by projecting them on to the selfishness of women, and in doing so is clearly alluding to women purity campaigners. In contrast Illingworth stimulates Gerald's 'discontent', or temptation – that disintegrative, racially inherited individualism which is the basis of progress – and promises to satisfy the desires this provokes. Illingworth's claim that this is the route to national as well as individual progress also demonstrates the threat that his philosophy poses to the restrictive English puritan mentality. These opposing attitudes are emphasised by being gendered (though only in the context of the family, since Mrs Allonby's dislike of marriage is complemented by an individualism as intense as Illingworth's) and through the class division between middle-class moralist and aristocratic libertine.

That marriage and the institution of the family are related specifically to English virtue is argued by Kelvil: 'It [home-life] is the mainstay of our moral system in England, Lady Stutfield. Without it *we would become like our neighbours*' (my emphasis).[55] In such a context, of course, the unmarried man is rendered immediately suspicious, not least because of his unrepresentativeness of the English: Lady Caroline, for example, claims that representation of England abroad by an unmarried man such as Lord Illingworth 'might lead to complications'.[56] For Illingworth, on the other hand, 'the happiness of a married man ... depends on the people he has not married'.[57]

All of which goes some way towards rendering plausible Lytton Strachey's account of the play following a 1907 revival of it. For Strachey, Beerbohm Tree (playing Illingworth)

> is a wicked Lord, staying in a country house, who has made up his mind to bugger one of the other guests – a handsome young man of twenty. The handsome young man is delighted; when his mother enters, sees his Lordship and recognises him as having copulated with her twenty years before, the result of which was – the handsome young man. She appeals to Lord Tree not to bugger his own son. He replies that that is an additional reason for doing it (oh! he's a *very* wicked Lord!).[58]

We might pursue Strachey's decoding of the play by noting that, at one point, Mrs Arbuthnot pointedly tells her son that 'Lord Illingworth is very good, I am sure, to interest himself in you for the moment'. This reinforces Strachey's interpretation, since the scene suggests a comparison between Illingworth's treatment of Mrs Arbuthnot and his present patronage of Gerald. Illingworth responds – hand on Gerald's shoulder – 'Gerald and I are great friends already.'[59] We should also note the specific term used by Mrs Arbuthnot to make this comparison: 'moment' was one of the key terms in aestheticism's manifesto. Notoriously Pater had concluded *The Renaissance* with the words: 'art comes to you proposing frankly to give nothing but the highest quality to your moments as they pass, and simply for those moments' sake',[60] thus celebrating the intensity of the experience divorced from moral claims. This is precisely the implication of Mrs Arbuthnot's remark: Illingworth will take his pleasures and move on.

The problem for Illingworth, though, is his former momentary interest in Mrs Arbuthnot herself. Unlike his interest in Gerald, *this* moment had implications: it led to pregnancy and to the demand for marriage – carrying the implication, for the dandy, that he must renounce his individualism (if he is to live up to his marriage vows). Illingworth's initial refusal leads to the uncompromising rejection of the possibility of any atonement on his part through his later offer of marriage, as Mrs Arbuthnot has become too attached to her sin in the form of Gerald. In fact Gerald embodies the paradox of her situation as both perpetual reminder of her transgression and object of her love: 'It is my dishonour that has bound you so closely to me. It is the price I paid for you – the price of body and soul – that makes me love you as I do.'[61] The 'price of body and soul' is clearly a reference to the ideal unity of aesthetic experience symbolised for aestheticism by Greek culture. It is this unity that Mrs Arbuthnot has renounced, and she demands a similar renunciation on the part of Gerald. In this same lengthy speech she laments the way that the world draws children from the influence of women into a more cosmopolitan environment from which Mrs Arbuthnot excludes herself on account of her own sense of shame, relegating her own activities to charity work under the aegis of the Church (the Church being 'the only house where sinners are made welcome'). Moreover, there is a strong hint that Mrs Arbuthnot's love for Gerald incorporates a suppressed sexual desire, which is therefore the counterpart of Lord Illingworth's coded attempt at seduction: at the point at which she tells Gerald that Hester, as his wife, must come first, she begs 'when you are away, Gerald ... with ... her – oh, think of me sometimes'.[62] Moreover, Mrs Arbuthnot passes on her mantle of moral guardian to Hester Worsley by sanctioning Gerald's marriage to her and at the same time referring to the coded theme of sexual object choice through a pointed substitution: 'Gerald, I cannot give you a father, but I have brought you a wife.'[63]

Wilde's appropriation in *A Woman of No Importance* of the crucial term 'moment' from what he regarded as his bible reflects on the relations of both aestheticism and male same-sex love to dominant English values. Aestheticism, in developing an elitist aura for itself and in voiding its relations to art objects of any moral significance, was rejecting the profoundly moralised relations which English society wanted to prescribe between art and its audiences.[64] Hence the emphasis on the 'uselessness' of art and the intensity of the individual's experience was at one level a dissident response. *A Woman of*

*No Importance* draws an analogy with this: male same-sex acts are coded as preserving the pristine intensity of the moment divorced from any moral claims. On the other hand, normative prescriptions on sexuality lead to familial claims and the consequent limitations on subjective experience and racial diversity which Wilde believed this entailed. If, as Kelvil claims, marriage is the basis of the English moral order – that which preserves it from the depravity of its malign 'neighbours' – 'buggery' is its negation, the ultimate outsider's threat to its integrity.

This, I would maintain, is a plausible decoding of the play, given the extent to which it draws on Wilde's preoccupations, but it is none the less important to remember that these preoccupations remained largely hidden from his audiences. Even if this interpretation helps to repudiate the largely sanitised, witty, yet tragically flawed figure Wilde has been made to cut in English and Irish culture until relatively recently, I am not attempting to make great claims for the play's subversiveness in its Victorian context. Strachey's decoding might have been available to the *cognoscenti* of Wilde's most intimate circle, but it was not one which would have occurred to many others.[65] In fact the play was largely uncontroversial, a qualified success both commercially and critically. According to Ellmann, the main offence it gave was to its first audience's patriotism (Wilde was booed, probably for the line 'England lies like a leper in purple', which he proceeded to delete).[66] Some of the reviews even praised the play's moral content – A. B. Walkley, for instance, found that 'the complete turning of tables on the cynical rascal of a father makes for righteousness'[67] – though others found the upright characters unconvincing: the *Saturday Review* suggested that 'Mr Wilde does not shine as a depictor of candour and innocence. His enthusiasms are flat and his moralisings tedious'.[68] This suggests a hunch on the part of the reviewer that Wilde was deliberately allowing his villain to upstage the virtuous characters whilst retaining a conventional moralistic framework, but that was as far as the suspicions went. Indeed Wilde's usual strategy was to hint at moral improprieties in his work whilst simultaneously denying that he was actually concealing anything. Rather, he claimed, any interpretation which discovered specific forms of corruption in his work was the product of the philistine and prurient middle-class psyche. This was his argument in relation to *Dorian Gray* – '*It is the spectator, and not life, that art really mirrors*'[69] – and one which he maintained in the dock, where he insisted that he could not be responsible for others' interpretations. Wilde did tread a precarious line in his work, deliberately aiming to be provocative, but also, on a personal level, needing to deflect attention from an agenda which ultimately had to remain undisclosed.

Unfortunately for Wilde, once he made Queensberry's allegations known, the vulgar proved adept at probing the symbol.

### The revenge of the philistines

> I do not profess to be an artist ... and when I hear you give evidence, I am glad I am not.
>
> Edward Carson to Wilde[70]

Lord Illingworth's ignominious exclusion at the end of *A Woman of No Importance* is one of those passages which apparently demonstrate Wilde's alleged prescience about his own fate. Rather, of course, it represents Wilde's recognition of the isolated and largely reviled position of the aesthete in Victorian society, a recognition which is maintained in the recriminatory letter to Alfred Douglas, *De Profundis*. After his prison sentence, Wilde did profess a purely formal penitence, but still insisted that he was a 'born antinomian'. In particular, he claimed to regret that aspect of his life which had entailed living for the moment, famously relating it to his prose style: 'What the paradox was to me in the sphere of thought, perversity became to me in the sphere of passion ... I took pleasure where it pleased me and passed on.'[71] As the reference to antinomianism indicates, Wilde did not abandon his determinist convictions in favour of moral self-castigation, and his repeated claim that everything that is realised is right indicates a resigned acceptance of events. *De Profundis* even maintains the specific elements of his deterministic convictions, since Wilde presents himself not only as the tragic victim of familial relations but also as the downtrodden figure in a racial contest. His prosecution, then, becomes a struggle between the qualities Wilde attached to competing races. In this way, the Oedipal antagonism between Alfred Douglas and Queensberry which ruined Wilde are finally made to connect with historic Anglo-Irish relations.

The Douglases are a family whose racial predisposition is towards self-ruin and the ruin of others, and Alfred is only the latest incarnation: 'You had yourself told me how many of your race there had been who had stained their hands in their own blood; your uncle certainly, your grandfather possibly; many others in the mad, bad line from which you come'; 'Through your father you come of a race, marriage with whom is horrible, friendship fatal, and that lays violent hands either on its own life or on the lives of others.'[72] In this context, Wilde represents Queensberry both as a social inferior and as an atavistic, unaesthetic racial throwback – precisely Anglo-Saxon and therefore pre-modern – brilliantly inverting the conventional English racist representations of the Irish as apes. The court itself takes on this very persona in its prosecution of Wilde as it vindicates the rule and continuing racial dominance of the philistine:

> I used to see your father bustling in and out [of the police court] in the hopes of attracting public attention, as if anyone could fail to note or remember the stableman's gait and dress, the bowed legs, the twitching hands, the hanging lower lip, the bestial and half-witted grin … I used to feel conscious of his presence, and the blank dreary walls of the great Court-room, the very air itself, seemed to me at times to be hung with multitudinous masks of that apelike face.[73]

Consequently Wilde depicts himself as racially antithetical to the Douglases. Hence his explanation of his extravagance towards Alfred Douglas – 'the virtues of prudence and thrift were not in my own nature or my own race' – as well as his indulgent tolerance, which was at least partly attributable to 'my own proverbial good-nature and Celtic laziness'.[74] And when Wilde admonishes Douglas's mother he invokes the bitterness of a more historic conflict, thus preserving the racialised philistine/aesthete dichotomy: 'I confess that it pains me when I hear of your mother's remarks about me, and I am sure that on reflection you will agree with me that if she has no word of regret or sorrow for the ruin your race has brought on mine it would be better if she remained silent.'[75] In this way Wilde formally completes his own version of his symbolic relations to his age by insisting on its integration into a larger narrative of British imperial repression.

'The ages live in history through their anachronisms.'[76] Wilde consciously exploited an ensemble of identifications which were conspicuously unEnglish – Catholic, dandy and Celt; criminal, sinner and idle artist – and his theorisation of them as related enabled him to make explicit – indeed visible – his dissident relations to the dominant culture. These personae were all deployed against the English puritanism and hegemony of the family of which he was a radical (if sexist) critic.

They were also, though, unintentionally revealing in terms of his relations to the society he inhabited, symptomatic through their disempowering archaisms and underdog connotations (however transgressive) of the power and integrity of the British imperial state and the moral relations it enforced. Indeed Wilde's assessment of the trials as a racial triumph for Anglo-Saxon philistinism was not entirely deluded, since the responses to his conviction quite self-consciously emphasised the necessity of maintaining the manly integrity of the nation. This is evident from the apparent fixation which developed with Wilde's hair. According to Hyde, one of the prostitutes who greeted his conviction outside the court exclaimed ''E'll 'ave 'is 'air cut *reglar now*!'[77] This may be a piece of 'colourful' apocrypha, but press coverage also focused on his hair as part of the relish that was taken in purging him of his affectations. In one account the prison regime imposes a more manly appearance on him: 'The prison barber, who is a man well used to his work, at once commenced to crop off with a pair of scissors Oscar's renowned and ever admired – at least by society – locks … at the present he looks an awful sight, more like a well-to-do butcher who has served a sentence for fraud than the great dramatic genius of the nineteenth century.'[78] This short passage is replete with a peculiarly English moralistic class triumphalism: Wilde's hair is taken – as it was no doubt intended – as metonymic of his contempt for puritanism, and the pointed reference to the barber's devotion to his work contrasts with the artist's idleness and luxury; great delight is therefore taken in the levelling of a figure previously lionised by an irresponsible elite to the status of a tradesman (albeit a dishonest one). Moreover, Wilde's specific form of punishment – two years' hard labour – was also presumably intended to correct his moral habits, and in this sense was savagely ironic, though to many it may have constituted a rather grim form of poetic justice. The artist who had celebrated 'doing nothing' because convinced of the unpredictability of action, was condemned to a regime of pointless exertion by a society committed to the redemptive value of work.

# Conclusion

WILDE'S adoption of an aristocratic persona, along with his scath-
ing attacks on the middle class, have helped to fix a notion in
our minds that the manliness he turned his back on was an essentially
'bourgeois' construction. However, it may be instructive to remember
that Wilde was only posing; his persecutor was the genuine article.

The perception that Victorian society and culture were thoroughly bourgeoisified in the nineteenth century must be contested,
not least in relation to questions of gender. Perry Anderson, for
instance, reminds us that the bourgeoisie 'did not have to overthrow
a feudal state in the nineteenth century, and it did not succeed in
becoming sole master of the new industrial society'. Consequently the
English bourgeoisie never went through a genuinely egalitarian phase
and did not displace the ideological legitimations on which aristocratic rule relied. The result, claims Anderson, was a hegemonic bloc
which was validated by a combination of traditionalism – the attachment to the past – and an empiricism which 'binds the future by fas-
tening it to the present'.[1] If we ignore this broader context in
discussions of manliness, the result is that the term tends to be reductively and even misleadlingly associated exclusively with a work ethic
which also determined an emphasis on sexual asceticism. Herbert
Sussman, for instance, argues that the 'definition of manhood as self-
discipline, as the ability to control male energy and to deploy this
power not for sexual but for productive purposes was clearly specific
to bourgeois man'.[2] Implicitly my argument suggests that such claims
are not so much wrong as inadequate, and that manly ideals were a
good deal more overdetermined than this suggests, bound up not
merely with particular class values but with perceptions of Englishness which emerged out of the counter-revolutionary, anti-egalitarian
culture of the late eighteenth and early nineteenth centuries. The

emphasis on manly self-control was therefore determined substantially by political, rather than fundamentally economic, forces, and the emphasis on stability remained ideologically crucial throughout the nineteenth century. It assisted, indeed, in stitching together England's sutured hegemony of capitalist and landed classes in opposition to radical working-class movements within England/Britain and anti-imperialist forces overseas.

In class terms, therefore, the dominant ideal of manliness in nineteenth-century culture might be described as hybrid, promoting national ideals which had a tendency, if anything, to subsume class differences. Indeed, in the culture of the hegemonic bloc the nation held a sacralised status which became even more pronounced as the century wore on. In part this status was no doubt indebted to the expansive 'spirit' of capitalism which brought about internal economic growth and, to a considerable extent, imperial expansion, thereby generating a sense of national and global purposiveness. But the manliness on which the achievement of a British historical destiny was presumed to rest often promoted ideals which were far from specifically bourgeois: chivalry and the heroic subordination of will to national purpose, for instance. Certainly, as Mark Girouard has amply documented, such patriotic values were frequently legitimated by traditionalist, even mythic, national sentiments;[3] they even reflected and encouraged national ambitions and racial solidarities which were explicitly disdainful of mere bourgeois individualism. At his theological college's debating society Gerard Manley Hopkins once argued the proposition that 'Eminence in arms is a better object of national ambition than eminence in commerce'.[4]

The inadequacy of accounts of manliness as a specifically bourgeois phenomenon is epitomised by many of the responses to the outbreak of war in 1914, responses which, as I have already implied, were not merely spontaneous, but were determined by the imperial context of late Victorian Britain. The war was popularly regarded, at least by the officer class, as the moment when Englishmen would prove their mettle, and the eagerness with which this challenge was faced was often indicative of a contempt for bourgeois normality, drawing on the kinds of expectations and ambitions bred in these officers by their public schools. The sentiments of one public schoolboy may be taken as reasonably typical: 'The follies, selfishness, luxury and general pettiness of the vile commercial sort of existence led by nine-tenths of the people of the world in peace time are replaced in war by a savagery that is at least honest and outspoken.' War meant no longer 'living for one's self' as the businessman or academic did.[5] Such sentiments were far removed from the elements which comprised the middle-class manly ideal, with its emphasis on mere moral rectitude and financial probity in the public world and on the family father as patriarch in the privacy of the home.

The context I have established for considering the development of manliness in nineteenth-century England is therefore a very broad one, and rather different from that emphasised in recent studies in this area. Grounded in an Anglican ethico-political sensibility which claimed to reconcile (Protestant) autonomy and (Catholic) submissiveness, ideals of manly self-possession became integral to a national/racial character which was believed to possess a historical and global purpose and was defined largely in opposition to its unstable and feminised European others, the Celts. The 'naturalness' of manly values resided in their largely undgomatic anathematisation of a generalisable atavistic principle of 'excess' – political, emotional, sexual – manifestations which were indicative of a lack of self-control which required quasi-patriarchal or even coercive correction. Recovering this context encourages us to reconsider the ways in which perceptions and representations of gender were inextricably bound up, not only with explicit debates about the relationship between men and women, but with other far-reaching questions of history, power and resistance.

# Notes

## Introduction

1 See *Gerard Manley Hopkins*, ed. Catherine Phillips (Oxford, Oxford University Press, 1986), pp. 146–8.

2 Hopkins wrote to his friend Robert Bridges that he was 'half inclined to hope the Hero of [the poem] may be killed in Afghanistan'. See *Letters to Robert Bridges*, ed. Claude Colleer Abbott (London, Oxford University Press, 1955), p. 92.

3 '(The Soldier)', *Hopkins*, p. 168.

4 *Further Letters of Gerard Manley Hopkins*, ed. Claude Colleer Abbott (London, Oxford University Press, 1956), pp. 366–7.

5 Most general accounts of nineteenth-century religion include discussions of anti-Catholicism. More detailed studies include: G. I. T. Machin, *The Catholic Questions in English Politics 1820 to 1830* (Oxford, Clarendon Press, 1964); E. R. Norman, *Anti-Catholicism in Victorian England* (London, Allen & Unwin, 1968), a valuable discussion with supporting documents; Walter L. Arnstein, *Protestant Versus Catholic in Mid-Victorian England: Mr Newdegate and the Nuns* (Columbia, University of Missouri Press, 1982). E. R. Norman's *The English Catholic Church in the Nineteenth Century* (Oxford, Clarendon Press, 1984) is obviously concerned with this, and John Wolfe's *God and Greater Britain: Religion and National Life in Britain and Ireland 1843–1945* (London, Routledge, 1994) includes a good deal of discussion on the subject.

6 David Hempton, *Religion and Political Culture in Britain and Ireland: From the Glorious Revolution to the Decline of Empire* (Cambridge, Cambridge University Press, 1996), p. 147.

7 Sandra Gilbert and Susan Gubar note Hopkins's masculinist poetics at the outset of *Madwoman in the Attic: The Woman Writer and the Nineteenth Century Literary Imagination* (New Haven, Yale University Press, 1979), pp. 3–4. For further reflections along these lines see Thaïs Morgan, 'Violence, creativity and the feminine: poetics and gender politics in Swinburne and Hopkins', in Antony H. Harrison and Beverley Taylor (eds), *Gender and Discourse in Victorian Literature* (DeKalb, Northern Illinois University Press, 1992), pp. 84–107. Jerome Bump, 'Hopkins, feminism and creativity: an overview', *Texas Studies*

*in Literature and Language*, 31:1 (1989), pp. 1–30 attempts to temper such perspectives.

8 Keith Richards, 'The Irish military tradition and the British empire', in Richards (ed.), *'An Irish Empire'?: Aspects of Ireland and the British Empire* (Manchester, Manchester University Press, 1996), pp. 94–5 & 102–3.

9 Charles Kingsley, *Westward Ho!*, vol. 1 (London, Macmillan, [1855] 1896), p. 179. See also C. J. W.-L. Wee's comments on the role of Ireland in this novel in 'Christian manliness and national identity: the problematic construction of a racially 'pure' nation', in Donald E. Hall (ed.), *Muscular Christianity: Embodying the Victorian Age* (Cambridge, Cambridge University Press, 1994), pp. 78–9.

10 *Punch*, 16 (1849), p. 206.

11 *Punch,* 19 (1850), p. 193.

12 'Lord John Russell's letter to the Bishop of Durham, 1850,' in E. R. Norman, *Anti-Catholicism*, pp. 160–1.

13 Wherever I refer to 'Britain' I do so in the recognition that this polity incorporated divisions as well as solidarities, and where I refer to a British identity I intend this to signify a dominant identity within this polity, one at least partly 'official' and centred on England. Any elision made in my argument between 'England' and 'Britain', or 'English' and 'British', is therefore symptomatic of this dominance.

14 Wolfe, *God and Greater Britain*, p. 113.

15 *Punch*, 19 (1850), p. 243.

16 Benedict Anderson, *Imagined Communities: Reflections on the Origin and Spread of Nationalism* (London, Verso, 1991), esp. chapters 1–3, pp. 1–46.

17 J. H. Newman, *St Bartholomew's Eve: A Tale of the Sixteenth Century* (1818–19); quoted in Sheridan Gilley, *Newman and His Age* (London, Darton, Longman and Todd, 1990), p. 32.

18 See Hugh A. MacDougall, *Racial Myth in English History* (Montreal/Hanover, Harvest House/University Press of New England, 1982). Broadly this account is supported by J. W. Burrow's account in *A Liberal Descent: The Victorians and the English Past* (Cambridge, Cambridge University Press, 1981), chapter 5, pp. 98–125.

19 See E. P. Thompson, *The Making of the English Working Class* (Harmondsworth, Penguin, 1968), chapter 4, pp. 84–110.

20 See Linda Colley, *Britons: Forging the Nation, 1707–1837* (New Haven, Yale University Press, 1992), chapter 1, esp. pp. 11–54.

21 *Ibid.*, p. 34.

22 See Roy Porter, 'The Enlightenment in England', in Roy Porter and Milulái Teich (eds), *The Enlightenment in National Context* (Cambridge, Cambridge University Press, 1981), p. 6.

23 Quoted by Keith Thomas in *Religion and the Decline of Magic* (Harmondsworth, Penguin 1978), p. 92.

24 Edmund Burke, 'Thoughts and details on scarcity', in *Works*, vol. 5 (London, Nimmo, 1899), p. 157.

25 Quoted in Thomas A. Boylan and Timothy P. Foley, *Political Economy and Colonial Ireland: The Propagation and Ideological Function of Economic Discourse in the Nineteenth Century* (London, Routledge, 1992), p. 145.

26 See John C. Hawley, 'Charles Kingsley and the Book of Nature', *Anglican and Episcopal History*, 61:4 (1991), pp. 461–79.

27 Charles Kingsley, 'Great cities and their influence for good or evil', in *Sanitary and Social Lectures and Essays* (London, Macmillan, [1857] 1892), p. 218.

28 James R. Moore, 'The crisis of faith: reformation versus revolution', in Moore (ed.), *Religion in Victorian England*, vol. 2: *Controversies* (Manchester and New York, Manchester University Press/Open University Press, 1988), esp. pp. 228–34.

29 Simone de Beauvoir, *The Second Sex* (Harmondsworth, Penguin, [1949] 1972), p. 15.

30 The classic account of the Protestant work ethic is obviously Weber's *The Protestant Ethic and the Spirit of Capitalism*, trans. Talcott Brown (London, Allen & Unwin, [1904–5] 1976). Christopher Hill's superb essay retains Weber's emphasis on the calling, but places a greater emphasis on the freedom of conscience offered by Protestantism: see 'Protestantism and the rise of capitalism', in *Change and Continuity in 17th Century England* (New Haven, Yale University Press, 1991), pp. 81–102.

31 Thomas Babington Macaulay, *The History of England*, vol. 2 (London, Longman, Brown, Green and Longmans, 1849), pp. 478–9.

32 Leonore Davidoff and Catherine Hall, *Family Fortunes: Men and Women of the English Middle Class, 1780–1850* (London, Hutchinson, 1987).

### Chapter 1

1 Thomas Paine, *Common Sense* (Harmondsworth, Penguin, [1776] 1986), p. 76.

2 George Woodcock, 'The meaning of revolution in Britain 1770–1800', in Ceri Crossley and Ian Small (eds), *The French Revolution and British Culture* (Oxford, Oxford University Press, 1989), pp. 7–8.

3 J. H. Newman, *Lectures on the Present Position of Catholics in England* (London, Longman, [1851] 1892), p. 295.

4 See R. S. Crane, 'Suggestions toward a genealogy of the "Man of Feeling"', *English Literary History*, 1:3 1934, pp. 205–30. On the Anglican bearing of Shaftesbury's arguments see, for instance, G. J. Barker-Benfield, *The Culture of Sensibility: Sex and Society in Eighteenth-century Britain* (Chicago, University of Chicago Press, 1992), p. 113.

5 Chris Jones, *Radical Sensibility: Literature and Ideas in the 1790s* (London, Routledge, 1993), p. 2.

6 See Crane, '"Man of Feeling"', p. 211.

7 On Hume and Smith, see Jones, *Radical Sensibility*, pp. 26–31.

8 See, for instance, the representations of Marie Antoinette in David Bindman (ed.), *In the Shadow of the Guillotine* (London, British Museum, 1989), pp. 150–3.

# Notes

9  Edmund Burke, *Reflections on the Revolution in France, Works*, vol. 3 (London, Nimmo, [1790] 1899), p. 337.

10  *Ibid.*, pp. 345–7.

11  See J. G. A. Pocock's comments on custom and usage in *The Machiavellian Moment: Florentine Political Thought and the Atlantic Republican Tradition* (Princeton, Princeton University Press, 1975), esp. pp. 13–17.

12  Joseph Butler, *The Analogy of Religion Natural and Revealed to the Constitution of Nature* (London, Macmillan, [1736] 1890), p. 81.

13  *Ibid.*, pp. 83–4.

14  Burke, *Reflections*, p. 456.

15  *Ibid.*, p. 458.

16  *Ibid.*, p. 491.

17  *Ibid.*, p. 494.

18  *Ibid.*, p. 357.

19  *Ibid.*, p. 276.

20  *Ibid.*, p. 316.

21  *Ibid.*, pp. 440–4.

22  Tony Tanner, *Jane Austen* (Houndmills, Macmillan, 1986), p. 27.

23  Jane Austen, *Mansfield Park* (Oxford, Oxford University Press, [1814], 1990), p. 12.

24  *Ibid.*, p. 19.

25  *Ibid.*, p. 14.

26  *Ibid.*, p. 84.

27  This is Raymond Williams's term. For his discussion of it see *The Country and the City* (London, Chatto & Windus, 1973), pp. 165–81.

28  Austen, *Mansfield Park*, p. 74. Alistair M. Duckworth discusses Maria's attitudes to Sotherton in the context of his overall suggestion that improvement is one element of the gentry's irresponsible rejection of tradition: see *The Improvement of the Estate: A Study of Jane Austen's Novels* (Baltimore, Johns Hopkins Press, 1971), pp. 36–80.

29  See Avrom Fleishman, *A Reading of Mansfield Park: An Essay in Critical Synthesis* (Minneapolis, University of Minnesota Press, 1967), p. 30.

30  Austen, *Mansfield Park*, pp. 311–13.

31  *Ibid.*, p. 288.

32  *Ibid.*, p. 8.

33  *Ibid.*, p. 30.

34  In relation to this passage D. D. Devlin claims that Austen is pointing to the superficiality of the Miss Bertrams' moral education whilst not holding in contempt their 'dignity and restraint' (*Jane Austen and Education* (London and Basingstoke, Macmillan, 1975), pp. 79–80). It seems to me that this underestimates the level of irony here.

35  Of course, the implications of this scene are in keeping with the conservative anti-European tenor of the book, since the play the actors choose is Kotzebue's *Lover's Vows*, whose message is 'the goodness of man, the legitimacy of his claims to equality, and the sanctity of his instincts as a guide to conduct'

# Notes

(Marilyn Butler, *Jane Austen and the War of Ideas*, 2nd ed. (Oxford, Clarendon Press, 1987), p. 233).

36 Roger Sales, *Jane Austen and Representations of Regency England* (London, Routledge, 1994), p. 128.

37 Warren Roberts, *Jane Austen and the French Revolution* (London, Macmillan, 1979), p. 142.

38 On this see also Oliver MacDonagh, *Jane Austen: Real and Imagined Worlds* (New Haven, Yale University Press, 1991), p. 14.

39 Sales, *Regency England*, p. 108.

40 Ellen Moers, *The Dandy: Brummell to Beerbohm* (London, Secker & Warburg, 1960), pp. 40–1.

41 Moers, in *The Dandy*, contradicts herself revealingly. On p. 20 she lists 'effeminacy' as one of the attributes of the dandy's refinement, but then goes on to claim that no one seems to have accused Beau Brummell of effeminacy (p. 36). On this latter occasion she seems to be referring to same-sex love, though she does not say so explicitly. On the perceived effeminacy of the aristocracy and what this signalled in relation to sexual practices see Alan Sinfield, *The Wilde Century: Effeminacy, Oscar Wilde and the Queer Moment* (London, Cassell, 1994), pp. 37–42.

42 On this see for instance Gerald Newman, *The Rise of English Nationalism: A Cultural History 1740–1830* (London, Weidenfeld and Nicolson, 1987), pp. 80–4.

43 I am drawing in a rather general way on J. G. A. Pocock's classic discussion. It is worth noting, though, that Pocock suggests that Augustan political economy witnessed the emergence of a commercial brand of civic virtue based on Protestant principles of frugality: *The Machiavellian Moment*, pp. 445–6. Clearly the ethos of the elite was at odds with this.

44 William Hazlitt, 'Brummelliana', in *Selected Writings* (Oxford, Oxford University Press, [1828] 1991), p. 160.

45 Hazlitt, 'On Fashion' [1818], in *ibid.*, p. 150.

46 Hazlitt, 'On Gusto' [1816], in *ibid.*, p. 267.

47 See Linda Colley, *Forging the Nation, 1707–1837* (New Haven, Yale University Press, 1992), pp. 147–93.

48 Newman, *English Nationalism*, pp. 127–33.

49 Austen, *Mansfield Park*, p. 401.

50 Terry Lovell, 'Jane Austen and the gentry: a study in literature and ideology', in *The Sociology of Literature: Applied Studies*, ed. Diana Laurenson (Keele, Sociological Monograph Review, 1978), p. 22. Lovell's argument is that Austen felt vulnerable because of her class position as a member of the lesser gentry, squeezed between the capitalist tenant farmers and the landowners who were consolidating their estates at this time.

51 See Roberts, *Austen and the French Revolution*, pp. 119–20 on the conservatism of Evangelicalism.

52 Austen, *Mansfield Park*, p. 324.

53 *Ibid.*, p. 418.

# Notes

54 This conclusion is broadly in agreement with that of Alistair Duckworth. See *The Improvement of the Estate*, p. 80.

55 S. T. Coleridge, *On the Constitution of the Church and State According to the Idea of Each, Works*, vol. 10, ed. John Colmer (London/Princeton, Routledge/Princeton University Press, [1830] 1976), pp. 78–9.

56 Gramsci suggests that, in England, 'The old land-owning aristocracy is joined to the industrialists by a kind of suture which is precisely that which in other countries unites the traditional intellectuals with the new dominant classes' (Antonio Gramsci, *Selections from Prison Notebooks*, ed. and trans. Quintin Hoare and Geoffrey Nowell-Smith (London, Lawrence and Wishart, 1971), p. 18).

57 Coleridge, *Church and State*, pp. 42–3.

58 *Ibid.*, pp. 43–4.

59 *Ibid.*, p. 54.

60 S. T. Coleridge, 'On civility', *Shorter Works and Fragments, II, Works*, vol. 11, ed. H. J. Jackson and J. R. de J. Jackson (Princeton, Princeton University Press, 1995), p. 1499.

61 On Arnold's place in this tradition see Ben Knights's discussion in *The Idea of the Clerisy in the Nineteenth Century* (Cambridge, Cambridge University Press, 1978), pp. 100–39.

62 In A *Liberal Descent: The Victorians and the English Past* (Cambridge, Cambridge University Press, 1981), pp. 120 J. W. Burrow describes the book as 'a watershed', influencing constitutional history for the rest of the century.

63 John Kemble, *The Saxons in England: A History of the English Commonwealth till the Period of the Norman Conquest* (London, Longman, Brown, Green and Longman, 1849), pp. v–vi.

64 *Ibid.*, p. 54.

65 Robert Knox, *The Races of Men: A Fragment* (London, Henry Renshaw, 1862), p. 69.

66 *Ibid.*, p. 327.

67 Isaac Taylor, *The Origin of the Aryans* (London, Walter Scott, 1889), p. 249.

68 See Seamus Deane's richly suggestive account of this opposition in *Strange Country: Modernity and Nationhood in Irish Writing Since 1790* (Oxford, Clarendon Press, 1997), pp. 3–18.

69 See Norma Clarke, 'Strenuous idleness: Thomas Carlyle and the man of letters as hero', in Michael Roper and John Tosh (eds), *Manful Assertions: Masculinities in Britain Since 1800* (London & New York, Routledge, 1991), pp. 25–43 for an account of Carlyle's attempts to reconcile his position as writer with the industrious, Calvinist example set by his father.

70 Fred Kaplan, *Thomas Carlyle: A Biography* (Berkeley, University of California Press, 1983), p. 112.

71 Thomas Carlyle, 'Signs of the times', in *Collected Works: Critical and Miscellaneous Essays II* (London, Chapman and Hall, 1896), p. 60: 'Not the external and physical alone is now managed by machinery, but the internal and spiritual also.'

72 *Ibid.*, p. 56.

73 See Hedva Ben-Israel, *English Historians on the French Revolution* (Cambridge, Cambridge University Press, 1968), p. 144–5; Ben-Israel's own view seems to be that Carlyle's devotion to fact above all else produces an unsystematic, even contradictory, narrative.

74 John Stuart Mill, 'Carlyle's French Revolution', in *Collected Works*, vol. 20: *Essays on French History and Historians*, eds. John M. Robson and Jack Stillinger (Toronto & Buffalo/London, University of Toronto Press/Routledge & Kegan Paul, [1837] 1985), pp. 158–60.

75 Thomas Carlyle, *The French Revolution* (Oxford, Oxford University Press, [1837] 1989), p. 221.

76 *Ibid.*, p. 223.

77 *Ibid.*, p. 225.

78 *Ibid.*, p. 452.

79 Peter Logan, *Nerves and Narratives: A Cultural History of Hysteria in Nineteenth Century British Prose* (Berkeley, University of California Press, 1997), p. 23. On the continuing assumption of female susceptibility to nervous excitation and hysteria in the mid-nineteenth century see Mary Poovey, *Uneven Developments: The Ideological Work of Gender in Mid-Victorian Britain* (London, Virago Press, 1989), p. 36–7.

80 See, for instance, Linda M. Shires, 'Of maenads, mothers and feminised males: Victorian readings of the French Revolution', in Shires (ed.), *Rewriting the Victorians: Theory, History and the Politics of Gender* (New York, Routledge, 1992), pp. 151–2 & 154; on Carlyle's account see also Herbert Sussman, *Victorian Masculinities: Manhood and Masculine Poetics in Early Victorian Literature and Art* (Cambridge, Cambridge University Press, 1995), pp. 21–2.

81 Carlyle, *French Revolution*, p. 262.

82 Bruce Haley, *The Healthy Body and Victorian Culture* (Cambridge Mass., Harvard University Press, 1978), pp. 31–2.

83 John Stuart Mill, 'Tennyson's Poems', in *Collected Works* vol. 1: *Autobiographical and Literary Essays*, ed. John M. Robson and Jack Stillinger (Toronto & Buffalo/London, University of Toronto Press/Routledge & Kegan Paul, [1835] 1981), pp. 413–14.

84 Charles Kingsley, 'Thoughts on Shelley and Byron', in *Literary and General Lectures and Essays* (London, Macmillan, [1853] 1890), pp. 47–8.

85 Edward Dowden, 'The French Revolution and literature', in *Studies in Literature 1789–1877* (London, Kegan Paul, Trench, Trübner, [1877] 1899) p. 28.

86 Dowden, 'The scientific movement and literature' [1877], in *ibid.*, pp. 111–13.

87 Charlotte Brontë, *Jane Eyre* (Oxford, Oxford University Press, [1847] 1990), p. 19.

88 Terry Eagleton, *Myths of Power: A Marxist Study of the Brontës* (London, Macmillan, 1975), p. 74.

89 Brontë, *Jane Eyre*, pp. 320–1.

90 *Ibid.*, pp. 441–3.

91 *Ibid.*, p. 474.

92 *Ibid.*, p. 146.

93 *Ibid.*, p. 325.

94 As Philip W. Martin points out, Rochester comes to accept that the fire was a punishment for his desire for Jane: *Mad Women in Romantic Writing* (Brighton, Harvester Press, 1987), p. 129.

95 Brontë, *Jane Eyre.* p, 115.

96 Sally Shuttleworth, *Charlotte Brontë and Victorian Psychology* (Cambridge, Cambridge University Press, 1986), p. 152.

97 Letter to Margaret Wooler, 31 March 1848, *The Brontës: Their Lives, Friendships and Correspondence*, 4 vols, ed. Thomas J. Wise and J. Alexander Symington (Oxford, Blackwell, [1933] 1980), vol. 2, p. 203.

98 Letter to W. S. Williams, 20 April 1848, *ibid.*, vol. 2, p. 203.

99 Brontë records receiving Kingsley's novel on 25 October 1850, and compares it with the 'far superior' poem in a letter to Mrs Gaskell on 6 August 1851, *ibid.*, vol. 3, pp. 174 and 268–9.

100 Helen Small, *Love's Madness: Medicine, the Novel, and Female Insanity, 1800–1865* (Oxford, Clarendon Press, 1996), pp. 154–78. This interpretation clearly contradicts Sally Shuttleworth's account in *Brontë and Victorian Psychology*, pp. 148–82, in which she argues that the text is far less assured in its progress. This, I think, results from basing her impressively detailed argument too exclusively on psychological texts.

101 The classic analysis along these lines is Sandra M. Gilbert and Susan Gubar, *The Madwoman in the Attic: The Woman Writer and the Nineteenth Century Literary Imagination* (New Haven, Yale University Press, 1979), pp. 336–71. Mary Poovey provides a more sophisticated account suggesting a similar process of displacement in *Uneven Developments*, pp. 126–48, though clearly this still conflicts with the view taken here.

102 See Philip W. Martin, *Mad Women*, pp. 129–30; also Elaine Showalter, *The Female Malady: Women, Madness and English Culture, 1830–1980* (London, Virago Press, 1987), pp. 68–9.

103 Brontë, *Jane Eyre*, p. 115.

104 *Ibid.*, p. 475.

105 Small, *Love's Madness*, p. 177.

106 See Rosemary Clark-Beattie, 'Fables of rebellion: anti-Catholicism and the structures of *Villette*', *English Literary History*, 53:4 (1986), pp. 821–47 for a detailed reading of the novel in these terms.

107 Charlotte Brontë, *Villette* (Oxford, Oxford University Press, [1853] 1990), pp. 90–1.

108 On this see Boyd Hilton's *The Age of Atonement: The Influences of Evangelicalism on Social and Economic Thought, 1785–1865* (Oxford, Clarendon Press, 1988), pp. 100–88.

## Chapter 2

1 Martin Luther, 'The freedom of a Christian', trans. W. A. Lambert and Harold

J. Grimm, in *Works,* vol. 31: *Career of the Reformer I,* ed. Harold J. Grim and Helmut T. Lehmann (Philadelphia, Muhlenberg Press, [1520] 1957), p. 359.

2 Charlotte Brontë, *Jane Eyre* (Oxford, Oxford University Press, [1847] 1993), pp. 390–1.

3 This is the interpretation which Norman Vance pursues in *The Sinews of the Spirit: The Ideal of Christian Manliness in Victorian Literature and Religious Thought* (Cambridge, Cambridge University Press, 1985).

4 Bruce Haley, *The Healthy Body and Victorian Culture* (Cambridge, Mass., Harvard University Press, 1978), p. 1.

5 Herbert Spencer, *Education: Intellectual, Moral and Physical* (London, Mainwaring, 1861), p. 190.

6 Thomas Carlyle, *Chartism,* in *Collected Works: Critical and Miscellaneous Essays IV* (London, Chapman and Hall), [1839] 1896), p. 145.

7 Karl Marx and Frederic Engels, *The Communist Manifesto,* in Karl Marx, *Selected Writings,* ed. David McLellan (Oxford, Oxford University Press, [1848] 1977), p. 238.

8 F. D. Maurice, *The Kingdom of Christ,* vol. 1 (London, Macmillan, [1842] 1883), p. 272.

9 Edward Norman, *The Victorian Christian Socialists* (Cambridge, Cambridge University Press, 1987), p. 21; see also Bernard M. G. Reardon, *Religious Thought in the Victorian Age: A Survey from Coleridge to Gore,* 2nd ed. (New York, Longmans, 1980), pp. 165–6.

10 Charles Kingsley, *His Letters and Memories of His Life,* ed. 'his wife' (London, Macmillan, [1876] 1890), p. 160. Seamus Deane suggests this was a widespread conviction: 'Protestant England had made 1688 possible; Catholic France had made 1789 and 1792 inevitable' (*The French Revolution and Enlightenment in England* (Cambridge, Mass., Harvard University Press, 1988), p. 22).

11 John Saville, *1848: The British State and the Chartist Movement* (Cambridge, Cambridge University Press, 1987).

12 Saville, *1848,* p. 109.

13 Saville, *1848,* p. 202.

14 Saville, *1848,* p. 164.

15 Kingsley, *Letters,* p. 311.

16 *Ibid.,* p. 130.

17 Susan Chitty, *The Beast and the Monk: A Life of Charles Kingsley* (London, Hodder & Stoughton, 1974), p. 133.

18 Charles Kingsley, *Alton Locke* (Oxford, Oxford University Press, [1850] 1983), p. 356.

19 *Ibid.,* pp. 196–206.

20 *Ibid.,* p. 305.

21 *Ibid.,* p. 307. Josephine Guy also notes the allusions to France (though not to Ireland) in *The Victorian Social-problem Novelists* (Houndmills, Macmillan, 1996), p. 174.

22 Kingsley, *Alton Locke,* p. 377.

23 Catherine Gallagher, *The Industrial Reformation of English Fiction: Social Discourse and Narrative Form, 1832–1867* (Chicago, Chicago University Press, 1987), chapter 4, pp. 88–110.

24 *Ibid.*, p. 107.

25 Kingsley, *Alton Locke*, p. 183.

26 *Ibid.*, p. 182.

27 *Ibid.*, p. 358.

28 *Ibid.*, p. 372.

29 *Ibid.*, p. 12.

30 *Ibid.*, p. 14.

31 *Ibid.*, p. 22.

32 *Ibid.*, p. 29.

33 Kingsley, *Letters*, p. 232.

34 Kingsley's sense of the monstrosity of the working class is therefore quite specific in its diagnosis. For a more general consideration of the alignment of radicalism with monstrosity and of physical with social health in his work see Donald E. Hall's 'On the making and unmaking of monsters: Christian socialism, muscular Christianity, and metaphorisation of class conflict', in Hall (ed.), *Muscular Christianity: Embodying the Victorian Age*, (Cambridge, Cambridge University Press, 1995), pp. 45–65.

35 Kingsley, *Alton Locke*, pp. 131–2.

36 Compare Paley's rather mechanical account 'Of the muscles', *Natural Theology, in Works*, vol. 4 (London, William Baynes, [1802] 1823), pp. 91–7, where the musculature merely provides further laborious evidence of design, rather than of the deity's intentions for his subjects.

37 Raymond Williams, *Culture and Society, Coleridge to Orwell* (London, Hogarth, [1958] 1993), p. 91.

38 *Ibid.*, p. 101.

39 Charles Kingsley, *Westward Ho!*, vol. 1 (London, Macmillan, [1855] 1896), pp. 14 & 16–17.

40 Robert Knox, *The Races of Men: A Fragment* (London, Henry Renshaw, [1850] 1862), p. 66.

41 Kingsley, *Yeast* (London, Macmillan, [1848] 1879), pp. iii–iv.

42 E. J. Hobsbawm, *The Age of Empire, 1875–1914* (London, Weidenfeld & Nicolson, 1987), p 178.

43 J. A. Mangan, *Athleticism in the Victorian and Edwardian Public School: The Emergence and Consolidation of an Educational Ideology* (Cambridge, Cambridge University Press, 1981), p. 86.

44 Philip Dodd, 'Englishness and the national culture', in Robert Colls and Philip Dodds (eds), *Englishness: Politics and Culture, 1880–1920* (Beckenham, Croom Helm, 1986), p. 4.

45 Archibald Maclaren, *A System of Physical Education, Theoretical and Practical* (1869); quoted in Haley, *Healthy Body*, p. 20.

46 See George M. Worth, 'Of muscles and manliness: some reflections on Thomas Hughes', in James R. Kincaid and Albert J. Kuhn (eds), *Victorian Literature and Society: Essays Presented to Richard D. Altick* (Cleveland, Ohio State

University Press, 1984), pp. 306–7.

47  Thomas Hughes, *Tom Brown's Schooldays* (Oxford, Oxford University Press, [1857] 1989), p. 282.

48  Boyd Hilton, 'Manliness, masculinity and mid-Victorian temperament', in Lawrence Goldman (ed.), *The Blind Victorian: Henry Fawcett and British Liberalism* (Cambridge, Cambridge University Press, 1989), p. 69.

49  H. H. Almond, 'The consecration of the body', in *Sermons by a Lay Headmaster* (Edinburgh, William Blackwood, 1886), pp. 173–5.

50  W. E. Bowen, *W. E. Bowen: A Memoir* (London, Longman, 1902), p. 331.

51  Mangan, *Athleticism*, p. 136. A more convincing presentation of this argument, is contained in his 'Social Darwinism and upper-class education in late Victorian and Edwardian England', in Mangan and James Walvin (eds), *Manliness and Morality: Middle-Class Masculinity in Britain and America, 1800–1940* (Manchester, Manchester University Press, 1987), pp. 135–59.

52  Vance, *Sinews*, pp. 190–1.

53  Thomas Hughes, *The Manliness of Christ* (London, Macmillan, 1879), p. 5.

54  *Ibid.*, pp. 25–6.

55  See Peter Bailey, *Leisure and Class in Victorian England: Rational Recreation and the Contest for Control, 1830–1885* (London, Methuen, 1987), pp. 138–44.

56  Michael Rosenthal, *The Character Factory: Baden-Powell's Boy Scouts and the Imperatives of Empire* (New York, Pantheon, 1986), esp. pp. 52–130.

57  *Ibid.*, p. 231. Interestingly John Springhall notes some examples of working-class resistance to these quasi-military movements in 'Building character in the British boy: the attempt to extend Christian Manliness to working-class adolescents, 1880–1914', in Mangan and Walvin (eds), *Manliness and Morality*, pp. 60–1.

58  Wilkie Collins, *Man and Wife* (Oxford, Oxford University Press, [1870] 1995), pp. 342–3.

59  Unsigned review in *Putnam's Magazine*, Sept. 1870, in Norman Page (ed.), *Wilkie Collins: The Critical Heritage* (London, Routledge & Kegan Paul, 1974), p. 187.

60  Wilkie Collins, *The Woman in White* (Oxford, Oxford University Press, [1860] 1980), pp. 373–4.

61  Collins, *Woman*, p. 373.

62  Jenny Bourne Taylor, *In the Secret Theatre of the Home: Wilkie Collins, Sensation Narrative and Nineteenth Century Psychology* (London, Routledge, 1988), p. 108.

63  See Mangan, *Athleticism*, esp. pp. 191–6. Mangan's *The Games Ethic and Imperialism: Aspects of the Diffusion of an Ideal* (Harmondsworth, Penguin, 1986), goes on to describe the diffusion of the ethic throughout the empire.

64  Daniel Pick notes that the concern with physical degeneration on the continent arose from fears about the influence of revolution on hereditary national character. See his *Faces of Degeneration: A European Disorder, c. 1848–1918* (Cambridge, Cambridge University Press, 1989), chapter 2, pp. 37–73.

65  See John C. Hawley, 'Charles Kingsley and literary theory of the 1850s', *Victo-*

*rian Literature and Culture*, 19 (1991), pp. 167–88.

66 On the other hand James Eli Adams has described some 'unexpected affinities' between Kingsley and Pater in 'Pater's Muscular Aestheticism', in Hall (ed.) *Muscular Christianity*, pp. 215–38.

67 Eve K. Sedgwick, Between Men: *English Literature and Male Homosocial Desire* (New York, Columbia University Press, 1985), p. 89.

68 Mangan, *Athleticism*, pp. 11–96.

69 Almond, *Sermons*, pp. 78–91.

70 Edward Thring, *Upingham Sermons*, vol. 1 (Cambridge, Deighton Bell, 1886), p. 307.

71 Haley, *Healthy* Body, p. 167.

72 See Mark Girouard, *The Return to Camelot: Chivalry and the English Gentleman* (New Haven, Yale University Press, 1981), chapter 11, pp. 166–76.

73 Jeffrey Richards covers this ground fairly comprehensively, though with strenuous efforts to disentangle sexual and non-sexual love, in '"Passing the love of women": manly love and Victorian society', in Mangan and Walvin (eds), *Manliness and Morality*, pp. 92–122.

74 This is the term Timothy D'Arch Smith appropriates to describe a range of writers on boy love at this time in *Love in Earnest: Some Notes on the Lives and Writings of English 'Uranian' Poets from 1889–1930* (London, Routledge & Kegan Paul, 1970).

75 Vance, *Sinews*, pp. 185–9.

76 Revd E. E. Bradford, *Stories of Life at Our Great Public Schools* (London, Arthur H. Stockwell, 1908), p. 191.

77 Bradford, *The New Chivalry* (London, Kegan, Paul, Trench Trübner, 1918), p. 65.

78 *Ibid.*, p. 31.

79 Bradford, *Passing the Love of Women* (London, Kegan Paul, 1913), pp. 28–32.

80 This is also argued by Linda Dowling, *Hellenism and Homosexuality in Victorian Oxford* (Ithaca, Cornell University Press, 1994), p. 115, though on different grounds.

81 Edward Carpenter, 'Homogenic Love', reproduced in Brian Reade (ed.), *Sexual Heretics: Male Homosexuality in English Literature from 1850–1900*, (London, Routledge & Kegan Paul, [1894] 1970), p. 344.

82 Charles Kains Jackson, 'The New Chivalry', in *ibid.*, pp. 315–16.

83 Alan Sinfield, *The Wilde Century: Effeminacy, Oscar Wilde and the Queer Moment* (London, Cassell, 1994), p. 110.

84 Alec Waugh, *Public School Life* (London, Collins, 1922), p. 158.

85 E. M. Forster, *The Longest Journey* (London, Edward Arnold, [1907] 1913), p. 52.

86 Gerard Manley Hopkins, 'To what serves mortal beauty?', in *Gerard Manley Hopkins*, ed. Catherine Phillips (Oxford, Oxford University Press, 1986), p. 167.

# Notes

## Chapter 3

1 Charles Kingsley, *Alton Locke* (Oxford, Oxford University Press, [1850] 1983), p. 156.

2 Kingsley, *Alton Locke* (London, Macmillan, [1862] 1889), p. 107.

3 See especially David Hilliard's influential 'UnEnglish and unmanly: Anglo-Catholicism and homosexuality', *Victorian Studies*, 25:2 (1983), pp. 181–200.

4 Ian Ker, *John Henry Newman: A Biography* (Oxford, Clarendon Press, 1989), p. viii.

5 *Ibid.*, p. 695.

6 This is partly the argument of Alan Sinfield in *Alfred Tennyson* (Oxford, Blackwell, 1986), pp. 143–53.

7 J. H. Newman, 'On the introduction of rationalistic principles into revealed religion', in *Essays Critical and Historical*, vol. 1 (London, Basil Montagu Pickering, [1835] 1875), p. 31.

8 *The Letters and Diaries of John Henry Newman*, vol. 2, ed. Ian Ker and Thomas Gornall (Oxford, Clarendon Press, 1979), pp. 263–6; also see Sheridan Gilley, *Newman and His Age* (London, Darton, Longman & Todd, 1990), p. 75.

9 Newman, *Loss and Gain* (Oxford, Oxford University Press, [1848] 1986), p. 293.

10 *Ibid.*, p. 294.

11 See Gilley, *Newman and His Age*, pp. 241 & 248; also, Ker, *John Henry Newman*, pp. 326–7 & 329.

12 Newman, *Essay on the Development of Christian Doctrine* (Harmondsworth, Penguin, [1845] 1974), p. 121.

13 *Ibid.*, p. 131.

14 Newman, *Lectures on the Present Position of Catholics in England* (London, Longman, [1851] 1892), pp. 70–1.

15 *Ibid.*, p. 88.

16 *Ibid.*, pp. 55–6.

17 Newman, *Letters and Diaries* vol. 2, pp. 118–19, 6 Feb. 1829.

18 I do not consider here Newman's experiences at the Catholic University in the 1850s, since I am principally interested in the effect of his religious disposition on his political attitudes to nationalism (English and Irish). His time in Ireland was largely spent mediating between the different factions in the Irish Catholic Church – principally as represented by the ultramontanist Archbishop Cullen and the nationalist MacHale. In this position of diplomat, and with his own views on University affairs, he was distrusted by both. The 1850s were also a relatively calm period in Irish history. Both Ker's and Gilley's biographies devote substantial space to these years, and Louis McRedmond, in *Thrown Among Strangers: John Henry Newman in Ireland* (Dublin, Veritas, 1990), provides a valuable – if obviously O'Connellite – account of the factions and politicking within the Irish Catholic Church at this time.

19 Newman, *Letters & Diaries* vol. 31, p. 195, 3 March 1887.

20 Newman, *Letters & Diaries* vol. 30, pp. 32–3, 19 Dec. 1881.

21 Newman, *Letters & Diaries* vol. 31, p. 24, 6 Feb. 1885.

# Notes

22 Newman, *Letters & Diaries* vol. 29, pp. 312–13, 8 Nov. 1880.

23 Newman, *Letters & Diaries* vol. 30, p. 12, 24 Oct. 1881.

24 Newman, *Letters & Diaries* vol. 31, pp. 250–1, 25 April 1888.

25 On this see Kevin Whelan's comments in 'An underground gentry?: Catholic middlemen in eighteenth century Ireland', *The Tree of Liberty: Radicalism, Catholicism and the Construction of an Irish Identity, 1760–1830* (Cork, Cork University Press, 1996), pp. 36–7; also Seamus Deane, *The French Revolution and Enlightenment in England* (Cambridge, Mass. and London, Harvard University Press, 1988), pp. 14–18.

26 'Mr Kingsley and Dr Newman. A correspondence on the question 'whether Dr Newman teaches that Truth is no virtue?", reproduced in Newman, *Apologia Pro Vita Sua*, ed. Martin J. Svaglic (Oxford, Clarendon Press, 1967), p. 341.

27 Oliver S. Buckton, '"An unnatural state": gender, "perversion", and Newman's *Apologia Pro Vita Sua', Victorian Studies*, 35:4 (1992), pp. 359–83.

28 This is the overall argument of Sinfield in *The Wilde Century: Effeminacy, Oscar Wilde and the Queer Moment* (London, Cassell, 1994).

29 Jonathan Dollimore, *Sexual Dissidence: Augustine to Wilde, Freud to Foucault* (Oxford, Clarendon Press, 1991), pp. 131–47.

30 *Norfolk News*, 24 September 1864; quoted in Hilliard, 'UnEnglish and unmanly', p. 192; my italics.

31 James Eli Adams also notes the anachronism involved in such arguments, though this is bound up with his argument about the peculiar appeal of Tractarian reserve, and seems to suggest that by the time of Kingsley's attack in the 1860s the sexual allegation was implicit: *Dandies and Dessert Saints: Styles of Victorian Masculinity* (New York, Cornell University Press, 1995), pp. 83–106.

32 Charles Kingsley, *His Letters and Memories of His Life*, ed. 'his wife' (London, Macmillan, [1876] 1890), p. 30.

33 Kingsley, 'What then does Dr Newman mean?', in Newman, *Apologia*, p. 360.

34 J. H. Newman, *The Idea of a University* (Oxford, Clarendon Press, [1852] 1976), p. 174. For a lengthier discussion of Newman's thoughts on the genleman see Robin Gilmour, *The Idea of a Gentleman in the Victorian Novel* (London, George Allen & Unwin, 1981), pp. 88–92.

35 Kingsley, 'What then', pp. 373–4.

36 *Ibid.*, p. 377.

37 See John Shelton Reed, '"A female movement": the feminisation of nineteenth century Anglo-Catholicism', *Anglican and Episcopal History*, 57 (1988), pp. 199–238.

38 Kingsley, *Letters*, pp. 303–4.

39 Martin Luther, 'The estate of marriage', trans. Walter I. Brandt, in *Works*, vol. 45: *The Christian in Society II*, ed. Walter I. Brandt and Helmut T. Lehman (Philadelphia, Muhlenberg Press, [1522] 1962), pp. 17–18; my emphasis.

40 See Keith Thomas, *Religion and the Decline of Magic*, (Penguin, Harmondsworth, 1978), p. 87.

41 Lawrence Stone, *The Family, Sex and Marriage in England, 1500–1864* (London, Weidenfeld & Nicolson, 1977), p. 625.

42 Michael Mason, *The Making of Victorian Sexual Attitudes* (Oxford, Oxford University Press, 1994), pp. 17–18.

43 Robert Browning, 'Fra Lippo Lippi', in *The Poetical Works of Robert Browning*, vol. 5: *Men and Women*, ed. Ian Jack and Robert Inglesfield (Oxford, Clarendon Press, 1995), pp. 35–53.

44 John Maynard, *Victorian Discourses on Sexuality and Religion* (Cambridge, Cambridge University Press, 1993), p. 118.

45 Kingsley 'What then', p. 383.

46 See Kingsley, 'The shaking of the heavens and the earth', in *Westminster Sermons* (London, Macmillan, [1874] 1894), pp. 94–7.

47 Quoted in Alan Hertz, 'The broad Church Militant and Newman's humiliation of Charles Kingsley', *Victorian Periodicals Review*, 19:4 (1986), p. 145.

48 Quoted in James Bentley, *Ritualism and Politics in Victorian Britain* (Oxford, Oxford University Press, 1978), p. 21.

49 Quoted in Geoffrey Faber, *Oxford Apostles: A Character Study of the Oxford Movement* (London, Faber, [1933] 1974), p. 33.

50 Faber, *Oxford Apostles*, p. 11.

51 *Ibid.*, p. 12.

52 *Ibid.*, p. 413.

53 *Ibid.*, p. 415–16.

54 Newman, *Apologia*, p. 20.

55 Newman, 'Poetry with reference to Aristotle's poetics', in *Essays Critical and Historical*, vol. 1 (London, Basil Montagu Pickering, [1828] 1871), p. 23.

56 Newman, 'The powers of nature', in *Parochial and Plain Sermons*, vol. 2 (London, Rivington, [1835] 1884), pp. 363.

57 The only psychology text Faber acknowledges in his book is J. R. Rees's *The Health of the Mind*. The only text I can trace which corresponds to this is dated 1951 (New York, W. W. Norton), i.e. after the publication of *Oxford Apostles*. I have therefore assumed that the book published by Rees in 1951 is an updated version. It certainly acknowledges Freud as the founding father of modern psychology and contains much pseudo-Freudian normative and normalising assertion. It, too, is notable for its assumption that there is a correspondence between racial and individual development, that each is a progression to a truer relation to reality, and, as part of this, the achievement of heterosexual union through marriage. Homosexuality figures as arrested development, and, implicitly therefore, represents a less than true relation to reality.

58 For a discussion of this see Jeffrey Weeks, *Sexuality and Its Discontents: Meanings, Myths and Modern Sexualities* (London and New York, Routledge & Kegan Paul, 1985), esp. pp. 149–56.

59 Sigmund Freud, *The Penguin Freud Library*, vol. 13: *Totem and Taboo: Some Points of Agreement Between the Mental Lives of Savages and Neurotics*, in *The Origins of Religion* (Harmondsworth, Penguin, [1913] 1985), p. 148.

60 Of course Freud cannot be entirely exonerated from such views, as he demonstrates in a 1910 footnote to the *Three Essays on Sexuality*: inverts 'identify themselves with a woman and take *themselves* as their sexual object. That is to say, they proceed from a narcissistic basis, and look for a young man who

resembles themselves and whom *they* may love as their mother loved *them*.' Freud, *The Penguin Freud Library*, vol. 7: *On Sexuality* (Harmondsworth, Penguin, [1905] 1977), p. 56. Indeed, Faber recapitulates this argument quite precisely with reference to Newman.

61 Rees, *Health of the Mind*, p. 126.

## Chapter 4

1 Terry Eagleton, 'Tennyson: politics and sexuality in *The Princess and In Memoriam*', in *1848: The Sociology of Literature* (University of Essex, 1978), p. 104.

2 Alfred Tennyson, *In Memoriam*, in *Tennyson: A Selected Edition*, ed. Christopher Ricks (Harlow, Longman, 1989), pp. 331–485, section II, ll. 1–4.

3 Elaine Jordan, *Alfred Lord Tennyson* (Hemel Hempstead, Harvester Wheatsheaf, 1988), p. 73. Jordan suggests that this contradiction is reconciled through Tennyson's identification with various feminine figures, but 'when sufficient authority over them has been gained, they can be figuratively speaking exchanged, and the bond between men created' (p. 78). My account may be seen as complementary to this.

4 Tess Cosslett, *The 'Scientific Movement' and Victorian Literature* (Brighton, Harvester Press, 1982), p. 48.

5 *Ibid*, p. 59.

6 Clearly most of *In Memoriam* was written prior to 1848, but some, at least, of the stanzas concerning revolution discussed above must have been penned in the aftermath of the events of that year. In section CXVII the reference to 'thrice again' indicates 1848, though Ricks's note suggests the section may have been revised in response to these events: *Tennyson*, p. 473n. It seems to me self-evident that the poem could hardly have been convincing in the unlikely event that the Chartists had been successful. Indeed, that *would* have wiped the smile off Hallam's face.

7 Entry for 24 Dec. 1867, *William Allingham's Diary* (Fontwell, Centaur Press, 1967), p. 167.

8 Oliver MacDonagh, *States of Mind: Two Centuries of Anglo-Irish Conflict, 1780–1980* (London, Pimlico, 1992), p. 32.

9 Charles Townshend, *Political Violence in Ireland: Government and Resistance Since 1848* (Oxford, Clarendon Press, 1983), pp. 101–2.

10 On the return of sectarianism post-1898, see Kevin Whelan's essay ''98 after '98: the politics of memory', *The Tree of Liberty: Radicalism and the Construction of Irish Identity 1760–1830* (Cork, Cork University Press, 1996), pp. 133–75. Specifically on O'Connellite sectarianism see, for instance, D. George Boyce, *Nationalism in Ireland*, 2nd ed. (London, Routledge, 1991), chapter 5, pp. 123–49.

11 *The Letters of Thomas Arnold the Younger*, ed. James Bertram (Auckland, Auckland University Press/Oxford University Press, 1980), p. 214.

12 Christopher Morash, *Writing the Irish Famine* (Oxford, Clarendon Press), 1995, pp. 13–17.

# Notes

13 This is partly the argument of Terry Eagleton in the title essay of *Heathcliff and the Great Hunger: Studies in Irish Culture* (London, Verso, 1995), pp. 1–26; see also Peter Miles's essay in *Wuthering Heights* (Houndmills, Macmillan, 1990), pp. 54–5.

14 Terry Eagleton, *Heathcliff*, p. 15.

15 Emily Brontë, *Wuthering Heights* (Oxford, Oxford University Press, [1847] 1981), p.196.

16 L. P. Curtis, *Anglo-Saxons and Celts: A Study of Anti-Irish Prejudice in Victorian England*, (Bridgeport, University of Bridgeport, 1968); also, *Apes and Angels: The Irishman in Victorian Caricature* (Newton Abbot, David & Charles, 1971). For further contributions see Sheridan Gilley, 'English Attitudes to the Irish in England, 1780–1900', in *Immigrants and Minorities in British Society*, ed. Colin Holmes (London, Allen & Unwin, 1978), pp. 81–110, who challenges the argument about the racial basis of English hostility as well as the extent to which it affected Irish people. Gilley often appears absurdly generous to some notorious English bigots, and his account has been queried on historical grounds by M. A. G. O Tuathaigh, in 'The Irish in nineteenth century Britain: problems of integration', *Royal Historical Society Transactions*, 31 (1981), pp. 160–1. Luke Gibbons also takes issue with Gilley in 'Race against time', in *Transformations in Irish Culture* (Cork, Cork University Press, 1996), pp. 149–63 on the grounds that Gilley's argument seems to assume that 'colonial rule had no role at all to play in fabricating the self-images of the Irish' (p. 156). R. F. Foster in the title essay of *Paddy and Mr Punch* (Harmondsworth, Allen Lane, 1993), pp. 171–94, argues that the picture of the Irish in Punch was more diverse than Curtis suggests and reflected historical events (as one might expect).

17 Chris Baldick, *In Frankenstein's Shadow: Myth Monstrosity and Nineteenth Century Writing* (Oxford, Clarendon Press, 1987), p. 10.

18 Thomas Carlyle, *Chartism*, in *Collected Works: Critical and Miscellaneous Essays IV*, (London, Chapman & Hall, [1839] 1896), p. 137.

19 Thomas Carlyle, *The French Revolution*, vol. 2 (Oxford, Oxford, Oxford University Press, [1837] 1989) p. 443.

20 Thomas Carlyle, *Reminiscences of My Irish Journey in 1849* (London, Sampson Low, Marstone, Searle and Rivington, 1882), p. v.

21 Carlyle remained concerned about this. See Seamus Deane, 'Irish national character, 1790–1900', in ed. Tom Dunne (ed.), *The Writer as Witness: Literature as Historical Evidence*, Historical Studies XVI (Cork, Cork University Press, 1987), p. 99.

22 Carlyle, *Chartism*, pp. 138–9.

23 *Ibid.*, p. 139.

24 *Ibid.*, p. 144.

25 Ken Caplan, *Thomas Carlyle: A Biography* (Berkeley, University of California Press, 1983), p. 338. For a more wide-ranging and generally more sympathetic account of Carlyle's views on Ireland than mine see Michael Goldberg, 'Carlyle and Ireland', *Canadian Journal of Irish Studies*, 5 (1979), pp. 4–25.

26 Carlyle, *Reminiscences*, p. 135.

27  *Ibid.*, p. 34.
28  *Ibid.*, p. 121.
29  *Ibid.*, pp. 135–9.
30  *Ibid.*, p. 215.
31  *Ibid.*, pp. 160–1.
32  *Ibid.*, p. 179.
33  *Ibid.*, p. 202.
34  *Ibid.*, p. 259.
35  *Ibid.*, p. 262.
36  Extract from a notebook of Ralph Waldo Emerson dated 5–6 May 1848, contained in *The Letters of Alfred Lord Tennyson*, vol. 1: *1821–1850*, ed. Cecil Y. Land and Edgar F. Shannon Jr (Oxford, Clarendon Press, 1982), p. 285.
37  Robert Bernard Martin, *Tennyson: The Unquiet Heart* (Oxford/London, Oxford University Press/Faber, 1980), pp. 318–19. Unfortunately Martin does not provide a reference for this.
38  Quoted in Christine Kinealy, *This Great Calamity: The Irish Famine, 1845–52* (Dublin, Gill & Macmillan, 1994), p. 34; for the persistence of such attitudes in the Peel administration see p. 38.
39  John Saville, *1848: The British State and the Chartist Movement* (Cambridge, Cambridge University Press, 1987), pp. 197–8.
40  This has been widely noted. See, for instance, Boyd Hilton, *The Age of Atonement: The Influences of Evangelicalism on Social and Economic Thought, 1785–1865* (Oxford, Clarendon Press, 1988), pp. 108–14; also Peter Gray, 'Potatoes and providence: British government's responses to the Great Famine', *Búllan: An Irish Studies Journal*, 1:1 (1994), pp. 75–90.
41  Thomas A. Boylan and Timothy P. Foley, *Political Economy and Colonial Ireland: The Propagation and Ideological Function of Economic Discourse in the Nineteenth Century* (London, Routledge, 1992), pp. 117–18.
42  For an account of the evolution of Mill's ideas and the controversy they provoked see E. D. Steele, 'J. S. Mill and the Irish question: reform, and the integrity of the empire, 1865–1870', in Alan O'Day (ed.), *Reactions to Irish Nationalism* (Dublin, Gill and Macmillan, 1987), pp. 205–36.
43  MacDonagh, *States of Mind*, p. 45.
44  John Stuart Mill, 'England and Ireland', in *Collected Works*, vol. 6: *Essays on England, Ireland and the Empire*, ed. John Robson (Toronto and Buffalo/London, University of Toronto/Routledge & Kegan Paul, [1868] 1982), p. 519.
45  Matthew Arnold, 'The incompatibles', in *The Complete Prose Works of Matthew Arnold*, vol. 9: *English Literature and Irish Politics*, ed. R. H. Super (Ann Arbor, University of Michigan Press, [1881] 1973), p. 254.
46  Curtis suggests 1860–90 as the most intense period of scientific racism: *Anglo-Saxons*, p. 27.
47  Alexander Somerville, *Letters from Ireland During the Famine of 1847*, ed. K. D. M. Snell (Blackrock, Irish Academic Press, 1994), p. 177.
48  *Ireland As It Is and As It Would Be Under Home Rule: Sixty-two Letters Written by the Special Commisssioner of the Birmingham Daily Gazette* (Birmingham,

Birmingham Daily Gazette, 1893), pp. 132–4.

49 Walter Walshe, *The Secret History of the Oxford Movement* (London, Swann Sonnenschein, 1898), pp. 362–3.

50 Nancy Stepan, *The Idea of Race in Science: Great Britain, 1800–1960* (London, Macmillan, 1982), p. 30.

51 Robert Knox, *The Races of Men: A Fragment* (London, Henry Renshaw, [1850] 1862), p. v.

52 *Ibid.*, p. 24.

53 Robert J. C. Young, *Colonial Desire: Hybridity in Theory, Culture and Race* (London, Routledge, 1995), p. 75. Young provides a valuable account of Arnold's interest in racial theory, arguing that Arnold subscribed to the view that racial types were permanent, not given to hybridisation (pp. 55–89). All of the racial theorists discussed in this chapter rejected the possibility of any permanent hybridity between races.

54 Frederic E. Faverty, *Matthew Arnold the Ethnologist* (Evanston, Northwestern University Press, 1951), p. 88.

55 Knox, *Races*, p. 25.

56 *Ibid.*, p. 27.

57 *Ibid.*, p. 379.

58 *Ibid.*, p. 318.

59 This is the distinction that Edward Said points to, though he is also clearly aware of the problems of drawing it too rigidly: *Culture and Imperialism* (London, Chatto & Windus, 1993), pp. 129–30.

60 Charles Kingsley, *His Letters and Memories of His Life*, ed. 'his wife' (London, Macmillan, [1876] 1890), p. 236.

61 John Beddoe, *The Races of Britain: A Contribution to the Anthropology of Western Europe* (Bristol/London, J. Arrowsmith/Trübner, 1885), pp. 9–12.

62 Knox, *Races*, pp. 319–20.

63 *Ibid.*, p. 320.

64 *Ibid.*, p. 329.

65 Arnold, 'From Easter to August', [1887]; quoted in Faverty, *Arnold the Ethnologist*, p. 142.

66 Arnold, 'On the study of Celtic literature', in *Prose Works*, vol. 3: *Lectures and Essays in Criticism*, ed. R. H. Super (Ann Arbor, University of Michigan Press, [1866] 1962), p. 344.

67 *Ibid.*, p. 328.

68 Oscar Wilde, 'The critic as artist', in *The Artist as Critic*, ed. Richard Ellmann (London, W. H. Allen, [1891] 1970), p. 369.

69 Arnold, 'Celtic literature', p. 347.

70 *Ibid.*, pp. 331–3.

71 *Ibid.*, p. 395.

72 David Lloyd, *Nationalism and Minor Literature: James Clarence Mangan and the Emergence of Irish Cultural Nationalism* (Berkeley, University of California Press, 1987), esp. pp. 6–19; see also Shaun Richards and David Cairns, *Writing Ireland: Colonialism, Nationalism and Culture* (Manchester, Manchester

University Press, 1988), p. 46, who see in Arnold's work an attempt to a utilise Celticism for the purposes of bourgeois hegemony.

73 Seamus Deane, *Strange Country: Modernity and Nationhood in Irish Writing Since 1790* (Oxford, Clarendon Press, 1997), p. 19.

74 For further comments on Arnold's indebtedness to Burke see Seamus Deane, *Celtic Revivals: Essays in Modern Irish Literature 1880–1980* (London, Faber, 1985), pp. 17–27.

75 Chris Baldick, *The Social Mission of English Criticism 1848–1932* (Oxford, Clarendon Press, 1983), pp. 49–50.

76 Matthew Arnold, 'La Reforme intellectuelle et morale de la France', in *Prose Works*, vol. 7: *God and the Bible*, ed. R. H. Super (Ann Arbor, University of Michigan Press, [1872] 1970), p. 45.

77 Declan Kiberd, *Inventing Ireland: The Literature of the Modern Nation* (London, Jonathan Cape, 1995), p. 25.

78 Arnold, 'Preface to *Irish Essays and Others*' [1882], in *Prose Works*, vol. 9, p. 315.

79 Arnold, 'Incompatibles', p. 253.

80 Park Honan, *Matthew Arnold: A Life* (New York, McGraw Hill, 1981), pp. 414–15.

81 Arnold, 'The nadir of liberalism', [1886], in *Prose Works*, vol. 11: The Last Word, ed. R. H. Super (Ann Arbor, University of Michigan Press, [1886] 1977), p. 60.

82 See Jenny Bourne Taylor, *In the Secret Theatre of Home: Wilkie Collins, Sensation Narrative, and Nineteenth Century Psychology* (London, Routledge, 1988), esp. pp. 2–15.

83 Arnold, 'Nadir', p. 67.

84 Oscar Wilde, 'The poets of '48', in *The Annotated Oscar Wilde*, ed. H. Montgomery Hyde (New York, Orbis, [1882] 1982), p. 374.

85 Grant Allen, 'The Celt in English art', *Fortnightly Review*, 55 (1891), p. 268.

86 *Ibid.*, p. 273.

87 For Foucault's definition of 'reverse discourse' in relation to sexuality see Michel Foucault, *The History of Sexuality: An Introduction* (Harmondsworth, Penguin, 1981), p. 101.

## Chapter 5

1 A. V. Dicey, *England's Case Against Home Rule* (Richmond, Richmond Publishing, [1886] 1973), p. 143.

2 Letter to Alexander Baillie, 23 Dec. 1886, *Further Letters of Gerard Manley Hopkins*, ed. Claude Colleer Abbott (London, Oxford University Press, 1956), p. 274.

3 See Robert Bernard Martin, *Gerard Manley Hopkins: A Very Private Life* (London, HarperCollins, 1991), pp. 363–4; also Norman White's substantially more detailed account in his *Hopkins: A Literary Biography* (Oxford, Clarendon Press, 1992), chapter 28, pp. 357–77.

# Notes

4  Hopkins, *Further Letters*, p. 183, 25 Dec. 1887.

5  Mary Daly, 'Dublin in the 1880s', *Hopkins Quarterly*, 14:1–4 (1987–8), pp. 100–1.

6  Charles Townshend, *Political Violence in Ireland: Government and Resistance Since 1848* (Oxford, Clarendon Press, 1983), p. 124.

7  F. S. L. Lyons, *Ireland Since the Famine* (London, Fontana, 1985), p. 179.

8  *Ibid.*, pp. 190–1.

9  Martin, *Hopkins*, pp. 368–71.

10  White, *Hopkins*, p. 383.

11  *Gerard Manley Hopkins*, ed. Catherine Phillips (Oxford, Oxford University Press, 1986), p. 166. For further reflections on Hopkins's 'multiple estrangements' as expressed in this and other poems see Matthew Campbell's 'Gerard Manley Hopkins and Ireland: "at a third / Remove"', *Bullán*, 3:1 (1997), pp. 45–55.

12  *The Sermons and Devotional Writings of Gerard Manley Hopkins*, ed. Christopher Devlin (London, Oxford University Press, 1959), p. 262.

13  *The Letters of Gerard Manley Hopkins to Robert Bridges*, ed. C. C. Abbott (London, Oxford University Press, 1935), p. 262, 28 Sept. 1887.

14  *Ibid.*, p. 265, 6 Nov. 1887.

15  *Hopkins*, p. 177.

16  Hopkins, *Letters to Bridges*, pp. 272–3, 10 Feb. 1888.

17  *Hopkins*, p. 178.

18  Hopkins, *Letters to Bridges*, p. 274 10 Feb. 1888.

19  White, *Hopkins*, p. 28.

20  Hopkins, *Further Letters*, p. 84, 19 Oct. 1863.

21  Alison G. Sulloway, *Gerard Manley Hopkins and the Victorian Temper* (London, Routledge & Kegan Paul, 1972), pp. 39–40.

22  Joseph Bristow has also noted this connection, though he writes about Hopkins's indebtedness to Christian Socialism – in many ways the precursor to Christian manliness. See his '"Churlsgrace": Gerard Manley Hopkins and the working-class male body', *English Literary History*, 59:3 (1992), pp. 693–711.

23  Hopkins, *Letters to Bridges*, p. 257, 30 July 1887.

24  Whilst at St Beuno's theological college Hopkins had moved a motion at the debating society declaring 'Eminence in arms is a better object of national ambition than eminence in commerce' (Alfred Thomas, *Hopkins the Jesuit: The Years of Training* (London, Oxford University Press, 1969), p. 247). He did, though, also speak against a motion declaring that 'There is no patriotism without some prospect of a fight or competition, a struggle with the foreigner' (Thomas, *Hopkins the Jesuit*, p. 249). This, of course, does not necessarily imply a contradiction on Hopkins's part.

25  White, *Hopkins*, p. 431.

26  Hopkins, *Further Letters*, p. 17, 1 June 1864.

27  Hopkins, *Sermons*, p. 48.

28  Hopkins, *Sermons*, p. 36.

29  Hopkins, *Letters to Bridges*, p. 95, 22 Oct. 1879.

30  'As kingfishers catch fire', in *Hopkins*, p. 129.

# Notes

31  Hopkins, *Letters to Bridges*, pp. 174–6, 3 Feb. 1883.

32  *The Correspondence of Gerard Manley Hopkins and Richard Watson Dixon*, ed. Claude Colleer Abbott (London, Oxford University Press, 1955), pp. 137–8, 3 July 1886.

33  Hopkins, *Further Letters*, p. 388, 6 May 1888.

34  Journal entry for the week following Christmas, 1873 in *The Journals and Papers of Gerard Manley Hopkins*, ed. Humphrey House and Graham Storey (London, Oxford University Press, 1959), p. 240.

35  Here I am largely indebted to Christopher Devlin's classic account in 'The image and the word', *The Tablet*, 11 (Feb.–March 1950), pp. 114–27.

36  Efrem Bettoni, *Duns Scotus: The Basic Principles of His Philosophy* (Washington, Catholic University of America Press, 1961), p. 63.

37  Hopkins, 'Poetry and verse' (fragment), *Journals*, p. 289.

38  Hopkins, *Letters to Bridges*, pp. 267–8, 6 Nov. 1887.

39  J. Hillis Miller, *The Disappearance of God: Five Nineteenth Century Writers* (Cambridge, Mass., Belknap Press, 1963), p. 283.

40  Hopkins, *Further Letters*, p. 373, 7 Nov. 1886.

41  William B. Thesing, 'Gerard Manley Hopkins's response to the city: the "composition of the crowd"', *Victorian Studies*, 30:3 (1987), pp. 397–9.

42  Retreat notes on 'Creation and redemption: the great sacrifice', in Hopkins, *Sermons*, p. 197, 8 Nov. 1881.

43  Hilary Fraser, *Beauty and Belief: Aestheticism and Religion in Victorian Literature* (Cambridge, Cambridge University Press, 1986), p. 92.

44  Hopkins, 'Contemplation for obtaining love', in *Sermons*, p. 194, 14 Aug. 1882.

45  Hopkins, *Journals*, p. 207, 21 April 1871.

46  *Hopkins*, p. 26.

47  *Ibid.*, p. 1.

48  *Ibid.*, pp. 110–19.

49  The British battleships known as dreadnoughts were not launched until 1906. However, the *OED* records: '1587 Drake *Desp* 27 Apr. in Hakluyt *Voy.* (1904) VI. p. xiv, A great leake sprange upon the Dreadnoughte'.

50  *Hopkins*, pp. 135–8.

51  Hopkins was hardly alone in this, as Gerald Roberts points out in 'Hopkins and the condition of England', *Hopkins Quarterly*, 14:1–4 (1987–8), pp. 112–26.

52  Hopkins, *Letters to Bridges*, pp. 127–8, 1 May 1881.

53  *Hopkins*, p. 184.

54  Hopkins, *Further Letters*, p. 195, 2 March 1889.

55  White, *Hopkins*, p. 389.

56  *Hopkins*, p. 175.

57  Hopkins, retreat notes, 1 Jan. 1889, *Sermons*, pp. 261–2.

58  Daniel A. Harris, *Inspirations Unbidden: The 'Terrible Sonnets' of Gerard Manley Hopkins* (Berkeley, University of California Press, 1982), p. 36.

59  Hopkins, *Further Letters*, p. 165, 9 Dec. 1884: 'for ivery word I delineate I disremember two'.

# Notes

## Chapter 6

1  Hopkins, *Further Letters of Gerad Manley Hopkins*, ed. Claude Colleer Abbot (London, Oxford University press, 1956), p. 155, 18 Oct. 1882.

2  For further reflections on this ambivalence and its relationship to others' forms of self-regulation at this time, see Peter Schwaab, 'Hopkins and the pushed peach', *Critical Quarterly*, ed. David Trotter, 37:3 (1995), pp. 43–60.

3  Peter Stallybrass and Allon White, *The Politics and Poetics of Transgression* (London, Methuen, 1986), p. 126.

4  *Ibid.*, p. 145.

5  *Gerard Manley Hopkins*, ed. Catherine Phillips (Oxford, Oxford University Press, 1986), p. 7.

6  Hopkins, *The Journals and Papers of Gerard Manley Hopkins*, ed. Humphrey House and Graham Storey (London, Oxford University Press, 1959), p. 8.

7  Hopkins, *Journal*, p. 15.

8  Hopkins, *Journal*, p. 16.

9  Hopkins, *The Letters of Gerard Manley Hopkins to Robert Bridges*, ed. C. C. Abbot (London, Oxford University Press, 1935), p. 299, 23 Feb. 1889.

10  *Hopkins*, p. 131.

11  *Ibid.*, pp. 111–12.

12  Robert Bernard Martin, *Gerard Manley Hopkins: A Very Private Life* (London, HarperCollins, 1991), p. 252.

13  In fact Hopkins believed that Protestantism underwrote sexual licence. Writing to Coventry Patmore about a *Saturday Review* article contrasting Protestant and Catholic ideas of a schoolboy, he claimed it 'came out with the frank truth, that it looked on chastity as a feminine virtue (=lewdness as a masculine one: it was not quite as raw as I put it, but this was the meaning)' (Hopkins, *Further Letters*, p. 308, 24 Sept. 1883).

14  *The Poems and Letters of Digby Mackworth Dolben, 1848–1867*, ed. Martin Cohen (Avebury, Avebury Press, 1981), pp. 27–8.

15  Quoted in Martin, *Hopkins*, p. 86; also in Norman White, *Hopkins: A Literary Biography* (Oxford, Clarendon Press, 1992), p. 109.

16  *The Early Poetic Manuscripts and Note-Books of Gerard Manley Hopkins in Facsimile*, ed. Norman H. Mackenzie (New York, Garland Publishing, 1989), pp. 157, 167, 186, 198 & 199.

17  *Hopkins*, p. 128.

18  Richard Dellamora, *Masculine Desire: The Sexual Politics of Victorian Aestheticism* (Chapel Hill, University of North Carolina Press, 1990), p. 53.

19  Hopkins, *Note-Books*, p. 198.

20  Hopkins, *Further Letters*, p. 58, undated [1872?].

## Chapter 7

1  Rupert Brooke, 'Peace', in *Collected Poems* (London, Sidgwick & Jackson, 1918), p. 5.

2  See Mark Girouard, *The Return to Camelot: Chivalry and the English Gentleman*

(New Haven, Yale University Press, 1981), pp. 276–82.

3  Ivor Gurney, 'To the Poet Before Battle', in *Severn & Somme. War's Embers*, ed. R. K. R. Thornton (Ashington/Manchester, Mid Northumberland Arts Groups/Carcanet Press, 1987), p. 23.

4  Joyce Kilmer, 'To certain poets', in Frederic W. Ziv (ed.), *The Valiant Muse* (New York, Putnam's, 1936), pp. 45–6.

5  Girouard, *Return to Camelot*, p. 170.

6  Quoted in Paul Fussell, *The Great War and Modern Memory* (Oxford, Oxford University Press, 1975), p. 301.

7  On the significance for aestheticism of developments in nineteenth-century materialist psychology see Ian Small, *Conditions for Criticism: Authority, Knowledge and Literature in the Late Nineteenth Century* (Oxford, Clarendon Press, 1991), chapter 3, pp. 64–88.

8  Oscar Wilde, *The Letters of Oscar Wilde*, ed. Rupert Hart-Davis (London, Hart-Davis, 1962), p. 21, 27 July 1876.

9  Perhaps not wholly, given Speranza's Catholic sympathies and her apparent baptism of her sons into the faith. See Richard Ellmann, *Oscar Wilde* (Harmondsworth, Penguin, 1988), pp. 18–19; also Davis Coakley, *The Importance of Being Irish* (Dublin, Town House, 1994), pp. 112–14.

10  Wilde, *Letters*, p. 20, 27 July 1876.

11  Letter and full anecdote are given in Ellmann, *Oscar Wilde*, pp. 90–1.

12  Gary Paterson reviews Wilde's Catholicism (somewhat moralistically) in 'Oscar Wilde and the Scarlet Woman', *Antigonish Review*, 85–6 (1991), pp. 241–54 concluding that it was initially an aspect of aestheticism and, later, of his decadence. Still more moralistic in its implications is Guy Willoughby's account of Wilde's identifications with the figure of Christ in *Art and Christhood: The Aesthetics of Oscar Wilde* (Cranbury, Associated University Presses, 1993). For some characteristically witty comments on gay men's identifications with Catholicism, see Eve Sedgwick's Epistemology of the Closet (Hemel Hempstead, Harvester Wheatsheaf, 1991), p. 140.

13  Oscar Wilde, *The Importance of Being Earnest*, in *Plays* (Harmondsworth, Penguin, [1895] 1986), p. 263.

14  *Ibid.*, p. 274.

15  Wilde, *Letters*, p. 218, June 1888.

16  Wilde, 'Mr Froude's Blue Book', in *The Artist as Critic*, ed. Richard Ellmann (London, W. H. Allen, [1889] 1970), p. 136.

17  Wilde, 'Sonnet to Liberty', in *Complete Works* (London, Collins, 1966), p. 709.

18  Wilde, 'Lord Arthur Savile's Crime', in *Complete Shorter Fiction* (Oxford, Oxford University Press, [1887] 1979), p. 33.

19  *Ibid.*, p. 44.

20  *Ibid.*, p. 45.

21  *Ibid.*, pp. 46–7.

22  Rodney Shewan's discussion – *Oscar Wilde: Art and Egotism* (London, Macmillan, 1977), pp. 27–31 – differs from mine in placing primary emphasis on what he calls 'the exemplary egoism of instinct'.

# Notes

23 *Oscar Wilde's Oxford Notebooks: A Portrait of Mind in the Making*, ed. Philip E. Smith and Michael S. Helfand (Oxford, Oxford University Press, 1989), p. 141.

24 *Ibid.*, p. 109.

25 For a detailed discussion of these influences see J. W. Burrow, *Evolution and Society: A Study in Victorian Social Theory* (Cambridge, Cambridge University Press, 1968), pp. 179–227.

26 On the influence of positivist thought on Wilde, see Bruce Haley, 'Wilde's decadence and the positivist tradition', *Victorian Studies*, 28:2 (1985), pp. 215–29; also Terry Eagleton, 'Oscar and George', in *Heathcliff and the Great Hunger: Studies in Irish Culture* (London, Verso, 1985), pp. 328–9.

27 Wilde, 'The Critic as Artist' [1891], in *The Artist as Critic*, p. 359.

28 See Smith and Helfand's introduction to Wilde, *Oxford Notebooks*, pp. 66–77, though their account tends to privilege the Hegelian dimension to Wilde's essay.

29 Wilde, 'Critic', p. 383.

30 Jonathan Dollimore constructs an anti-essentialist Wilde: see *Sexual Dissidence: Augustine to Wilde, Freud to Foucault* (Oxford, Clarendon Press, 1991), esp. pp. 3–18. Though Terry Eagleton recognises that Wilde's dissolution of the autonomous ego is indebted to evolutionism, he makes this the basis of a comparison with Roland Barthes, in 'Oscar and George', pp. 328–9. Lawrence Danson in *Wilde's Intentions: The Artist in his Criticism* (Oxford, Clarendon Press, 1997), pp. 18–19 sees a contradiction between Wilde's self-fashioning and his emphasis on heredity, whereas this reading suggests Wilde believed that heredity made pluralistic identities possible.

31 Linda Dowling, *Hellenism and Homosexuality in Victorian Oxford* (Ithaca, Cornell University Press, 1994), p. 116.

32 H. Montgomery Hyde, *Famous Trials 7: Oscar Wilde* (Harmondsworth, Penguin, 1962), p. 201.

33 Walter Pater, 'Winckelmann', in *The Renaissance: Studies in Art and Poetry*, ed. Donald L. Hill (Berkeley, University of California Press, [1867] 1980), esp. pp. 176–7.

34 We know that Wilde read *Greek Poets* when it was first published (Ellmann, *Oscar Wilde*, p. 31). Given his interest in Symonds's work and the company he kept, it is likely – though not certain – that he came across *Greek Ethics*.

35 J. A. Symonds, *Studies of the Greek Poets*, 3rd ed. (London, A. & C. Black, [1873] 1920), p. 554.

36 *Ibid.*, p. 571.

37 J. A. Symonds, *A Problem in Greek Ethics* (London, privately printed, [1873] 1908), p. 17.

38 *Ibid.*, p. 59.

39 Wilde, 'Critic', p. 396.

40 Wilde, 'Pen, Pencil and Poison' [1889], in The Artist as Critic, p. 324.

41 Hyde, *Trials* (Harmondsworth, Penguin), 1962, p. 108.

42 Quoted in John Stokes, 'Wilde at bay: the diaries of George Ives', *English*

*Literature in Transition 1880–1920*, 26:3 (1983), p. 184.

43  For an analysis of the contribution of Maudsley to moral norms see Ed Cohen, *Talk on the Wilde Side: Toward a Genealogy of a Discourse on Male Sexualities* (New York and London, Routledge, 1993), pp. 58–66.

44  Max Nordau, *Degeneration* (Lincoln and London, University of Nebraska Press, [1895] 1993), pp. 42–3.

45  *Ibid.*, p. 259.

46  Wilde, *Letters*, p. 402, 2 July 1896.

47  This is most clearly indicated in the letters from Rome, which, as with the earlier letter from Ireland, demonstrate Wilde's sense that Catholicism was compatible with same-sex desire. See *ibid.*, pp. 820–5.

48  See Kerry Powell, *Oscar Wilde and the Theatre of the 1890s* (Cambridge, Cambridge University Press, 1990), chapter 6, pp. 89–107.

49  Wilde, *A Woman of No Importance*, in *Plays* (Harmondsworth, Penguin, [1893] 1954), p. 89.

50  Frank Mort, *Dangerous Sexualities: Medico-moral Politics in England Since 1830* (London, Routledge, 1987), pp. 126–30.

51  *Ibid.*, p. 113.

52  J. S. Mill, *On Liberty,* in *Collected Works of John Stuart Mill*, vol. 18: *Essays on Politics and Society* (Toronto/London, University of Toronto Press/Routledge & Kegan Paul, [1859] 1977), p. 275. This was the only work of Mill Wilde thought worth reading (see Wilde, *The Artist as Critic*, p. 27).

53  Wilde, *Woman*, p. 103.

54  *Ibid.*, pp. 111–12.

55  *Ibid.*, p. 89.

56  *Ibid.*, p. 81.

57  *Ibid.*, p. 117.

58  Quoted in Ellmann, *Oscar Wilde*, p. 357n. I am grateful to Alan Sinfield for drawing my attention to this.

59  Wilde, *Woman*, p. 108.

60  Pater, 'Conclusion' [1868], in *The Renaissance*, p. 190.

61  Wilde, *Woman*, p. 136.

62  *Ibid.*, p. 138.

63  *Ibid.*, p. 138.

64  See Josephine M. Guy, *The British Avant Garde: The Theory and Politics of Tradition* (Hemel Hempstead, Harvester Wheatsheaf, 1991), pp. 88–93.

65  Patricia Flanagan Behrendt makes a similar point in *Oscar Wilde: Eros and Aesthetics* (Houndmills, Macmillan, 1991), p. 156, though she does insist that the dandy figure is covertly queer. Alan Sinfield, on the other hand, warns against seeing homosexuality as the truth of Wilde's dandies, since this depends on anachronistically reading the plays in the light of the trials ('"Effeminacy" and "femininity": sexual politics in Wilde's comedies', *Modern Drama*, 37 (1994), pp. 34–52). Joseph Bristow appears to adopt a similar line: see *Effeminate England: Homoerotic Writing after 1895* (New York, Columbia University Press, 1995), pp. 41–2.

66 Ellmann, *Oscar Wilde*, p. 360.

67 A. B. Walkley in the *Speaker*, 29 April 1893, in *Oscar Wilde: The Critical Heritage*, ed. Karl Beckson (London, Routledge & Kegan Paul, 1970), p. 152.

68 Unsigned review, *Saturday Review*, 6 May 1893, in *ibid.*, p. 153.

69 Wilde, *The Picture of Dorian Gray* (Oxford, Oxford University Press, [1891] 1992), p. xxiv.

70 Hyde, *Trials*, p. 116.

71 Wilde, *Letters*, p. 466.

72 *Ibid.*, pp. 435 & 440.

73 *Ibid.*, p. 492.

74 *Ibid.*, pp. 427 & 429.

75 *Ibid.*, p. 501.

76 Wilde, 'Phrases and philosophies for the use of the young', [1894] in *The Artist as Critic*, p. 434.

77 Hyde, *Trials*, p. 273.

78 *The Illustrated Police Budget*, 1 June 1985, in Jonathan Goodman (comp.), *The Oscar Wilde File* (London, W. H. Allen, 1988), p. 131. Goodman also reproduces a cartoon from *The Morning*, 6 June 1895, which also focuses on Wilde's prison haircut, p. 137.

## Conclusion

1 Perry Anderson, 'Origins of the present crisis', in *English Questions* (London, Verso, [1964] 1992), p. 31. The Nairn–Anderson theses have been challenged recently by Ellen Meiksins Wood in *The Pristine Culture of Capitalism: A Historical Essay on Old Regimes and Modern States* (London, Verso, 1991). Despite the brilliance of the argument, it does not have the explanatory reach of Anderson's, nor does it deal fully with the obvious tensions which Anderson rightly suggests are endemic to English culture and society.

2 Herbert Sussman, *Victorian Masculinities: Manhood and Masculine Poetics in Early Victorian Literature and Art* (Cambridge, Cambridge University Press, 1995), p. 11.

3 Mark Girouard, *The Return to Camelot: Chivalry and the English Gentleman* (New Haven, Yale University Press, 1981).

4 Quoted in Alfred Thomas, *Hopkins the Jesuit: The Years of Training* (London, Oxford University Press, 1969), p. 247.

5 Paul Jones, *War Letters of a Public Schoolboy* (London, Cassell, 1918), p. 253.

# Index

absolutism 10
aestheticism and art 64, 119,
    147–8
  Newman 94
  Wilde 148–50, 155–9, 163–4,
    165
Allen, Grant 119
Allingham, William 102
Almond, Hely Hutchinson 59–60,
    65
Anderson, Benedict 7
Anderson, Perry 168, 197
Anglican Church 13, 15–16, 26;
    habit 18
  ritualism 6, 113
Anglicanism 170
  in C. Brontë 40–5
Anglo-Catholicism 72–86, 91–3, 121
Anglo-Saxons/Saxons 10, 33–4, 57,
    103, 108, 114–16, 119, 125
  Mark 33
antinomianism 165
Arnold, Matthew 32, 112, 116–19,
    189
  *Culture and Anarchy* 118
  *Irish Essays* 118
  'The Nadir of Liberalism' 118–19,
    120
  *On the Study of Celtic Literature*
    116–17
  *St Paul and Protestantism* 117

Arnold, Thomas (headmaster of
    Rugby) 59
Arnold, Thomas, the younger 104
art *see* aestheticism and art
*Artist, The* 69
asceticism 83, 88, 130, 140–1, 168
  *see also* celibacy
athleticism 59–70, 147
Austen, Jane: *Mansfield Park* 21–9,
    30, 39
authority 10, 14, 15, 93, 97, 149
autonomy 11, 15, 170
  *see also* freedom
*Awful Disclosures of Maria Monk*
    (anonymous) 82

Baden-Powell, 1st Baron 62
Baldick, Chris 106
Beddoe, John 115
Belgium 112
Bettoni, Efrem 129
Bible 77
  David and Jonathan 65–6
*Birmingham Daily Gazette* 112
Blachford, Lord 79
body, male:
  of Christ 126–30, 138
  dismemberment 135–8
  eroticised 64–70, 147–8
  and games ethic 46–7, 55–64
  Hopkins on 122–5, 139